THE
ESSENTIAL
FLY
TIER

BOOKS BY J. EDSON LEONARD

FLIES

FLY ROD CASTING

BAIT ROD CASTING

FEATHER IN THE BREEZE

THE ESSENTIAL FLY TIER

THE ESSENTIAL FLY TIER

J. Edson Leonard

Illustrated by the Author

THE LYONS PRESS

Guilford, Connecticut

An imprint of The Globe Pequot Press

The Essential Fly Tier

---

by J. Edson Leonard

The Lyons Press is an imprint of The Globe Pequot Press

10 9 8 7 6 5 4 3 2 1

Printed in the United States of America

ISBN 1–58574–616–9

Library of Congress Cataloging-in-Publication data is available on file.

For Page

Who, for 30 years, has been wife,
helpmate, executive vice president, counsel, and a
pretty good fisher to boot.

Acknowledgments

My sincere appreciation to John Veniard,
Surrey, England, for lists of hook calibrations,
and to Eric Peper for
his boundless enthusiasm and good advice.

PREFACE

Fly tying is both an art form and a science: an art form of necessity and a science by evolution. Perhaps its *best* quality is filling that awful limbo of the sportsman's fifth season—the time falling between the last of deer season and the first of trout season—for it is then that the fly rods, impatient to go, fairly twist in their cases, and the fly chest buzzes with dozens of flies still untried from last season.

As an art form, fly tying caught the royal eye of kings, who commissioned their own fly tiers to conceive of patterns ornate as the sovereign escutcheons. As a science, it has caught the eye of the aquatic biologist who fishes and the fly fisher who reads aquatic biology; the medical doctor, the mechanic, the policeman, the nuclear physicist, the janitor, the businessman, the student, even the housewife. And lo, the writers! My bookshelves sag from the weight of their treatises, compendiums, and analyses. Most of them are excellent. Many are most scholarly, some magnificently illustrated, others replete with supporting scientific charts and diagrams. Each, in one way or another, has its own fascination; each has its place.

To show how to make a better fly, one that will float better, sink faster, reflect light better, twitch better, last longer; one that is more like its natural counterpart, whether nymph, dun, or spinner; shrimp, spearing, sculpin, sow bug, or sand eel; one that will bring fish to strike as no other fly has done—that is the ultimate aim of books on fly tying. Yet tying a fly to imitate the natural insect, or whatever, is one thing. But tying a fly that will catch fish is quite another. One might think that the two are one and the same. They are not. There is a keen distinction between them. That distinction plagues the fisher-tier, always has and probably always will. It is the angler's choice, and his alone, how far to go, one way or the other.

This book treats the *types* of flies more than the patterns, although there is a section devoted to the best known patterns for most fish that will "take the fly." It considers various approaches to achieving the same effects. Most important, perhaps, it stresses fundamentals throughout, a quality that in our time has lost so much favor. We all know the chap who can cast a country mile with his $300 rod but seldom catches a fish, very likely because he has become so addicted to professionalism that he cannot bend his rationale to cope with simple things. The tackle houses thrive on this fellow!

Certainly there are many anglers who will disagree with contentions appearing in this book, denouncing them for what may seem oversimplification. So be it. But it is not hard to be an apologist for simplicity, even in tying a fly. One of the best brown trout flies I ever contrived was hackled with clippings from my beard and tailed with four guard hairs from my cat.

J. Edson Leonard
Barrington, Rhode Island

CONTENTS

HOOKS

One would think that hooks designed for fly tying would have changed appreciably in the past twenty-five years, but that is not the case. With the exception of the stainless-steel saltwater hooks, the "point-up" weedless hook, and the continued miniaturization of the midge hook (to size 28), little new has come from the hook machines of Great Britain and continental Europe. There is really little need for it. The hook spectrum now spans lengths from 7X-short to 8X-long, diameters from 4X-fine to 3X-stout, shapes of every worthwhile kind, and points and barbs for anything with fins.

Some firms have merged with others, some have disappeared, at least as far as I can determine, and relatively few new ones exist. Hook making, for centuries a highly safeguarded craft, is most specialized, and the critical balance between cost and price determines, as it does in all enterprises, who stays in business. Those firms that have survived continue to offer good products.

England and Norway have cornered the hook market. For many decades both have produced hooks of quality, and whatever standards exist today are the results of their know-how, acquired from solid experience.

Years ago I made a vigorous and exhaustive effort to arrive at some sort of standard, or set of standards, based on then existing practices, tolerances, gauges, and shapes, and those characteristics peculiar to the hooks produced in the 1930s. The diversity in tempering, wire gauge, flattening and drawing, bronzing and plating, tapering, pointing, and barbing made the task a difficult one. And it was during that effort that I resolved that the cries of the fly tier for new and different hooks would drive any hook manufacturer berserk if he tried to accommodate such requests,

1

set up his machines for short runs, and still show a profit for his endeavors.

Perhaps, in the final analysis, a few salient points did emerge from those studies. For trout flies, the weight and shape of the hook are more critical than its outright strength, a term of various definitions to be sure. What with leader points testing as little as ¾-pound tensile strength, the actual strength of the smallest hooks is relatively minor. As the sizes become larger, the need for greater strength increases.

Hardness, a doubtful measure of strength, has useful limits; after a certain value is reached, hardness becomes brittleness, the product of poor carbon control and improper tempering. You can determine this by placing a hook in your fly vise and giving it several lateral movements with pliers. A brittle hook probably will break. Brittleness is relative, however, and its main disadvantages are two: If the hook is offset, that is, if the point and shank are not in the same line of draft, it may fracture or break from the forces of the closed jaws of the vise. A fracture is worse than a break: It is not always detectable, and the hook may survive the tying of a fly but may break later in the mouth of a good fish. Moreover, a brittle hook point may break off from the slightest impact with a hard object, such as a ferrule or line guide during casting, or with a rock and the like. This emphasizes the added value of the straight bend, in which the point does not project—up, down, to the left or to the right.

Nomenclature

The hook parts described here are illustrated in Figure 1 and in subsequent figures in detail. Included are shape, size, shank, gape, bend (offset), spear, point, barb, eye, cross section and gauge. Available standards for current manufacture are shown in tabular form.

For hundreds of years the term "pattern" has been accepted as the index to the hook type. I, for one, find the term vague because it frequently includes several characteristics, which makes comparison of one hook with another difficult. For example, two characteristics—"bend," which is really the lateral offset given the return bend, and the "curvature" of the hook—are often both referred to as "bend," without distinction. For this reason, I prefer the word "shape" for the curvature of the hook

Kirbed　　　　　Straight　　　　　Reverse

BEND (OFFSET)

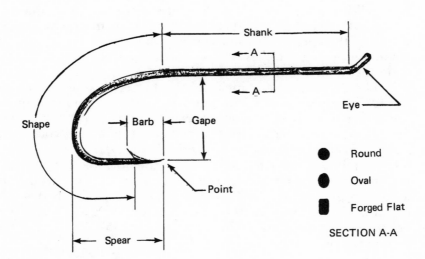

FIG. 1.　HOOK NOMENCLATURE

and call "bend" the offset only. Any style of hook may or may not have a bend without its shape being altered; therefore, for purposes of describing and comparing its properties, the terms "shape" and "bend" should be considered separately. They are in this book, and there certainly will be repercussion from many fronts for it!

Shape

The shape is the key to any hook. Many have been developed for better holding and penetrating—some round, some parabolic, others even square. Each is claimed to have its own advantages. Modern shapes are almost always round or parabolic. The gradual curvature from the straight shank minimizes stress risers that develop from bending at acute angles during forming. Figure 2 illustrates the many shapes described in detail.

The *round* shape includes the Model Perfect, the Viking, and less well-known shapes. It is distinctly roundish in profile, and some makes have an almost constant radius from the shank to the origin of the spear. This shape is justifiably popular for all flies, for its roundness reduces leverage in the mouth of the fish, which is no mean advantage.

The *parabolic* shape includes the Limerick, the Sproat, and the O'Shaughnessy, favorites that have survived man's innovations for many decades. The Limerick is more parabolic than the Sproat, its curvature ending rather abruptly at the root of the spear. It is more popular in the larger sizes, say, from size 10 up. If it has a failing, it is the tendency to slot the hole made by the hook penetrating the fish's mouth, the result of leverage inherent in the long, straight spear. The Limerick, however, probably has more eye appeal, and looks more "fishy" than anything else with a barb. In some quarters, tying a salmon fly on any hook shape other than a Limerick is pure sacrilege!

The *Sproat* has a more gradual parabolic curvature and a slightly shorter spear than the Limerick. It is a graceful shape, appealing to the fly dresser for the slight curvature at the rear of the shank, which makes for a lifelike body contour, particularly in nymphs and wet flies. Some manufacturers make the Sproat very similar to the Limerick. But the two shapes are distinctly different when made to traditional standards.

The *O'Shaughnessy* is characterized by its parabolic curvature, falling between those of the Limerick and the Sproat, and by its

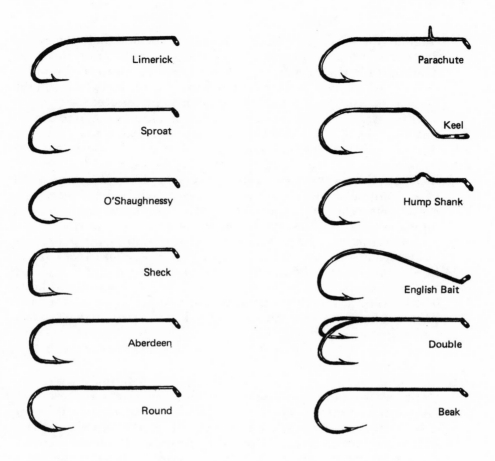

Limerick

Sproat

O'Shaughnessy

Sheck

Aberdeen

Round

Parachute

Keel

Hump Shank

English Bait

Double

Beak

FIG. 2. HOOK SHAPES

JEL

singularly inward curve at the root of the spear, which places the draft line of the point slightly inside the outer surface of the hook. Theoretically this placement allows more resistance to bending and ensures better hold once the fish is on, although the slight S-curve in the spear is believed slower to penetrate.

The *Square* shape now is seldom seen although at one time it was a style leader. It is best represented by the *Sneck,* featuring the tight corner radii at the end of the shank and the beginning of the straight spear. Here again, the straightness of the spear adversely increases the leverage when the hook is set. From the standpoint of eye appeal alone, the Sneck leaves much to be desired, although its relatively longer straight shank allows for dressing longer straight bodies—if that is important to the tier.

The *Aberdeen* is also squarish but has another property, not generally associated with shape, that sets it apart from other hooks: the ability to bend without breaking. Usually of fine gauge and soft temper, the Aberdeen is used largely for deep-sinking, lead-headed jigs on the premise that, if hooked on the bottom, the jig can be retrieved because the hook will bend. It withstands reshaping with pliers.

Size

Hook size is relative because the so-called standards and scales of measurement differ. To the eye, two hooks made by different manufacturers may appear the same in length and shape; yet, when precisely measured, they differ. This difference is sometimes traceable to proprietary interests on the part of the hook maker. Making a hook slightly longer or shorter than "standard" and giving it a new name, without declaring its specifications, may be good business, and the fly tier may stand to profit by it if he uses the hook properly. But, for the purposes of comparing hook sizes, certain definite standard specifications are to be considered: shape, shank length and cross section. Bend is left out of account here, for lateral offset does not affect size measurement. The eye is excluded from measurement as well.

The length of a hook is measured from immediately behind the eye to the perpendicular line falling on the outer edge of the curved portion, or "shape." The relation between the gape (the space between the point and the shank) and the length, so measured, is the only real means for establishing a standard size scale. The proportions of length-to-gape-to-wire gauge are fixed. As

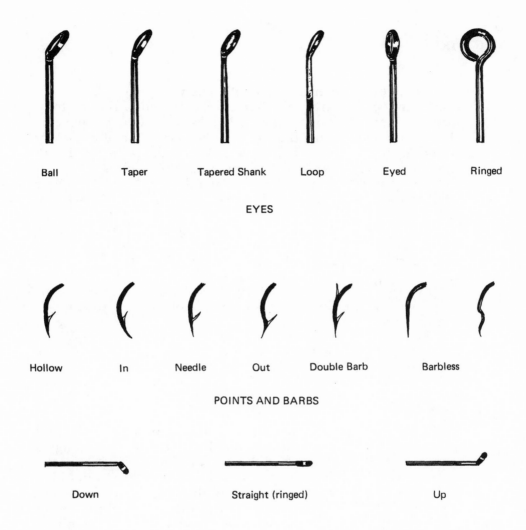

Ball   Taper   Tapered Shank   Loop   Eyed   Ringed

EYES

Hollow   In   Needle   Out   Double Barb   Barbless

POINTS AND BARBS

Down   Straight (ringed)   Up

FIG. 3. HOOK EYES, POINTS, AND BARBS

JEL

size increases, so do the gape, length, and wire gauge. Any deviation from the standard scale characterizes the hook as fine, stout, long-shanked, or short-shanked. Hooks with shanks longer or shorter and wire gauge finer or stouter than those of a hook of standard dimensions are designated by numbers suffixed with the letter X, to indicate how many times the hook is longer or shorter, stouter or finer than the standard dimension. These designations will be explained under *Shank* and *Cross Section* that follow..

Figure 4 shows the exact measurements for hooks, according to the standard British Redditch scale, perhaps the best-known and most-used system of measurement. Sizes from 24 to 13 are scaled by 32nds of an inch; from 12 to 4 by 16ths; from 3 to 5/0 by 8ths; from 6/0 to 10/0 by 4ths. Figure 4 expresses the lengths from size 24 to size 4 in 32nds of an inch to simplify comparisons.

Figure 6 illustrates the difference between the Low-Water Salmon and Salmon Dry-fly hooks. Regular salmon hooks are scaled to the Redditch Standard.

Shank

The shank is the straight part of the hook extending from behind the eye to where the curvature of the shape begins. Shank lengths vary from very short, in which the eye is almost directly above the point, to very long, in which the hook looks more like a one-sided hairpin than a hook. Measurement of this length is expressed in units of X, 1X, 2X, 3X, and so on representing the number of times the shank is shorter or longer than that of the standard shank *for that hook size.* The number before X indicates the interval between this size and the larger or smaller standard size. Examples: a 3X-long shank in size 10 has the shank length of a standard 7; a 4X-long size 8 has the shank length of a standard size 4, and a 5X-short size 8 has the shank length of a standard 13. Despite the use of odd numbers as the means for determining shank lengths, most manufacturers produce hooks in even sizes only, up to size 1. The shortest at present is 5X, the longest 8X; but some 10X-long hooks have been made in the past. They are impractical. A hook, theoretically of one shape, wire gauge, and size, can exist in as many as 14 shank lengths. Surprisingly, there are good uses for every one. Unfortunately, shank lengths for the same standard-size hook may vary among manufacturers. Two firms, for exam-

SIZE	ACTUAL LENGTH	LGTH. IN.	WIRE DIA.
1/0		1-1/2	.048
1-1/2		1-3/8	.045
1		1-1/4	.042
2		1-1/8	.040
3		1	.037
4		30	.035
5		28	.033
6		26	.030
7		24	.029
8		22	.027
9		20	.026
10		18	.024
11		16	.023
12		14	.022
13		12	.020
14		11	.018
15		10	.017
16		9	.016
17		8	.015
18		7	.014
20		6	.012
22		5	.011
24		4	.010

(32nds.)

FIG. 4. REDDITCH STANDARD

ple, may make size 10 round shape hooks in slightly different shank lengths and, by comparison, their long- and short-shank hooks will perpetuate that same variation. A 6X-long size 8 by one manufacturer may be a 5X-long size 8 according to another and 7X-long size 8 according to still another.

In X designations for shank length only, the gape, shape and gauge remain the same as in the basic standard.

Several shank configurations, some recent, have improved the tying of nymphs, parachute dry flies, cork-bodied hair bugs, and streamers with the hook points up, each to be described later at length. They are illustrated in Figure 2. The new "bait hook," which features a sickle-shaped shank, aligning the point with the eye, is a really great hook for tying arched-body nymphs and shrimp. It is successful for fish that have fleshy mouths. The novel pin-like extension on the new parachute hook rises at right angles to the shank, simplifying the previously difficult-to-tie parachute. The vertical piece is integral to the shank. The hump shank, which has a hairpin-like hump, was designed to provide greater bearing surface for the hook within cork and wood bodies, and to reduce the tendency of the hook to rotate. The new Keel Hook, which has the shank bent in the form of a step, places the center of gravity well below the draft line; the hook rides point up and is, for the most part, snagless, if not "weedless."

Gape

Gape (see Figure 1) is the space between the point and the shank and is one of the dimensions that determines the size of the hook. Some makers have marketed hooks with wide gapes, using standard size numbers as a reference: wide-gape 10, 12 and so on. For all practical purposes, there is little difference between a wide-gape hook and one the next size larger in a finer wire gauge. A wide-gape size 10, for example, is proportionately the same as a 2X-short size 8 2X-fine.

Bend

As stated earlier, the terms "bend, "pattern" and "shape" are often used interchangeably. "Bend" properly refers to the lateral offset—right or left—of the spear, the return portion of the hook containing the barb and point. Look at the hook from the bottom, holding the shank between the fingers. If the spear and shank are

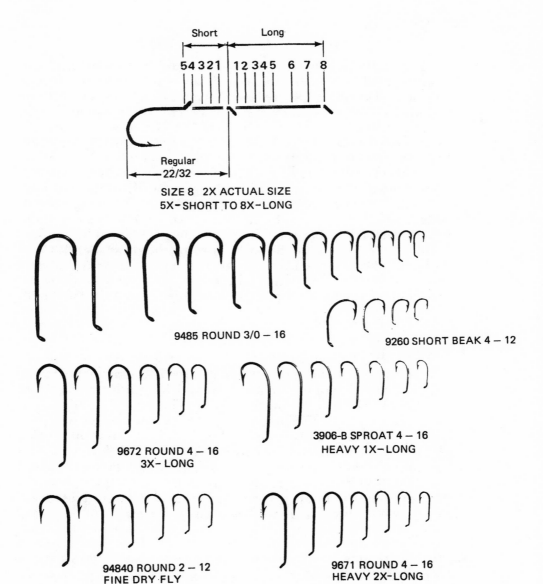

Short   Long

5 4 3 2 1   1 2 3 4 5   6   7   8

Regular
— 22/32 —

SIZE 8   2X ACTUAL SIZE
5X–SHORT TO 8X–LONG

9485 ROUND 3/0 – 16

9260 SHORT BEAK 4 – 12

9672 ROUND 4 – 16
3X– LONG

3906-B SPROAT 4 – 16
HEAVY 1X–LONG

94840 ROUND 2 – 12
FINE DRY FLY

9671 ROUND 4 – 16
HEAVY 2X–LONG

POPULAR MUSTAD HOOKS

FIG. 5. TYPICAL HOOK DESIGNS

JEL

exactly parallel, there is no offset, and the hook is called "straight." If the point inclines to the left, the hook is called Kirbed, if to the right, reversed. Figure 1 illustrates all three conditions. Here is an example of precise specifications for an item of apparent trivial importance! Whether the bend is to the right or to the left, it is still offset. Other than inclining the shank toward or away from the tier when the hook is placed in the vise, the only effect of the left or right offset is to point the angle of the hook toward or away from the angler, which depends upon whether he is casting to his left or right. I prefer a straight hook, except for the striped bass, which has a tough, cartilaginous mouth and is capable of holding a streamer horizontally in its jaws and too often escaping the barb. Turning the spear slightly to the left or right with needle-nosed pliers is a good remedy, but only the least amount of bend is necessary. In nearly all other fly fishing, a straight bend penetrates deeper than an offset bend.

Spear

The Spear, illustrated in Figure 1, is not usually defined in hook nomenclature, although it is perhaps the most essential part of a hook. Consisting of the return band, which includes the barb and the point, it is the real "business" end. The Round, Sproat, Limerick, Sneck, and O'Shaughnessy shapes have differing spear configurations, claims for each being that penetration, setting and holding power are superior. The Limerick has a straight spear, penetrates well and sets deep. The Sproat is not so straight, but the Sneck is. The Round has a short, straight spear, the O'Shaughnessy almost an S-curve. The advantages and disadvantages will be explained in the section on Leverage.

Point

The point of any hook (see Figure 3) must be as sharp as the manufacturer can produce and the angler can maintain with his hone. It is the most critical part of the hook, being the weakest. Dull or distorted points fail to penetrate, and, the harder the fish's mouth, the harder it is for the angler to set the hook. With the fine caliber of tackle today—the soft-action rods and gossamer-like leader points—the point on a trout-fly hook just has to be sharp. If it isn't, throw the fly away. Don't waste time tying flies on or using hooks whose points are less than needle sharp.

SIZE	LENGTH IN.		
	REDDITCH STD.	LOW—WATER	DRYFLY
10/0	3-1/4		
9/0	3	3-1/2	
8/0	2-3/4	3-1/8	
7/0	2-1/2	2-5/8	
6/0	2-1/4	2-3/8	
5/0	2	2-1/8	
4/0	1-7/8	2	
3/0	1-3/4	1-7/8	
2/0	1-5/8	1-3/4	
1/0	1-1/2	1-5/8	
1-1/2	1-3/8		
1	1-1/4	1-1/2	
2	1-1/8	1-5/16	
3	1	1-1/4	
4	15/16	1-3/16	1-1/4
5	7/8	1-1/8	
6	13/16	1	1-1/8
7	3/4	7/8	
8	11/16	13/16	1
9	5/8	3/4	7/8
10	9/16	11/16	3/4
11	1/2	5/8	
12	7/16	9/16	5/8

FIG. 6. EQUIVALENT LENGTHS—SALMON HOOKS

The *Hollow Point* is ground to a fine point by machine. It is characterized by the smooth inner radius extending from the tip of the barb to the hook point. Well-made Hollow Points are extremely sharp, and some of the finest hooks have them.

The *Needle Point,* as the name suggests, is like the point on a sewing needle. It is recognized by its slender, conical taper and the absence of the gradual radius typical of the Hollow Point. The barb appears to have been sliced and rises at an angle. Some manufacturers hollow-grind needle points slightly.

The *In-Point* is called Beak, Claw and other names by their makers for the inward curve of the point, which, in most designs, is in line with the eye. Many flyrodders prefer this point for flies; I do not, preferring the draft line of the point parallel with the shank. The In-Point is better suited to hollow grinding than the conical needle type.

The *Out-Point* seldom is seen now. The point projects outward and is objectionable because the draft line is not parallel with the shank. Some claim that it has excellent penetration, but fine-wire hooks, like those for trout flies, with out points customarily do not hold.

The *Superior Point* is the "as machined" point of a low-grade hook and is production-made for bait fishing. It is not included here except to identify it. Superior Points are unfit for fly tying.

Barb

The barb (see Figure 3) has one function: to prevent the hook from disengaging after penetrating. The ideal barb is tapered to prevent making a hole oversize , yet is high enough not to back out easily.

Double Barbs have been featured on salmon fly hooks in England for many years, and there is continuing discussion about the penetrating and holding power of a hook with an additional barb on the outer surface and behind the conventional inner barb. Long considered superior in some quarters for holding *large* salmon, the double-barbed hook still presents the probability that the second barb will enlarge the hole already made by the first making it easier for fish to back out. Moreover, penetration of hard cartilage is doubly difficult.

Barbless hooks are used mainly in hatchery fishing, where the release of the fish unharmed is the objective by some conservation-minded anglers. An S-shape curve replaces the regular barb, greatly diminishing the holding power of the hook. Another type has a conventional shape but no barb. A fish hooked can be released easily, simply by giving it slack line.

Eye

The eye of the hook is far more than just the receiving end for attaching the leader. Hooks for flies, especially, have eyes designed for specific purposes. The eye may be tapered to reduce the weight of a fine-wire hook, or it may be of the same gauge as the wire in the shank to add weight. Eyes may be straight or turned up or down. Some makers bend eyes quite sharply, others only a few degrees, the latter being better for fly tying; finishing the head is easier, and the lesser angle makes for a neater-looking fly. The smaller angle also reduces stress risers that occur when the hook is formed.

The following types of eyes and their accepted designations are illustrated in Figure 3:

TURN-DOWN EYE (T.D.E.): The eye is bent down from the shank.

TURN-UP EYE (T.U.E.): The eye is bent up from the shank.

RING EYE (R.E.): The eye projects straight in the horizontal plane.

EYED (E.): The eye projects straight in the vertical plane.

LOOP EYE (L.E.): The eye is oval in shape, bent up or down, the wire tapered and bent back along the shank to be covered with tying thread when finishing the head of the fly.

BALL EYE (B.E.): The eye is bent up or down or is straight in the horizontal or vertical planes and is of the same gauge as the shank.

TAPER EYE (T.E.): There are two types. In the first, the taper to a finer wire gauge is confined to the eye itself. In the second, the taper begins in the shank behind the eye. Taper reduces weight and the diameter of the eye.

Cross Section

In a hook, as in any beam or structural member, the cross section is the form and dimension of the part and determines resistance to bending. There is much to be said about it, for a hook is subjected to lateral forces when solidly set in a fish's mouth. In round wire hooks, the cross section (gauge of the wire), is a strictly controlled standard in wire drawing. The bending strength of round wire is uniformly the same in any direction, but the bending strength of a rectangular or oval wire is not. Hooks that are forged (flattened) during forming have increased resistance to bending through the longer dimension but reduced resistance through the shorter. Consequently, the forged hook is weaker laterally but stronger vertically—from the shank through the shape. This means that a forged hook, solidly placed in the hard cartilage of a fish's mouth, is more apt to fail from a lateral load than is a round wire hook. Figure 1 shows the three cross-sectional shapes.

Cross section is relatively unimportant in small hooks for trout but is significant in long-shank streamers and flies when strong leverage from the side is the rule, rather than the exception.

Decrease and increase in cross section (gauge) is numerically designated as to how many times the wire is larger or smaller than the wire of a standard hook of the same size. For example, a 2X-stout No. 6 hook has the wire diameter of a No. 4 two sizes larger; a 3X-fine No. 10 hook has the wire diameter of a No. 13, three sizes smaller. There are practical limits. At present 4X-fine dry-fly hooks are available and border on being too delicate for all but the most skillful, gentle-handed anglers. At the opposite side of the scale is the 4X-stout, a pretty robust cross section for any hook.

Stout hooks sink faster than regular-gauge hooks and therefore do not require lead-wire wrapping, as a regular hook would, to reach the bottom of fast-water streams. Steelhead flies are typical of the stout-wire, short-shank hook. Such hooks are naturally very strong and find favor among fishers seeking striped bass, big pike and bass. The greater bearing surface of a stout hook minimizes slotting and tearing in soft-mouthed fish such as the weakfish, the favorite of many a fly fisherman.

Double Hooks

The controversy about the advantages claimed for the double hook over the single hook goes on. It may never be resolved, especially among salmon fishermen. Double hooks (see Figure 2) remain popular for salmon flies in some regions. They are effective for fish with fleshy mouths, questionable for those with hard jaws such as the striped bass. Keep in mind that we are dealing with fly rods, not casting rods with sufficient backbone to drive a nail into a board. Penetration is the first concern. *More* than twice the force to set a single hook is necessary to set a double hook. Large-sized double hooks, say larger than No. 4, are difficult to set with the fly rod, but a No. 8 or 10 double hook will penetrate quite easily, the additional effort hardly being realized. I do not use double hooks, but that is my personal choice; I may be prejudiced. I would not think of trying to ram home the barbs of a double hook into a striped bass, one of my favorite fly-rod fish.

On the plus side, the double hook has a better sink rate than a single hook, and its extra weight is preferred by many anglers for this reason.

Finish and Plating

Hooks for fly tying are produced from tempered high-carbon steel and, of late, from stainless steel. The carbon-steel hooks are bronzed, tinned or lacquered black to resist corrosion. Stainless-steel hooks require no exterior treatment. Tradition about finishes is just as strong as about shapes, bends and points. The salmon wet fly in Limerick shape is almost always tied on a black hook, and few trout flies are tied on anything but bronzed hooks, except that steelhead flies tied on gold-plated hooks appear with growing frequency. By all means, use the right finished hook. A bronzed hook has a short life in salt water, and a gold-plated hook is so obvious in a delicate dry fly that it seems to negate the effort of attempting to tie a lifelike imitation of an insect.

Bronzed hooks are for freshwater. By far the greatest percentage of hooks is bronzed. Some manufacturers claim they double-bronze hooks for longer life of the point.

Black-lacquered (Japanned) hooks are standard for salmon-fly hooks. The finish is durable in freshwater and resists brackish water moderately well.

Tinned hooks resist saltwater corrosion better than any plating I have found so far. They are superior to either nickel- or gold-plating and, in my opinion, are the best *finish* for saltwater flies. The round-shape Kendall is a good example.

Nickel-plated hooks are bright and withstand salt water fairly well. I have never had one yet that did not checker, then chip, leaving the steel exposed to corrosive attack, although I once favored this finish for brackish-water fishing.

Gold-plated hooks also are bright and excellent for steelhead flies. For resistance to saltwater corrosion I would rate them slightly below nickel-plated hooks.

Stainless-steel hooks are not plated. They are comprised of steel alloyed with chromium or chromium and nickel to make them resistant to corrosion. I have checked several makes and found them to be magnetic, therefore suspect that in many cases their alloys are martensitic, consisting of no more than 2.5 percent nickel (if any) and perhaps 13.0 percent chromium, with carbon content appropriate for the alloy.

The great migrations of inland fly fishers to the sea, the tidal rivers and estuaries, led to the development of hooks that would not corrode in salt water. At first, nickel hooks appeared. They did not corrode, nor did they hold a point or sharpen well. The recent advent of the stainless-steel hook has proved the answer, for it has high hardness and strength without being brittle. The hook sharpens beautifully with a pocket hone, and is virtually impervious to saltwater corrosion.

The subject of hooks for fly tying is broad, taking into account the combinations of shape, shank, gape, spear, barb, point, eye, bend, finish, and cross section. Add the powerful influences of tradition and personal preference, and it becomes vast. Add further the peculiarities and differences among standards, and it becomes still vaster.

Through the years there have been many attempts to modify hooks. Novelty, more than improvement, has resulted. Barbs, for example, have been sliced on the outside, instead of on the inside; there have been twin barbs, one on each side. Gapes have been increased and decreased. Hooks have been enameled the approximate hues of insect's bodies. Cross sections of several odd configurations have been tried. Many other novel treatments have appeared from time to time but, like the others, were weeded out, victims of tradition. Nevertheless, man's efforts to create new and better ways to make a hook and surer ways to hook a fish are to be applauded, for that, really, is what fishing is all about.

Leverage

As mentioned in the paragraphs on Cross Section, a hook, firmly set in a fish's jaw, becomes a cantilevered beam, subject to surprisingly great stresses from both the movement of the fish and the force exerted by the fly rod. Some authors have treated the subject in a worthwhile manner, yet I am continually amazed at the lack of interest many otherwise well-informed anglers—and fly tiers—show when the basic mechanics of hook design arises. As long as the point is sharp and the eye is open for inserting the leader tip, they are satisfied, it seems. No matter how beautifully tied the fly, however, if the hook is poor or worthless, so is the fly. Beautiful feathers never yet held a fish.

A fly of any type is a *moving* lure, and the characteristics of a hook in a moving lure are certainly different from those of a bait hook. The geometry of the bait hook too often has left marked influences on the design of fly hooks, although the modes of hooking are entirely different. To be effective, any fly hook should be capable of hooking and holding a fish striking it from any direction. That is quite an order. It means that, first, the point must penetrate, regardless of the angle of the strike and with the least resistance; second, the barb must follow the point quickly, without enlarging the hole made by the point, and must not back out; third, the shape and spear must exert the least possible leverage on the set point and barb, and, fourth, the line of draft should be parallel to the hook shank, to minimize twist, rotation, and eventual release of the hook by the fish.

One might think that *any* hook made by a reputable maker would possess those properties. That is not so, because not all hooks sold for fly-tying purposes, regardless of how well made they are, have the ideal characteristics for moving lures.

A point having an in (negative) or an out (positive) bend exerts extra resistance upon entry and a shearing effect as it progresses into the tissue of the fish's mouth. The result is easier backing out of the hole, which has become enlarged from the corkscrew effect of the offset. But a point parallel to the shank will enter cleanly, with minimum resistance. The barb can follow without enlarging the hole, seat solidly, and be resistant to backing out.

Offset (bend) is positive, whether left or right, and resists penetration laterally, as an in- or an out-point resists it vertically. Instead of penetrating hard cartilage, it may deflect, particularly if the offset points away from the position of the angler.

A very long spear, which includes both point and barb, responds adversely to lateral force because its length increases the leverage laterally on the point, a tendency to rotate, tear and loosen resulting.

As I see it, the hook made of round wire with a round shape, without offset and having a needle or hollow-ground point and a moderately long spear, is the hook for the serious-minded fly tier. That is the hook on which to spend the time to make a good fly.

Matching Hook and Fly

Tradition influences the makeup of a fly, and it begins with the hook. Some of this tradition is well founded; some isn't. It is too often based more on notion than on fact, like the insistence that a turn-up eye is better than a down eye for dry flies, or that a Limerick hook is the only correct shape for a salmon fly.

From the practical standpoint, there is an advantage in using the best-designed hook for certain fishing conditions. The type of fly, that is, dry fly, wet fly, nymph, streamer; the fish to be caught, whether it has a fleshy or cartilaginous mouth; the nature of the water to be fished, placid, or turbulent, ought to be considered before selecting the hook to match the fly. In some cases, the fly has to match the hook! A dry fly, for example, will become a very wet fly if tied on a heavy-weight wet-fly hook; conversely, a wet fly tied on a fine-wire dry-fly hook is apt to float if cast upstream.

Trout dry-fly hooks are of regular, 1X-, 2X- and 3X-fine wire gauge for minimal weight. They are fished with the lightest of leaders, and their strength properties, considerably below those of heavy-gauge hooks, are compensated for by light tackle. The eyes on regular-gauge hooks may be up or down, tapered or untapered. Those in the 2X- and 3X-fine-wire hooks generally are not tapered. Lengths may be longer or shorter, to suit specific types of flies, as will be discussed later. Offsets are not preferred as a rule, except that in rough, fast-flowing water an offset is sometimes considered *by some,* surer hooking for fish that must strike quickly before the fly has swept past.

Trout wet-fly hooks are of regular, 1X- and 2X-stout-wire gauge, to ensure sinking. The eyes may be tapered, which makes for neater heads perhaps, but the ball eye, having the same wire diameter as the shank, is preferred for its slightly extra weight. As with the dry-fly hook, the lengths may be shorter or longer—1X, 2X, 3X—to meet the requirements of the fly to be tied. Offsets are a matter of preference.

Steelhead wet-fly hooks are in a class by themselves, for they are extra heavy to sink well and stout enough to withstand the power of the vigorous steelhead. Here a fine-wire hook has no place. The short-shank, oversized hook has, for it makes possible the tying of a small fly on a large hook. No wonder many steelheaders refer to their hooks as "irons." They dress size 8 wet flies on 5X-short size-4 and -2 hooks!

Trout nymph hooks are the same as wet-fly hooks, although there have been serious efforts of late to set them apart by slightly altering the length, shape and eye. Actually, suitable nymph hooks exist among any of the well-made standard configurations. Lengths to 6X are sometimes needed to accommodate long bodies simulating some naturals. A solid percentage of fishers prefer offsets, but again that is a matter of choice. The eyes are generally ball eye for weight, turned up or down. Recently developed sickle-shaped hooks are widely arched for tying curved bodies peculiar to some nymphs and larvae. They do not have up or down eyes but, nevertheless, are extremely effective. As such, they attest to the fact that the traditionally right up or down eye is not sacred.

Trout streamer hooks are simply long-shank, wet-fly hooks. They may be up- or down-eyed. Wire gauge depends upon the streamer. If it is to be slim and sparse for use with a fine leader, the regular-gauge wire is preferred; if full bodied and intended to sink quickly, 2X- or 3X-stout wire is better.

Salmon dry-fly hooks are traditionally black, fine wire and loop-eyed. Recent trends have proved that the standard bronzed trout-fly hook serves equally well, although die-hards look upon the bronzed hook as the toy of the heretic and espouse the time-worn theory that the wire end, which is not completely closed in forming the eye, will cut the inner turns of the leader where it is knotted. Well-made hooks are totally closed, and the edges of the wire are not exposed to cut the leader. The loop eye of the classic salmon hook, of course, has no edge in the eye because the return bend of the eye extends down the shank and is sealed as the fly is tied and the head formed. Black or bronzed finishes are optional. Local preferences, although steeped in tradition, may be a good cause for choosing black hooks for specific times.

Salmon wet-fly hooks, perhaps the most rakish and appealing hooks made, are basically of two kinds: light-weight, for low-water fishing and regular weight, usually 2X-stout in the salmon hook vernacular. They feature the traditional loop eye, black finish and Limerick shape. The low-water hook is often 1X-fine gauge and 2X-long. Recent designs have the up or down eye (looped) in bronze finish, which seems to be denting the popularity of the black hook.

The Salmon double hook has a large following in some sections. It is almost always black-finished and has all the qualities of a good salmon hook, including a turned-up eye. It seems to be most popular in the smaller sizes—from 6 to 10—in which the problem of double penetration is minimal

Spinner fly hooks are ring-eyed for attachment to spinners. Up or down eyes naturally cock the fly out of line, and the straight ring eye is more effective as a universal joint. The weight of the hook is not critical. If the hook is sufficiently strong and the point sharp, almost any well made ring-eye hook of proper size will do. Length depends upon the character of the fly to be tied. Offset is standard among most manufacturers, probably because the ring eye is a volume-marketed bait hook. The best grades are available with straight bends, however. Don't save nickels per hundred by buying cheap, ring-eye hooks.

Bass wet-fly hooks are simply trout wet-fly hooks in larger sizes—from 4 to 3/0. Refinements such as tapered eyes and fine wire are unnecessary. A faster sink rate is the only reason to use heavy-gauge wire. A good hook of regular wire will hold any smallmouth or largemouth bass caught with the fly rod. Shank lengths to 3X and 4X are commonly used, depending upon the nature of the fly.

Bass dry-fly hooks are the larger trout-fly hooks in sizes ranging from 10 to 4. The majority are in sizes 6 and 8 to 3X- and 4X-long. Regular wire is preferred over fine wire, for the bass has crushing jaws. Tapered eyes make for neater heads. There is no need for offset.

Bass-streamer hooks are the same as trout-streamer hooks. The size is larger but trout-size streamers are often as effective for bass as they are for trout, because the minnows inhabiting trout and bass waters are frequently of the same size. Ring eyes are versatile, for they are adaptable to spinner couplings.

Pike-and Muskie-streamer hooks must be strong and sharp above all else. Long points for sure penetration and stout wire to resist bending are needed. Because the streamers for these long-billed fellows are the longest of all the freshwater fly-rod lures, the hooks are 4X- and 6X-long. There is a sense of proportion to be considered here, however. Seldom is a hook larger than 3/0 needed to hold any freshwater fish, especially with a fly rod. A slight offset may have its place in these large lures; driving the hook home in these bony-mouthed fish is difficult, no matter what the circumstances, and the corkscrew effect of the offset hook, as commanded by a powerful fly rod, is in order.

Cork- and Hair-body lures run the gamut from miniatures for panfish to large ones, verging on the size of a Ping-Pong ball, for largemouth bass. Smallmouth like the middle-sized bugs, from size 4 to size 1. Regular wire hooks with turned-down eyes are entirely satisfactory. Hump shanks (see Figure 2) are preferred for cork bugs, the hump adding bearing surface which reduces rotation of the hook shank within the body. Offsets are unnecessary, but the hook must be large enough to extend well beyond the diameter of the body.

Saltwater-fly hooks: resistance to saltwater corrosion, strength, and long points are essential. With only one exception—the slight offset for striped bass—straight bends are first choice. The 2X-stout up to size 1/0, in stainless steel or tinned finish, have proved superior. The nickel- and gold-plated finishes just do not survive. The stainless hook has one unresolvable failing: it is so resistant to corrosion that it will not deteriorate in the mouth of a fish that has broken free—something to keep in mind if you are conservation minded. Otherwise, in my book at least, the stainless steel-hook, so far, is unexcelled.

THE TIER'S BENCH

Ideally, the fly tier will have a place set aside for tying and storing materials. A small rigid table and a suitable cabinet with shallow drawers are desirable, as is a draftman's extensible light. Lacking these, the contemplative tier can get by with any household table, ordinary stationery envelopes for storing feathers, hair, body materials and the like, and a table lamp. If the bug bites hard enough, (and it usually does), the tier eventually will manage to find a sequestered spot, probably the spare room, the walls of which he will soon cover with framed examples of his skill, art prints and photographs. When the bug bites, it bites hard!

But a word of caution: The fly tier is too often prey for gimmick makers. People who never tied a fly invent devices for better fly tying. Only the tier himself will know if those devices are really worth their price, unfortunately only after he has discarded many of them.

Few tools specifically designed for fly tying are genuinely needed, regardless of the flies to be tied—from the tiniest midge to the largest saltwater streamer.

Vise

The first consideration is the vise, the costliest tool on the bench. Bargain hunting is futile. If you buy a "cheapie" you'll end up buying a good one to replace it. Any vise worth a second glance should be rugged and of sufficient mass to secure the hook with no apology. Of late, some makes reveal cheapening; the essential parts are of minimal stock and spring when the vise is tightened. Avoid them. Look for solid, machined parts, forged or cast, well finished and of ample dimension. *Some styles are reversible for left-handers.*

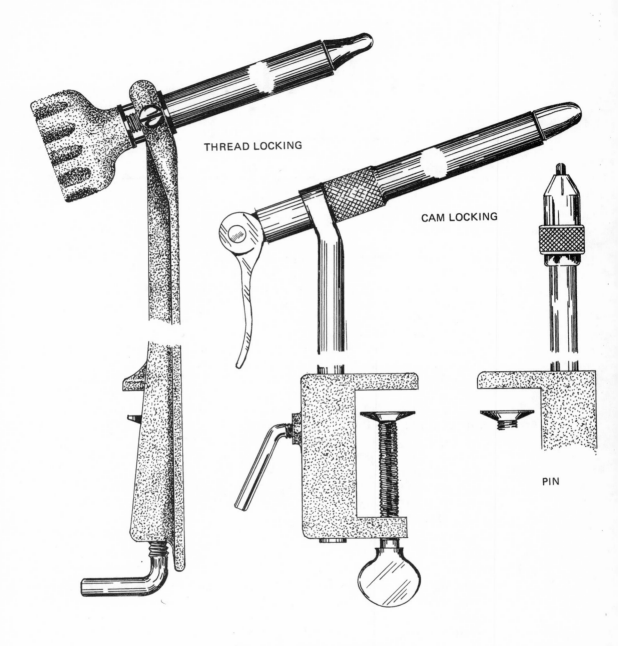

THREAD LOCKING

CAM LOCKING

PIN

FIG. 7. FLY VISES

JEL

A vise consists of three basic parts: the jaw-closing mechanism, the body, and the table clamp (see Figure 7). Jaw-closing mechanisms are of four kinds. The first features a knob-controlled thread, which causes the jaws to retract toward the hand knob and to close as it is turned. The jaws close from the taper in the jaw housing or sleeve. Powerful force is exerted on the jaws, and the hook becomes well clamped.

The second works on the principle of cam rotation. The jaws and jaw housing are similar to those of the first type, but the force from a lever-operated cam retracts the jaws into the closed position. The force is adjustable by a spacer-locking nut, which increases or decreases the angle of contact between the surfaces of the cam and jaw mechanism.

The third is the old jeweler's pin vise. It's shortcomings are many, and at best it is moderately useful for only small work.

The fourth is a simple type, consisting of a thumbscrew or wing-nut clamping action. A threaded wing-nut, lock, near the end of the jaws—too near for good tying—forces the jaws closed. It is good to have for a spare.

Vise bodies that are forged in one piece, ordinarily L- or T-shape in cross section and tapered toward the upper end, are rugged and a comfort to use. They are of fixed height, extending approximately six or eight inches above the table top. Some tiers like adjustable height and prefer, instead of the forged body, a round, vertical shaft that is position-locked by a thumbscrew.

There are several kinds of bases and clamps. The first, standard for one-piece forged bodies, is clamped to the table top by a screw-threaded lever. The second is pedestal-mounted, typical of the vise with a round shaft body, which terminates in a collared socket for permanent attachment to the table top by wood screws. The third accommodates height adjustment of the body shaft. It consists of a U-shaped bracket that slips over the edge of the table, a levered screw for clamping, and a horizontal thumb screw for holding the shaft at the desired height. Some designs require drilling a hole in the table for the protrusion of the shaft when it is lowered.

Trays for holding bottles of cement, spools of thread, small tools, hooks and other small items have been added for convenience. They are fine for those who like them or will learn to; I prefer a simple vise and keep those items the trays were designed to hold some distance from the immediate tying area.

Pedestal types with heavy bases are useful. They require no

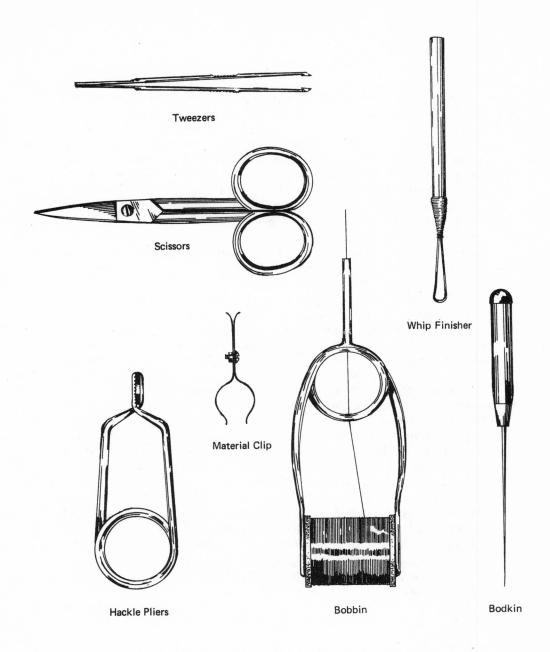

Tweezers

Scissors

Whip Finisher

Material Clip

Hackle Pliers

Bobbin

Bodkin

FIG. 8. OTHER TOOLS

JEL

clamps or direct mounting to the table, and they are portable, a decided advantage.

Swivel heads allow for turning the vise, for viewing the fly from all directions, a handy feature. One type swivels 360 degrees in a socket at the base. Another is hinged at the top and is adjustable vertically only. In any case, the degree of angularity, and the need for revolving the vise, to view better the work in progress, are the choice of the tier. One advantage of the swiveled vise is that it eliminates the need for a mirror to see what occurs on the far side of the fly while it is being tied.

Bobbin

Bobbins are thread holders made in a variety of shapes and sizes, to fit the hand. Their purpose is to hold the spool of thread at a fixed tension below the breaking strength of the thread and to add sufficient weight to hold the tying thread taut but to release it as needed during tying. Tension is usually adjustable in most designs, but fixed in some of the simple wishbone types, which depend upon preset spring pressure in the frame for tension. The majority are wishbone shape; but at least one is L-shaped, having the tension adjustment on the end of the lower leg. Some tiers do not care for the bobbin and use, instead, the old-fashioned rubber button, a friction device hardly more than a soft-faced thumbtack stuck into the edge of the table. Years ago I contrived a gadget that still works perfectly—a small brass clip fastened to the body of my vise. It maintains tension well, is out of the way and requires no preparation or maintenance.

The bobbin may hang from the hook, or it may rest in a bobbin holder as a sort of "third hand" extending on a shaft clamped to the vise body. Many tiers like the bobbin and bobbin holder. I consider both just other objects to strike when tying a fly.

Material Clip

The material clip is one auxiliary that I have found most useful for holding material to be tied later to the left and out of the way. It slips over the jaw housing. The upper edges are rounded and bent outward to receive and hold body materials that must be tied in first but not wound until other tying operations are completed. Although the material clip projects above the top of the vise, it is still an asset. If you are handy with small tools, you can make one easily from a strip of spring brass.

Hackle Pliers

In the beginning hackle pliers are necessary. As the tier becomes accomplished, he will use them less, except for winding hackle on the smallest flies. Pliers have sufficient weight to hold the un-wound hackle below the hook and to keep it from unwinding, when one phase of work must be stopped and another started.

Sizes, spring tension, and jaw faces vary with the manufacturer. The "trout" size is about 2¼ inches long, the "large" size 3 inches. One style has a once-around, circular loop bent in the spring frame for additional tension. Rubber tubing on the grips prevents slipping in the hand. The shape and surfaces of the jaw faces are important. Some jaws have interlocking notches for holding hackle feathers and the like. Sharp notches may cut the end of the hackle quill, usually during the last turn or two of winding the hackle: sometimes a near disaster. One type of pliers features one rubber-faced and one notched jaw, a good combination that prevents slippage without cutting fiber and quill. Another type has both jaws faced with rubber. But pliers are inexpensive; try several kinds until you find the one that suits your hand and style of tying. One works well for one tier but not for another.

Scissors

Good scissors are essential for good fly tying. Have one pair fine enough for close trimming in tight spots and another for coarse work that soon would spring the blades of the fine scissors. Scissors that do not close well and cut cleanly are worthless. Manicure and pedicure scissors of the best grade are satisfactory, provided they are well fitted, are of good steel, and are sharply ground. The average dime-store variety just does not qualify. Those sold by fly-material suppliers are the best in the long run, because they have straight, stepped-down, ground points for precise cutting.

Small diagonal wire cutters are necessary for cutting materials too coarse for scissors—wing quills, monofilament, tail feathers, and those items that will spring the blades of the best scissors in a hurry. Pedicure cutters with angular tips are good for all but the coarsest materials.

Tweezers

You will need tweezers for sorting, plucking feathers, removing small items from corners, and otherwise handling materials too small to be manipulated by hand. Buy good ones, with angular jaws for plucking. As with scissors, cheap ones are next to worthless, for they spring under force and close only partially, if at all.

Bodkin

The uses for the bodkin (dubbing needle) are many: roughing fur bodies, separating the fibers of wing quills into sections for tying, ferreting out hackle whisks that have been tied over, clearing the hook eye of cement or varnish, and applying cement to the head knot. A large sewing needle makes an excellent bodkin for most purposes. Inserted into the end of a slender plastic shaft, the tip of a ball-point pen, for example, it becomes one of the most-used tools on the table. Heat the large end of the needle, and burn a hole in the tip of the shaft. Wrap the end of the needle with fine working thread, and cement it. When the cement is tacky, insert the needle into the hole, and seal the tip with another drop of cement.

A shoemaker's needle is good for a rigid dubbing needle, and a small screwdriver ground to a slender, pointed tip is about the closest approach to a manufactured bodkin that there is.

Mirror

A mirror for viewing the far side of the fly being tied has found favor among some tiers. It is not really needed, however, if the vise is equipped with a swivel base that permits viewing the work from all directions. A mirror may be confusing when reflecting far and near motion. I have found it to be in the way, despite the adjustable arm which is clamped to the shaft of the vise.

Whip Finisher

The head of a fly must not unwind. It is foolish to take the trouble of tying a good fly then neglect to finish the head properly with a secure knot. The half hitch is suitable for temporarily holding the winding thread between phases of tying but certainly is not dependable as a head knot. Both the half hitch and jam knot depend upon saturation of the thread by cement or varnish for holding. The whip finish, if properly tied, will not unravel; if merely touched with the cement or varnish, it will last the life of the fly.

Mechanical whip finishers are on the market, but I prefer to make my own. It works successfully on all sizes of flies, is light and compact and is free of wire extensions and gadgets to manipulate. Many times I have met the challenge to prove that it will form secure heads on flies as small as size 20.

A whip knot is a wrapped-over knot; that is, the end of the tying thread is pulled under several turns wrapped around it. Essentially a loop of thread will do the job. For large flies one needs nothing else. A better tool is that same loop of thread fastened to a round, thin shaft, a meat skewer or a 4-inch length of stiff, insulated electric wire. Old, discarded manicure sets sometimes contain small handles that can be reworked for the purpose. Make two while you are at it; one having the loop of fine thread about ½ inch in length, the other having the loop of coarser thread (the smaller the better) about 1 inch. Bind the ends of the loop to the handle with winding thread, and coat with cement or lacquer.

Tying the whip finish is easy. After completing the head winding, hold the whip finisher in the left hand over the top of the fly, the loop resting on the head. Wind four turns around the loop, cut the thread, leaving about 4 inches to pass through the loop. Press on the windings with the left forefinger to keep them tight, and pass the tip of the thread through the loop. The whip finisher will be dangling, but don't worry about that. Grasp the tip of the thread with the right hand, the handle of the whip finisher with the left. Pull the loop under the windings, and trim off the tail of the thread. Cement or varnish the head.

Razor Blades

The single-edge razor blade is the best, the easiest obtained, the sharpest, and the cheapest of all thread-cutting tools. It seems a waste of effort to try to find a substitute. A blade reserved for cutting the tying thread will last a long time. When it becomes dull, throw it away.

FLY NOMENCLATURE

Compared with the salmon fly, trout flies and bass flies have few parts: tail, body, ribbing, hackle, wings, and sometimes jungle-cock shoulders. Many successful patterns consist only of tail, body, and hackle; but the fully dressed salmon fly stands apart, for it has nearly two dozen parts. Tradition held them inviolable by name and order until some years ago, when common sense on the parts of both the fly tier and the angler substituted available materials for those rare and costly ones and transcended much of that tradition.

Doubtless, the classic salmon fly was fit for a king; it became the object of contrived complication, its patterns shrouded in secrecy, often at the king's urging, so history tells. However, for sheer beauty, the product of painstaking selection and arrangement of fibers and sections from the crests, tippets, breast feathers, wing quills, and herled plumes of brilliant birds, and the dubbing of furs from no less than the ermine and mink, the dressing of the salmon fly remains one of the finest of the fine arts, bar none.

The classic salmon fly includes the full spectrum of fly parts. It is well to know it even though the average tier seldom is concerned with more than seven or eight of the parts. Starting from the end of the shank and in the order they appear these parts are:

> TAG: Usually tinsel tied on directly above the rear part of the barb; in some patterns it extends slightly down the curvature of the hook.
> TIP: Floss or tinsel tied immediately in front of the tag, *under* the tail fibers in salmon flies but usually *around* them in trout flies.
> TAIL: Any of various feather or hair whisks projecting

33

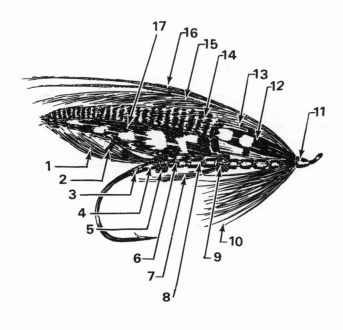

1. Tail
2. Tail Topping
3. Tag
4. Tip
5. Butt
6. Tinsel Ribbing
7. Trailer
8. Body
9. Center Joint (Ruff)
10. Hackle
11. Head
12. Cheek
13. Shoulder
14. Upper Wing
15. Crest (Topping)
16. Horns
17. Under Wing

FIG. 9. PARTS OF A FLY

JEL

beyond the curve of the hook; it may slant up or down or project straight, according to the pattern and type of fly.

TAIL TOPPING: The topmost fibers of the tail; most often of contrasting color, barring and shorter than the tail fibers. Fibers from the golden pheasant, Amherst pheasant, black-barred woodduck are good examples.

BUTT: Peacock herl, ostrich herl, sometimes chenille, or a trimmed hackle feather, tied in directly above the hook point.

AFT BODY: The rear half of the body proper; approximately one half the length of the shank and separated from the forebody by the center joint, which is similar to the butt; often ribbed with tinsel or other contrasting material.

AFT-BODY RIBBING: Tinsel or other material spiralled between the butt and the center joint.

TRAILER: Feather fibers tied on the top and bottom of the body at mid-length immediately behind the center joint. Pheasant crests are the most called for, although hackle whisks and duck-throat fibers are specified for some patterns.

CENTER JOINT (RUFF): The same material as the butt and tied at the center of the body.

FOREBODY: The half body between the center joint and the base of the wing; may or may not be the same color or material as the aft body.

FOREBODY RIBBING: Similar to the aft-body ribbing; may be of a different color.

HACKLE: One or more kinds of feathers, hair, nylon, or fur attached in a bunch at the throat of a fly, as in the wet fly; wound vertically as in the typical dry fly and some wet flies; wound horizontally as in the parachute fly, or spirally up the body as in the palmer type of fly. Combinations of two colors and types to produce mottling are common. Strips of Mylar, lengths of rubber bands, and shreds of wool are specified for certain patterns.

> *Backing (shoulder) hackle:* The principal hackle tied behind the eye of the hook; in some patterns it may be palmered or started near the tag of the fly and wound

spirally up the body, ending with two or three turns at the front of the body.

Beard hackle: The barbules of a hackle feather or the fibers from a breast feather bunched together and tied at the throat of the fly; also of the barbules of a hackle wound around the hook and gathered by windings at the throat.

Collar hackle: Occupies the space immediately behind the head of the fly; when used, it is different in color and markings from backing hackle in front of which it is tied.

Palmer hackle: Wound spirally up the body and is spaced to let the color and texture of the body show through; tied tip first at the rear of the body and spiralled toward the front.

Parachute hackle: Tied in the horizontal plane around the base of the wings; gives the dry fly a low silhouette and supports the fly weight by means of the barbules, most of which rest upon the water surface.

Reverse hackle: Tied with the bright (convex) side of the feather facing the rear, so that the barbules slant forward, better flotation and silhouette resulting, so claim many dry-fly fishers.

Split (stripped) hackle: Has all the barbules removed from one side of the feather to reduce the bulk of the winding; frequently tied in pairs of contrasting hues, as in some trout and salmon wet flies, to produce multicolored effects.

WING: Fibers from the body plumage or wing feathers of a bird, hackle (whisks or whole feathers), strands of nylon and similar whisks extending from behind the eye of the hook approximately vertically (as in the dry fly) or slanted horizontally (as in the wet fly). This term is appropriate for the wings of dry flies and wet flies that resemble natural insects but is hardly appropriate when applied to the hair and feather streamers, some three and four inches long, tied to represent minnows.

Closed wings: Slant over the body of the fly in a vertical plane, in typical wet-fly fashion, the inner surfaces together.

Cocked wings: Upright and divided, typical of the traditional dry fly. Cocked forward wings slant forward of the hook eye, a favorite type some years ago.

Cut wings: Hackle feathers or wing-quill sections that have been shaped with scissors, clippers, or fly tier's wing cutters; a recent favorite but many years old.

Dee wings: Long, narrow, slightly divided and tied in the horizontal plane; a low-water salmon-fly type.

Divided wings: Upright, as in the dry fly, or slanted over the body, as in the wet fly. If made of wing-quill fibers, the wings are tied with the curvature outward; earlier standards required that the wings have double-fiber layers, two per wing.

Down wings: Flat (horizontal) and slanting over the fly body to represent the natural position of the roof-like wings of the caddisfly; sometimes tied tip first for easier handling, but the fibers invariably splay.

Fan wings: Breast feathers tied with the outer (curved) sides back to back. Only practical for dry flies.

Feather wings: A devious term that can mean the wings formed from the fiber sections cut from any wing quills or, more appropriately, two whole breast or flank feathers tied vertically over the fly body.

Flat wings: Tied horizontally lengthwise, one on top of the other, to simulate the wings of the stonefly.

Forward wings: Divided and similar to cocked wings but slant further beyond the eye of the hook.

Hackle wings: Consist of the barbules of a hackle feather tied on in a bunch, the same effect being attained by winding the hackle, then trimming the bottom with scissors.

Hackle-tip wings: The tipmost part of the hackle or the whole smaller feathers found at the top of the cape. Versatile, the hackle tip is tied as a spent wing, sail wing, vibrator, down, flat, or closed wing.

Hair wings: Made of hair from any of the many animal skins used in fly tying. Position, angle and bulk are determined by the type of fly.

Inner wings: In some fancy flies, are the inside layers over which the outer wings are tied, a veiled effect resulting, when the outer wing is sparsely fibered.

Married-feather wings: Sections cut from two or more dissimilar feathers, the edge barbules of which are joined by stroking the sections between the thumb and forefinger.

Matched wings: Wing feathers that have equal texture, shape, color and markings.

Mixed wings: Combinations of several hackle feathers or sections of body plumage, feather fibers or hair, and the like, to create laminate effects or indistinct blends.

Outer wings: Sparse fiber wings tied over the inner wings, to "veil" or change the appearance of the inner wing, giving the whole an alive appearance from the opening and closing of the outer wing, when the fly is twitched through the water.

Reverse wings: Tied tip first, the object to minimize the bulk where the wings are tied to the hook; the butts are trimmed to suit. Used in down-wing wet flies.

Rolled wings: Made by rubbing breast or flank plumage between the palms of the hands, to straighten the natural lay of the feather. No matching is necessary because the fibers are tied like hair. Most effective for dry and wet flies; some tiers like to separate the fibers with tying thread into two parts, to form divided wings.

Sail wings: Single hackle-tip feathers tied upright. Offering little air resistance, the sail wing settles lightly on the water and is well adapted to sparse, lightly-hackled dry flies.

Side wings: Narrow, and short and fastened along the side of the body like the wings on caddis pupae.

Single wings: Paired wings having a single layer of fibers in each; most trout-fly wings are of this sort (see "divided wings").

Spent wings: Rest outstretched on the water surface and represent the wings of spent female mayflies which have oviposited. Hackle tips are preferred, for they are less dense than the fibers from a wing feather and are more easily tied.

Spey wings: Long, narrow strips of mallard tied down-wing style; a low-water salmon-fly type.

Strip wings: Similar to married feather wings, but the barbules along the edges are not joined; strip wings are easier to tie, yet none of the banded effect is lost.

Under wing: The lower fibers or hair in a two-color or two-layered wing.

Upper wing: The upper fibers or hair in a two-color or two-layered wing.

Upright wings: Vertical wings, as in the typical dry fly.

Veil: An outer feather covering the wing proper; tied sparse of fine-fibered breast and side plumage.

Vibrator wings: Hackle tips that project forward on a wet fly, their purpose to quiver from the flow of water and bend back intermittently during the retrieve.

TOPPING: The top covering, generally pheasant crest or peacock sword or herl placed over the wing proper; often two crests tied on each side of the wing and extending along its top edge.

HORNS: Two contrasting feather fibers placed over the wing(s) or topping. Brown mallard and woodduck are popular as are single fibers from pheasant and turkey tails.

SHOULDER: Pheasant tippet, jungle cock eye-feather, woodduck breast or flank feather or similar plumage tied next to the wing. Triangular tippets make good imitations of minnows' gills.

CHEEK: The outermost section of the wing placed over the shoulder, often for gill effect in streamer flies.

HEAD: The closeout portion of the fly immediately behind the hook eye. Sufficient space should be allowed for securing the last part tied: the whip knot. In salmon flies the head is often finished with peacock herl or chenille.

MATERIALS

Where tradition once dictated the use of a fiber or two from a rare bird to lend a certain claimed attractiveness to a fly, common sense bolstered by ingenuity now has set a new trend in thinking about what is really necessary in the makeup of a fly. It is timely that regulations prohibiting import and export of certain bird and animal skins were enacted in recent years. For centuries the clamor by furriers, milliners and, yes, fly tiers, for exotic bird skins and animal hides has caused many creatures to suffer near extinction. There was much criticism of those governments limiting or even halting the trade in feathers and fur as being purely political and the means of price fixing. Regardless of whether the criticism is justified, out of these limitations has come the realization, at least to a good many fly tiers, that maybe the prescribed four hairs from the belly of an ape, so essential for the tails of the genuine low-water Mugwump, are not so essential after all. One might wonder what those tails might have been in the first place, had not some enterprising fellow had an ape to pluck them from; the chances are good, in my humble opinion, that they very well may have been four, five, even six or more hairs or fibers from any other critter, dead, mounted, or just passing by. The concoction of a genuine, original fly pattern is a curious thing! I know only too well: I've been at it for nearly 50 years.

Tying Thread

Tying threads are spooled nylon and silk having high strength for their diameter. Nylon is waterproof, resists weather and use well, does not fade quickly, and is slightly elastic. Silk, the original thread for fly tying, and still preferred by some tiers, is not so weather resistant as nylon and has lower breaking strength, is not

41

elastic, but ties well. For extremely fine work it remains superior to nylon in the hands of a skillful tier.

Sizes range from .002- to .008-inch diameter and even larger. The real need for thread larger than .005 inch is rare. The table compares thread size with the corresponding hook size. Relative breaking strength is not shown because it doesn't mean very much. The finest thread that will survive tying is the best. Contrary to some opinions, the fine threads hold materials more firmly than do the coarse threads and with less tendency to rotate them out of position. The heads are smaller and neater, lending the flies a better overall appearance. Tiers new at the game are cautious about tying with thread they think may break too easily, but they soon see the advantage of using the finer threads as their skills improve.

SIZE	DIAMETER (INCHES)	HOOK SIZE
7/0	.002	20–28
6/0	.003	14–20
5/0	.004	6–14
4/0	.005	1/0–6
3/0	.006	1/0 and larger

Several flat threads are available. They are excellent for nymphs, and many tiers use them regularly because they tie well and reduce bulk. Prewaxed threads also are available and have found wide acceptance. Colors range from white through black, and some sizes are multicolored. Cotton has no use in tying thread. In the long run, nylon is the solid choice for nearly every purpose.

The use of nylon monofilament as tying thread began a few years ago. The diameter is very fine, about .004 inch, and the thread ties well. It has a tendency to be slightly springy, but after tying a few flies with it the tier will see its values. Being virtually transparent, it is perfect for counterwinding naturally weak bodies such as peacock herl, ostrich herl, and some quill bodies. I have used it for counterwinding tubular Mylar bodies on saltwater flies and streamers.

Some tiers have a naturally light touch, others develop it; still others don't have it, never acquire it, and must resort to heavier thread. Regardless, learn to minimize the number of turns necessary for securing the materials to the hook and winding between operations. Excessive winding does not contribute to the strength of the fly; it merely makes it bulky, an objectionable by-product of overdoing a good thing. When you have determined the finest thread that suits your mode of tying—and only you can do that —continue to use that thread. After tying several dozen flies, try a smaller size thread. If it works well, adopt it as your standard for flies of comparable size.

Wax

Waxing tying thread is desirable for two reasons: It makes the thread adhesive so it will stay in place, and fur dubbing sticks to it. Most of the cake wax sold by supply houses is good, having sufficient resin to treat the thread thoroughly. Shoemaker's wax is excellent, although too tacky for fine work.

There are many recipes for making tier's wax, but they are hardly worth the effort when such good waxes are available for pennies from firms catering to the fly tier. Some tiers have used ordinary furniture and automobile waxes, others varnish, the excess of which they remove with a cloth.

I still like to wax the thread I use—a few feet at a time —stroking the thread another time or two when dubbing fur bodies.

Cements, Varnishes, Lacquers

The unwinding of the head knot is best prevented by a small amount of cement, varnish, or lacquer. Cements are probably more popular for finishing heads than are varnishes, although the latter have much to be said for them. All types of head finishes have undergone changes in recent years, resulting in increased resistance to water absorption.

For finishing the heads of small flies, any dependable cement, varnish, or one of several lacquers will do nicely. The greatest source of permanence in the head of a fly is traceable to the head knot itself, not to the coating applied to it. Not that a good penetrating sealant is unnecessary; it is *added* assurance that the final tying operation—the knot—will not unwind.

To penetrate well, a cement, lacquer, or varnish must be thin. Otherwise, they will just coat the surface. The ideal sealant will penetrate *and* coat. The tier will have to determine the proper consistency from experience, by thinning the solution, as needed, with the right thinner. Nitrate and toluene are bases for several cements produced today, and they should be thinned only with appropriate thinners. Don't second-guess the maker and the supplier by assuming any thinner will work. There is no gain, economically or otherwise.

Cements are water-clear or black. Water-clear is probably preferred for small flies; the black adds eye appeal to larger flies.

Bakelite resin varnishes are excellent and the choice of countless tiers, for penetration and slower drying. I believe they adhere to waxed thread better than do cements, forming a solid seal. Bakelite resin is said to retain some elasticity and to resist chipping. The surface, especially after a second coat, is glossy and resists salt water to boot. Again, use only the specified thinner. The color of the varnish is amber. Applied to yellow, olive, and white tying threads, it adds natural translucency to the head of a fly—even a small one.

Celluloid enamels are gaining favor, particularly for finishing the heads of larger flies more suitable for "glossing" than those of small flies. Salmon flies are a good example. Celluloid enamel is good for coating the body of a silk-body streamer with tinsel ribbing. Salt water has the penchant for changing the color of silk and tarnishing, if not destroying, tinsel. Two coats of clear celluloid enamel will lessen that reaction. Colors range from white to black.

Lacquers include fingernail polish, which many tiers use successfully. Thinned with polish thinner, it is suitable for trout flies, although some scoff at the idea. A bottle of polish and one of thinner are available in all five-and-dime stores for about one dollar. In addition to the clear, colors include bizarre hues that may interest some tiers. Clear is the choice for most purposes.

Remember, the final head knot determines whether the head windings will or will not unwind. I know two competent tiers who use no sealant at all; they whip-knot the head and depend on it!

Suppliers bottle varnishes, cements and thinners in 1-ounce and pint sizes. The 1-ounce size is right for the bench. Because all are air drying they should be sealed. Keep the cap screwed on tightly. When tying, this is an inconvenience, and one way to offset it is to remove the paper sealing gasket in the cap, puncture it with a pointed tool slightly larger than the dubbing needle you will use to apply the sealant, then replace the gasket on the mouth of the bottle. Withdrawing the dubbing needle through the hole in the gasket removes excess cement.

Caution!! The described solutions contain allergens for some individuals. Consider this if you are sensitive to certain chemical compounds. One of my fishing buddies is an allergenic, and he likes to tie flies. For years he hunted for a cement, lacquer, varnish—anything that would seal the heads of flies and not cause his face to swell up like a blimp. He never did and finally quit the search. Today he ties one of the sweetest striper streamers in the country, held together with waxed thread and nothing else!

Cleaners, Dyes

Bird and animal skins for the tier are nearly always cleaned at the source of supply before being packaged and stored—another good reason for buying from reputable concerns. Hunters' trophies—ducks and pheasants, which are so richly feathered, the choice rooster and hen necks not easily come by these days and maybe a bucktail or two have to be cleaned at home. Hot water and kitchen soap powder will do well. Continue washing and rinsing until the material is free of dirt and oil. Squeeze dry between towels, then dip in a cleaning solution, and rinse several times. With luck, bird skins will not be so badly matted with blood that they cannot be plucked and the feathers stored in small cardboard boxes for final sorting and labeling.

Supply houses know best how to dye materials, and I suggest that you purchase whatever dyed materials you need from them. But, if you want to dye materials at home, be prepared for disappointments until you have struggled with a few capes, tails and feathers. Years ago a *true* red and a *bright* yellow were hard to find. Both eluded the dyer using a kitchen pot and a packet of dye crystals. I finally settled for picric acid for the yellow, because the yellow was reproducible; but picric acid dyes not only the materials to be dyed but the dyer as well. I always had trouble getting red to turn out red. With modern dyes, however, about every color, hue, and shade are attainable. The directions that are printed on the package are easy to follow, and with a little care in handling the materials to be dyed good results can be expected, after a few tries. However, I still believe it is hard to beat a man at his own game, and I buy items that must be dyed from a supplier on whom I can rely.

If your wife is amenable, you might wheedle her into parting with a few kitchen items such as porcelain-lined trays, soup spoons, tongs, and the like. You'll need two trays, one for soaking the materials before putting them in the dye bath, the other for the dye bath itself. Tinned pans are not recommended, nor are plain steel ones; their surfaces may react unfavorably to the dye solution. Use the porcelain-lined or stainless pans. Add stainless soup spoons and tongs, an ordinary conical sieve for straining rinse water from loose feathers, a stack of newspapers, and you are ready for business.

Plan ahead to dye similar materials. Rooster necks and hen necks can be dyed together. Duck and goose plumage and that of other water fowl can be dyed together as well. But do not mix the two if you expect uniformity of color. Water fowl naturally have more oil in their makeup than do poultry and upland fowl. Pheasants are more like poultry in that respect, and their feathers can be dyed along with the chicken variety.

If capes, skins, wings, and other materials are not thoroughly cleaned, you will waste time trying to get good dye results. Be sure to soak them thoroughly in plain kitchen detergent or soap powder. Rinse them well before soaking them in the dye solution. Keep the material damp until it is dyed.

Add the dye crystals to the water after it has boiled. The high temperature will dissolve the dye fast. A "fixer," to make the color fast, is necessary. Vinegar, which contains acetic acid, is as good as any other. Try two tablespoons for a starter. Let the water cool, or add cold water to the mix until it is finger hot.

Immerse the materials (all of one kind) in the dye bath, and keep circulating them until the right hue appears on the feathers. This is the nub of it all. If you have put too many dye crystals in the bath, the hue may be too dark; it is better to start with a pale hue and to bring it up to full tone by adding dye crystals.

As soon as the material is the right hue, remove it from the bath, and rinse it well. Nothing is better than the kitchen sink, if you can convince your wife. Remember, she has to *try* to pick up the fluff and down you leave in strange places with the vacuum cleaner, and removing the pink, olive, dun and insect-green stains in the bottom of the sink may not be the joys of her day, regardless of her usually good humor.

Squeeze the material dry. Hackle capes squeeze well between several layers of newspaper. Lay them out, skin side down, on dry newspaper to dry thoroughly. Loose feathers should be rinsed in the sieve and also placed between the folds of newspaper to dry. If the hues appear too light, repeat the dye process, depending upon time to correct the lightness of the material. If necessary, add more dye crystals; but be careful! Dye works fast the second time around. Use the tongs frequently to remove the material for checking the depth of color.

Unfortunately, even with the best of care through the entire process, you will probably be surprised with the results. Material when wet appears several hues darker than when dry. But that is one of the natural problems you must expect until you become an old hand at the game—and a solid reason for buying materials already dyed by professionals who know the ingredients of time, mix and pre- and post-treatments.

Skin shrivels and becomes brittle after being dyed, which is particularly objectionable in hackle capes. Mix a little glycerine with water, and soak the dyed necks until the skin is pliant; dry, and place them separately in plastic bags until needed.

Bucktails, calf tails, squirrel tails, and the like are treated in the same way. Cleaning and soaking them well are the first considerations. Remove them occasionally from the dye bath, to check the color depth.

Bleaches

Bleaching can be as tricky as dyeing, but for different reasons. Household Clorox and hydrogen peroxide are the accepted standard solutions for dissolving the flues from peacock herl and the trimmed stems of hackles to be used for quill bodies. Hydrogen peroxide makes skin brittle as it bleaches and can be a harmful solution if not checked frequently. Clorox, on the other hand, is less embrittling and is the better choice. A half-and-half solution, half Clorox and half water, is adequate to bleach peacock-eye quills and to dissolve the greenish-metallic flues on the edges. A good arrester of the bleaching action is warm water to which baking soda has been added. The same water-and-glycerine combination used to restore the pliancy of hackle necks is equally good for restoring the flexibility of quills for bodies. A good example is the hackle stem of a brown hackle, the stubble of which, after cutting, is subjected to the Clorox treatment and dissolved. Normally, the quill would be too brittle to use, but, once soaked in the glycerine-water mix, it will return to its natural flexibility.

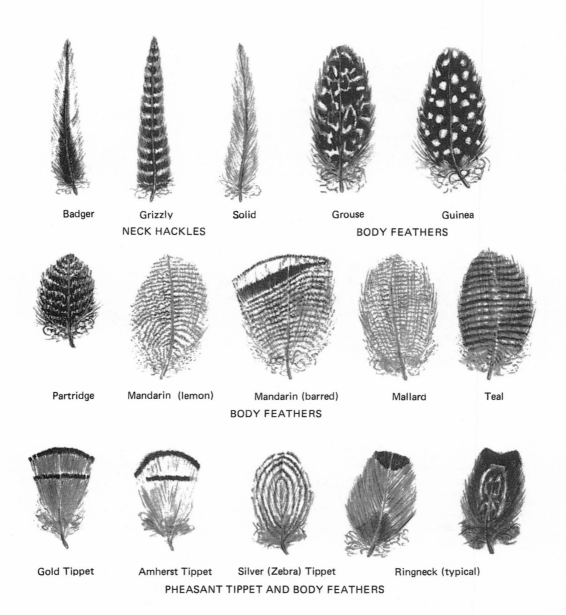

Badger   Grizzly   Solid   Grouse   Guinea

NECK HACKLES   BODY FEATHERS

Partridge   Mandarin (lemon)   Mandarin (barred)   Mallard   Teal

BODY FEATHERS

Gold Tippet   Amherst Tippet   Silver (Zebra) Tippet   Ringneck (typical)

PHEASANT TIPPET AND BODY FEATHERS

FIG. 10. BASIC HACKLE AND BODY FEATHERS

JEL

Hackle

In the fly-tying vernacular, hackle is a major subject about which there has been, is, and likely always will be, profound disagreement on its every facet, from color to quality—even the proper name for the bird from which it is plucked or skinned. The term "hackle" is generally accepted to mean the whisks forming the ruff behind the eye of the hook. But hackle is also wound around the body of the fly for many patterns, is bunched at the throat of the fly and even appears in separate sections in the makeup of others. Many anglers but fewer tiers believe that hackle must be a neck feather from a cock or a hen chicken. That is not so. Hackle can be the fibers from any bird, the hair from any animal, or the equivalent from man-made materials.

To the trouter, hackle represents the six legs of an insect. To the basser it may represent the movement of gills on a streamer fly. Either is correct, although a six-legged dry fly probably will not float, and the gill movement imparted by shoulder hackle on a streamer is debatable. But the opening and closing of hackle around the body of a fly can change the overall hue, from the fish's point of view.

Hackle is ample on dry flies, to make them float, and this will be discussed at length later, for other values must be considered. It is sparse on wet flies, to give them lifelike swimming action like that of the natural insect, crustacean, and minnow they purportedly imitate, and to make them sink rapidly.

Body Hackle

Nearly any bird plumage—wing, body, or tail—of appropriate texture and size is suitable for wet-fly hackle. Examples are breast and throat feathers, small feathers on the outer sides of wings, rump feathers, crests, and tippets. Excellent mottling and barring, not available in ordinary gamecock, rooster, and hen hackles are found in such feathers; yet surprisingly few tiers use them to full advantage, preferring, instead, to paw through piles of poultry necks in search of barrings, and markings they never will find, simply because chickens do not grow hackles that way.

The following list includes both body and neck feathers suitable for hackling wet flies and some dry flies, the latter requiring special techniques to be described later. This list by no means includes all body feathers; it just gives you an idea of the *kinds* of feathers that are good wet-fly hackle, hardly making a dent in the piles of body feathers one could wade through. There is no end in sight either—so don't despair if you have no snipe feathers to hackle a special pattern. There are others just as "snipey," and if you do not know what they are you will find out sooner or later. That's half the fun of the game.

BLACK: crow, black Leghorns, black Minorca hen chickens, blackbird

BLUE DUN: coot and partridge

BROWN: Rhode Island Red hen chickens, partridge, golden pheasant

BUFF: partridge, buff Leghorn hen, chickens, snipe

CINNAMON: partridge, blue chatterer

DEEP RED: golden pheasant, Amherst pheasant, ring-necked pheasant

GOLDEN YELLOW: golden pheasant, Amherst pheasant

GRAY BARRED: gray mallard, teal (darker than mallard), other ducks in lesser amounts

IRON BLUE: starling, coot

METALLIC BLUE: peacock, Amherst pheasant

METALLIC GREEN: peacock, golden pheasant, Amherst pheasant, some ducks (but you will have to look for the feathers on ducks)

METALLIC PURPLISH BLUE: starling

POLKA DOT: guinea (white dots on gray to black)

WHITE TO CREAM: white Leghorn hen chickens, Amherst pheasant, wild and domestic ducks, geese

WHITE-BLACK BARRED: Ripon (zebra) pheasant, light irregular markings

Cock Hackle

With few exceptions, dry-fly hackle comes from the neck and cape feathers of gamecocks and roosters, especially the former. Domestic roosters are sometimes as good, if they have the much-sought narrow, glossy, stiff hackle typical of the gamecock. As a rule, they tend to longer-fibered, webbier hackle. However, there is no fixed level for evaluation. Much depends upon the individual bird, the breed, and time of year the hackle is plucked. One of the finest capes I ever had once glistened on a sassy, strutting

Rhode Island Red rooster. As I recall, that cape was in my materials chest for many years. I used the hackles sparingly, for they were magnificent, the perfect mahogany red-brown for the Coachman, and the spades made exceptional tails; four fibers would make the fly bounce when it was dropped on the table top. I have paid premium prices for imported necks that were of poorer quality, not one having the color or the texture of the hackles from that Rhode Island Red. Perhaps the only other hackle that might have been equal to the Red's belonged to an old Rajah of a grizzly that I saw nestled against the weatherboarding of one of the houses at the site of the restored Pilgrim Village in Plymouth. There he sat, his entourage of hens peacefully napping nearby; then, as if the town crier, he stretched upright, surveyed his environs, and emitted a hoarse, jerky squawk, not at all like a rooster's crow, and fanned a span of dusty-silver hackles the size of a kitchen colander. What a cascade of translucent, ice-bright dry-fly hackle that fell back into place after that rusty bray! I could not reach the old fellow, but my fingers itched to snatch a few 12s and 14s from his feathered mane.

Despite the standards commonly set for grading a dry-fly neck, some erroneous, there are two values that are often overlooked: diameter of the fiber and the overall luster. A hackle with whisks 2 or 3 times the diameter of those on a so-called top-notch cape would be ideal. There is none, but keep looking. One day you may find a freak neck and be fortunate.

Thick-fibered, lustrous hackle is firm and springy. A few turns of it on a dry fly are superior to 6 or 7 turns of fine, weak hackle, regardless of how rare or costly it may be. Even though the barnyard rooster (like my Rhode Island Red) has generally oversized hackle, don't be fooled into rejecting it just for that reason. Trimmed to size, it is even better, although hordes of anglers will disagree! Another feature which I believe is overemphasized is the absence of web down the center along the stem. Some excellent hackle has this slight web and, if the fibers are lustrous and of ample thickness, is superior to much of the so-called "better" hackle having no web at all. The web allows for bending quite like a spring-loaded beam, a definite advantage in supporting the weight of the dry fly.

By color, natural cock hackles may be described as solids and mixed. The following list includes most available cock necks and some "freak" necks that appear sporadically on suppliers' lists.

Solid Hues

WHITE: Rarely pure white, usually ranging from near white through ivory.

CREAM: White, chosen for its creamy hue.

PALE GINGER: An indefinite hue generally described as "between cream and buff."

GINGER: Also an indefinite hue, likened to natural leather.

DARK GINGER: Light brown with a touch of natural red.

BROWN: Hard to define, although it is one of the common colors called for in fly tying. It falls between dark ginger and dark brown and varies from bird to bird.

DARK BROWN: Rich, dark, reddish brown (Rhode Island Red), usually referred to as "Coachman brown" for its mahogany tones.

BLACK: A near, but not true, black.

Mixed Hues

BADGER: Ivory to white, with a black stripe along the stem of the feather.

FURNACE: Often called Cock-y Bondhu. A true furnace hackle is brown with a black stripe along the stem of the feather. Some authorities claim the Cock-y Bondhu differs from furnace in having black tips; others disagree, considering the two to be the same. I have found both on the same neck. The quality is seldom good, and the black center that evolves from winding can be simulated with a trimmed black hackle anyway.

DARK GRIZZLY: A gray with dark-gray cross barring.

LIGHT GRIZZLY: Barred like dark grizzly and often called "chinchilla" or "salt and pepper."

RED GRIZZLY: Barred like other grizzly but on a brown background; alias cree.

GINGER VARIANT: Pale to dark ginger with whitish barring.

HONEY DUN: Honey color with darker, often grayish, areas along the stem; if of darker hue, generally called "brassy dun," another nonspecific hue.

FREAKS: Furnace and badger are freaks that are available most of the time. There are many others: Nairobi, dun badger, fiery-brown mixtures, multivariants, duns, blue duns, bronze and rusty duns, olive and iron-blue duns, all rather scarce and difficult to duplicate. Most can be equaled by tying two ordinary hackles having colors and markings that, when blended, produce the same tonality as the freaks.

VARIANT: Any hackle feather having irregular barrings or spots, which can be of many hues. Without a modifier the term is indefinite.

Dyed Hues

When dyed, any solid or mixed-hue hackle becomes entirely different, for the dye affects both light and dark areas, creating interesting tones. A blue dun may become goldish, a ginger blue or greenish; this unpredictability is what makes dyeing feathers interesting. The chances are you never will repeat the hues you produce, mainly because the material you will dye will seldom, if ever, be exactly the same from lot to lot. Some tiers have a "thing" about using natural, undyed hackle, saying that dyes alter the translucency of the feather. I am not one to stand in judgment on the subject, except to point out that one such perfectionist became almost obsessed with a particular cape I once had, which, as a joke, I professed was a natural undyed cape from India. It really was an ordinary but excellent ginger that I had toned to a brassy dun, probably beyond duplication. Yet he contended that the success he had with the Gordon Quills he tied with the hackles I had given him from that cape was traceable to the natural, undyed feathers! I never told him the truth of the matter, because he had such fixed notions about using only undyed hackle. Telling him would have shattered his whole point of view about the Gordon Quill.

Dun is the term once assigned to brownish-gray, which is difficult to separate from "rusty-dun" hues. Of late the term has come to mean solid gray of a rather light cast.

Blue Dun has replaced "dun," the blue indicating the absence of brownish cast. This hue is difficult to define, tiers and suppliers disagreeing on the color density. Some interpret it to mean almost water-clear, others pale gray, some gray with a blue cast.

Iron-Blue Dun has been known as many shades: brownish dark gray, blue-gray with a plum hue, deep slate gray. Today it is generally accepted as meaning deep slate gray.

Bronze is another term that has been loosely used to describe the colors "bronze dun," "bronze blue" and others. The bronze effect results from tinting ginger hackle with blue or green dyes; it is interesting but hard to reproduce.

Wine falls into the same category as "bronze." We might ask, "Sherry" or "Burgundy"? Without a modifier the word means nothing. "Claret" is a common synonym.

Instead of concerning yourself with the exactness of a hue—exactness, that is, within the scope of definition—you will profit from the simple practice of mixing two hackles, sometimes three, to produce that hue: a blue dun and a ginger, a grizzly and a ginger for example. The effects are more insect-like because the six legs of most aquatic insects have not one hue but several, some even barred and splotched. Tradition has strongly influenced the tier toward selecting hackle according to vague standards, the natural result being the repetition of the "purity" of a fly pattern, more and more of passing interest.

The spectral colors—blue, orange, green, red, and yellow—featured on many wet flies are repeatable, owing to more tolerance for slight variations in hue. Patterns requiring such bright colors are effective for their contrasts and often bizarre arrangements.

Hackle can play tricks on the eye. An unplucked neck emits the full density of color because the feathers are layered. A single feather held to the light will be lighter in tone and, depending upon its luster or lack of it, may differ greatly from your expectations. This merely emphasizes that the exactness of hue is largely in the eye of the viewer.

Saddle Hackle

Saddle hackles are long, lustrous, fine-stemmed feathers located beyond the cape. They are often clear, resilient, and closely fibered, and are either overlooked or disregarded by certain dry-fly fanciers: overlooked because they are not part of the neck, disregarded because they are longer fibered than most neck hackles. Having fine stems, they tie well and occupy small space on the hook for the flotation they give the fly. If they have a failing (and this depends on the age of the bird from which they were taken), it is the tendency to break during winding. Experience will minimize such breakage. The tips of the smaller ones are not too large for size-14 and -16 dry flies, probably the most popular sizes in the average dry-fly box. I have tied as many as five dry flies with one saddle hackle!

Undyed or natural saddle hackle ranges in color from white to near black. The outer side is more lustrous than the inner and may appear lighter in hue. The difference is the lack of luster on the inner side. Solid and mottled colors are difficult to describe because they vary from bird to bird. Brown, for example, the most ordinary color, is of many casts. For general purposes, saddle and neck hackles have the same hues. I believe it is fair to state, however, that hues vary from lot to lot.

I have thought many times about developing a color spectrum for the recognition of hues for fly tying. Color reproduction being what is it, I long since abandoned the idea. However, through the course of your career as an angler-fly tier, you probably will resort to blending mixed solid and mottled hackles to simulate the legs of insects; the exactness of one color will be relative at best. You certainly cannot depend upon the colored illustrations in a book.

If you know a poultry farmer well, you may be in luck. Good hackle comes from the Leghorn, Cochin, Wyandotte, Plymouth Rock and Rhode Island Red strains. Roosters may be hard to catch, but, when they are in prime condition, their feathers glisten in the sun; they will yield many good hackles. Plucking may seem a problem, but at least you can get what you need. Roosters regenerate new hackle quickly, offering two or three pluckings a year. Some have been known to enjoy the process: They crowed!

Hair Hackle

Hair is good for hackling both wet and dry flies: bucktail, bear, squirrel tail, groundhog, ox, moose mane, skunk and dozens of others can be used successfully. Resiliency differs from kind to kind, but even the stiffer ones are good, if tied properly, ox hair and moose mane are excellent examples. Tying methods differ, as explained in the sections on tying the wet fly and dry fly.

Ox, skunk, moose, and caribou have solid colors; badger, groundhog, raccoon, gray and dark-gray variations. Squirrel and bear hairs are popular and are available in light and dark; some are even white.

Evaluating dry-fly hackle is relatively easy, although some professionals would have you believe it is difficult. Look, first, for luster; second, for narrow feathers in wild cocks (not so narrow in domestic roosters, but the narrower the better); third, for resiliency and thickness of each fiber; fourth, for the right angular appearance of each fiber when the feather is curved, the tip touching the butt.

Body Materials

Probably everything within reason that can be wound on a hook shank has been used to form a body of one kind or another. As expected, recent developments in synthetics have led to effects not otherwise attainable; the adaptation of polypropylene, which has a low specific gravity, as a dubbing material is a good example. Translucency has been improved, as has durability of materials in both storage and in the makeup of a fly.

Body materials can be categorized as fuzzy or smooth. Fuzzy ones include animal fur, chenille, peacock herl, ostrich herl, wool, kapok, clipped animal hair, and some synthetic materials. Smooth ones include silk, fiber quills from bird plumage, porcupine quills, flat nylon, tinsel, straw, plastic strip and raffia, to name but a few. Smooth bodies may be segmented to simulate the banding of the body of an insect; bird-fiber quills, moose mane, caribou hair, peccary bristles, porcupine quills, monofilament leader material, alternating bands of light and dark animal hair and the like are popular.

Fuzzy Bodies

Fur that has been dubbed to the tying thread after being combed or shredded has been the choice for trout wet and dry flies and salmon flies for hundreds of years. Fur from water-frequenting animals is water resistant, from terrestrial animals generally water absorbent. Even the water-absorbent furs make good dry-fly bodies when dressed with modern flotants. Fur captures air particles that act as prisms, refracting light rays as no other material does.

The following furs are selected for their hue, texture and translucency:

ANGORA GOAT (MOHAIR): cream, long-fibered
BADGER: cream, for Light Cahill, Light Hendrickson, Little Marryat
BEAR: Polar—white to cream (very translucent); black—warm light brown; brown—ruddy brown
BEAVER: dark brown
CHINCHILLA: silver gray
ERMINE (WEASEL): white
FITCH: ruddy tan to cream

FOX BELLY: cream, for Light Cahill, Light Hendrickson, Little Marryat
FOX TAIL: white, pale gray, medium gray, silver gray
GOAT: white and gray
LYNX TAIL: white, light buff and cream to dark gray
MARTEN: cream to dark brown
MINK: tan to brown
MOHAIR (ANGORA GOAT): cream, long-fibered
MOLE: dark gray for Dark Cahill; also ruddy tan
MONKEY: gray to black
MUSKRAT: blue-gray, for Dark Cahill
OPOSSUM: pale buff to cream for Light Cahill, Light Hendrickson, Little Marryat
OTTER: cream
RABBIT: white to black, also angora, a long, silky fur
RACCOON: gray and brown
SEAL: black, white, and ruddy brown (very translucent)
SHEEP WOOL: cream to black
SKUNK: near black and black-brown
SQUIRREL: gray-dun, ruddy gray to tan
WOODCHUCK: near black

Spun natural fur and wool: These are prepared and carded for tying, eliminating the need to dub them onto the tying thread. Both are popular.

Spun synthetic fur and wool: Man-made materials, which have simplified the search by fly tiers for the texture, quality and color in fly-body materials. Nylon and polypropylene head the list. *Nylon yarn* is usually three-strand for separation into finer sections for small or slim bodies. *Nylon wool* is carded or spooled two-strand. It is similar to yarn but forms a more compact body.

Polypropylene: This man-made material makes exceptionally good dubbing, because its specific gravity is less than that of water. The carded yarn is a little more difficult to handle, being stiffer than other processed materials. A newer form, prepared in pressed sheets, offers the advantage of being used like natural fur dubbing. The material is shredded from the edge of the sheet, and the shreds are dubbed like fur. It is clean, and stores flat in an envelope.

Acrylic fiber: Another, new synthetic, highly water resistant. It ties well.

Kapok: Kapok is Java cotton, the silky fluff found on the seeds of the silk-cotton tree of tropical America, Africa and the

East Indies. It is best known as a filling for mattresses and life jackets. Kapok probably is the most water resistant of all the natural products, being several times more buoyant than cork. Compressible and workable, it is ideal as a filler under silk-floss bodies or as dubbing on the tying thread.

Herl: The short flues branching from the stems of the tail feathers of the peacock, ostrich, and emu are the fly tier's *herl.* Those of the peacock are metallic green and bronze, those of the ostrich and emu dusty white. The fibers comprising the "eye" of the peacock tail are not so thickly herled as those farther down the stalk and are best suited to light- and dark-banded bodies. The thickly herled fibers are wrapped around the hook shank like dubbed tying thread. Ostrich and emu herl is similar but duller and less resilient. The flues are longer. All herl may break easily when it is being wound. Instead of using a single strand, use three or four. If one breaks, catch the broken end, and wind it under the others. Herl is excellent body material, having been specified for many patterns for trout, salmon and bass flies for hundreds of years.

Trimmed Hackle: Hackle can be trimmed the length of herl flues, or it can be wound on the hook and trimmed to shape. Either way works well, although neater appearance comes from trimming the hackle first.

Chenille: This is a manufactured material, fluffy and fast winding. Originally of silk and cellulite, it now is made of nontarnishing Mylar and of gold and silver tinsel with a thread core. Silk chenille is resilient and admits light through its fibers. Chenille is widely used for all kinds of fly bodies, for egg sacs at the tips of trout flies, and for spiraling tinsel bodies. Bands of alternating colors effectively represent the dark and light segments of bees and wasps.

Supply houses list chenille in four or five sizes (diameters), the smallest for trout dry and wet flies, the largest for bass and salmon flies. Chenille is not practical for hooks smaller than size 16; it occupies too much space between the barb and the shank. Spun fur or wool is better, even for forming the egg sac on a small dry fly.

Smooth Bodies

Patterns having smooth bodies are legion for trout dry and wet flies and salmon and bass flies, many of the oldest and still most reliable being dressed with floss ribbed with gold or silver tinsel.

Smaller trout flies designed to represent natural insects have quill bodies usually of peacock tail fibers, stripped cock neck hackle, or the quill fibers from certain bird wings, tail feathers and body plumage.

Silk floss is the traditional standard for hundreds of smooth-body patterns. Originally it was available twisted, requiring unraveling before tying. Current styles are flat, to reduce bulk and simplify body tapering, hallmarks of the well-tied fly. It is now carded and spooled. Some floss changes color when wet, becoming darker than when wound. Clear lacquer or celluloid enamel will preserve the original color, but the tier should experiment with several hues of the desired color, for both lacquer and celluloid enamel bring out the depth of any hue. Years ago, enameling the hook shank white was popular to produce translucency of silk bodies that had been saturated with dry-fly oil. Some tiers still follow this practice. Others wrap the shank with tinsel or Mylar before applying the silk.

Wool yarn makes good smooth bodies and becomes somewhat translucent when saturated with dry-fly oil. It fluffs slightly if lightly scraped with a razor blade. So treated, it rivals wool dubbing in quality, although yarn is disliked by many, possibly for reasons not founded in fact. One of its real advantages is it will not appreciably change color.

Raffia is the grass-like fiber from the palm *Raphia pedunculata,* found in the Malagasy Republic. It is long-fibered, ties well and is inexpensive. Smooth and strong, it has been favored for many years for the bodies of large mayflies and stoneflies. It is often listed as African grass.

Straw is seldom used today. It is best ribbed with fine fly-tying monofilament or gold wire to prevent fraying. Straw becomes water soaked after continued use, if not coated with lacquer or clear enamel. I like it especially wrapped over kapok.

Tinsel was originally jewelers' material and quite naturally became a fly tier's standard for adding glitter to fly bodies. It is produced from metal as flat tape, round cord (spiraled over a thread core), round or oval wire, machine-embossed tape, and 3-strand twist in silver, gold, and copper. It comes in yellow, blue, red, pink, and other colors, the availability of each color depending upon the supply house. Sizes range from fine wire to approximately $5/64$-inch width and from .001- to .005-inch thickness.

Tinsel retains its natural brightness in most freshwater but discolors in brackish and salt water. Coating the tinsel with waterproof lacquer or cement will allay its reaction to salt.

Tinsel wire is used for numerous patterns of trout flies, the best-known, perhaps, being the Gordon Quill, the body of which is counterwound with the fine gold wire for reinforcement. The added sparkle from the gold wire has been a point of argument for years. Is it needed? Or is the sparkle simply a side benefit? Other patterns similarly tied but lacking the gold wire are equally effective, and if well made they do not fray or unwind. Wire is featured on nymph bodies as well. It contributes to the illusion of body segments of the natural insect. Spiraled on the body, it adds the brightness conferred by the gases surrounding the natural midge as it emerges.

Fine, flat tinsel about $1/64$-inch wide is for ribbing and building a solid tinsel trout-fly body or streamer. It is most suitable for hooks in sizes 10 to 20. Smaller hooks are too short for ribbing with flat tinsel; the round wire is better. Medium, flat tinsel approximately $1/32$-inch wide is best for ribbing bodies in sizes 8 through 2. Wide, flat tinsel (approximately $3/64$- to $5/64$-inch wide) is for flies size 1 and larger. Embossed tinsel is flat, having indentations that scatter light reflections and is about $1/32$-inch wide. Round, thread-core tinsels have fine diameter for ribbing trout flies and smaller salmon flies.

Including the many types available from the best sources, tinsels divide dimensionally as indicated in the following table:

Type and Width in .000 inch.	Typical Use	Hook Size
Wire: .005, .006	Counterwinding quill bodies and ribbing small flies	28–8
Round thread: .007, .010	Ribbing and solid segmented bodies	14–8
Oval: .020, .022 .030, .035 .040, .058	Ribbing and solid segmented bodies	12–6 5–2 1 and larger
Twist: .010, .016 .020, .022	Ribbing	14–8 10–6
Embossed: .030	Ribbing and solid bodies	12–6

(*Table continued*)

Flat:		
.012, .015		20–16
.023		14–10
.030		8, 6
.040, .043	Ribbing and solid bodies	6, 4
.045, .048, .052		4–1
.060		1/0 and larger
.072, .075		largest salmon flies and streamers

Mylar is a recent development. A plastic foil, it does not tarnish and is well suited to dry flies for its light weight. It is offered by most suppliers in the narrow ¹/₃₂-inch width, the most popular, but is available in sheets for hand cutting. Mylar is also prepared as woven cord similar to fabric-covered electric-light wire. The cotton core is easily removed from the end of the cord, leaving the Mylar in a herringbone tube, which is slipped over the hook shank from the eye. The cord is made in large and small diameters. In addition to having become a standard in the tackle-supply houses, Mylar is also sold for apparel decoration in dry-goods stores. The herringbone weave scintillates like fish scales, adding much to the attractiveness of minnow-like streamers.

Plastics of many kinds have been tried by fly tiers. Few have survived the test, possibly because they are opaque. Yet, I have seen mayfly patterns with bodies made from vinyl-covered electric wire. The wire had been pulled out and the vinyl covering slipped over the hook eye and down the shank. The tail fibers were hackle whisks inserted in the opening at the rear.

In the 1930s man-made cellulosic fibers, long-chain polymers synthesized by combining carbon, hydrogen, and oxygen with other elements, were first produced under high pressure. The chances are that the scientists and chemists who devised that first polymerization process were not thinking about leaders and fly bodies at the time. Nevertheless, the flyrodder was casting with synthetic leaders shortly thereafter and experimenting a little later, using the new stuff for making fly bodies. Films of such material stripped in ³/₃₂-inch widths are superb for "quill" bodies. Originally developed for the textile industry, they, too, found their way into the fly tier's bag of tricks. The strips are easily separated into narrower widths for segmenting bodies. The lighter colors of pale gray, straw, and olive, are translucent.

Wind the basic color full width; then band the segments with the narrower strip. Of lighter density than even polypropylene, polyurethane is ideal for "quilling" dry-fly bodies and rivals the best of animal fibers in both appearance and durability. It is perfect for the flat-body nymph.

Mohair, previously described as a material for fuzzy bodies, is equally good for smooth bodies. When not dubbed like fur, the fibers are long and wind like floss. Mohair is durable and quite insectlike in the finished fly.

Rubber bands, pink, light green, amber, and brown, form excellent bodies for trout wet flies and simulate well the banding of the natural insect's body. Coating the finished body with lacquer or cement checkers the rubber in time. The untreated surface is better in all respects.

Heat-shrinkable tubing, one of the recent products for sealing the exposed connections in electrical wiring, has interesting and useful properties. The shrink rate is about 2 to 1 and is obtained by holding a hot object such as a small soldering iron a short distance from the tubing, or by immersing the material in hot water. (I've even used a match). The size range is limited, which is probably the reason why this tubing is not more widely used in fly tying. Colors are black and white only. If some enterprising concern were to introduce the material in colors, there would be a new fad in wet-fly bodies. It also makes a neat head on streamer flies.

Segmented Bodies

Many, if not the majority, of patterns for trout flies call for segmented bodies to simulate those of natural insects. Floss or wool, ribbed with tying thread or another material, is an example. Better effects are possible with quills and some animal hair.

Peacock-eye and herl quills are undoubtedly the favorites for segmented bodies. Each quill fiber has short, metallic-green barbs that, when stripped, reveal a tannish hue that contrasts with the hue of the unbarbed side. The resulting tan and brown bands are very similar to the banding of an insect's body. The herl fibers are darker than the fibers from the eye of the feather and offer little contrast. They are useful, nevertheless, natural or dyed. Many difficult-to-get hues of natural insect bodies are obtained by dying herl fibers yellow, which turns them olive; red, which turns them plum, or green, which turns them slate-olive. The fibers from the eye of the feather dye well, producing the pastel hues, and they can be bleached lighter if soaked in hydrogen peroxide or Clorox. Fine wire or monofilament counterwound around a peacock-quill body will prevent it from unwinding or breaking.

Feather-quill fibers from most birds make excellent smaller trout-fly bodies. The short, stiff fibers from a duck's wing feather are strong and conveniently tapered at the tip for tying to the hook and are edged with a contrasting hue—and sometimes density—contributing to the desired segmented effect. They may appear too short at first glance, but when carefully wound with the aid of tweezers, these short fibers form superb bodies to size 12. They make up for being short by their width and strength. The short, stiff fibers on the narrow side of duck and goose flight feathers, the fibers from the turkey tail and pheasant tail, and those from the common barnyard chicken are unbeatable sources for body quill. I am always surprised that so many tiers either ignore them or simply do not know about them. They are easy to use and need no de-fluing.

Body-feather stems are another source for quill material. All birds have an abundance of medium and small body feathers the center stems of which are ideal for segmented bodies. They are easily stripped of their fibers and they tie well. First strip them; then soak them in water before flattening them between the thumbnail and forefinger. Those with dark edges can be stroked so that the dark and light edges become parallel on one side of the stem, resulting in well defined bands when the quills are wound. These quills are actually flattened tubes and contain both the pith of the feather and some air; therefore they contribute significantly to the flotation of the larger dry flies. They are unsurpassed for nymph bodies. Dyeing produces unequaled two-tone effects.

Hackle-feather stems from the wild cock and the common rooster—and the hen, as well—when stripped of the hackle barbules, make fine two-tone bodies. The sides that are exposed after stripping are lighter in hue than the unstripped portions. Before tying, soak the stripped fibers in warm water (some tiers add glycerine); when they have softened, pull them between the thumbnail and forefinger, to flatten them. Dyed hackle-feather stems prepared in this manner are ideal for forming segmented bodies on dry flies. Another use is ribbing. A floss body ribbed with a hackle stem is, in every sense of the word, a segmented quill body.

Stripped quill, the shell stripped from the stems or center quills

in wing feathers is a fine source for segmented bodies, despite all
the time necessary to strip and prepare it for winding. Cut across
the stem with a razor blade, and make a short, lengthwise slice.
Grasp the edge of the slice with fine, needle-nose pliers, and peel
the shell toward the base of the feather. The pith inside the stem
may cling to the stripping, but this can be removed easily by
scraping. A few attempts with the razor blade will show how wide
and deep to cut the stem, and as many times with the pliers will
show how to peel the shell most effectively. The color of the
stripped quill is usually grayish, except that it shades to near
translucency at the origin of the feather. Banding is not well
defined because there is little, if any, contrast lengthwise. White
feather stems yield nearly translucent quill. Wound over red,
green, yellow, or brown tying thread or floss, such quill "coats" the
fly body quite like the chitin of the natural insect.

Porcupine quill is well structured for dry-fly bodies. Flexible,
light, hollow, and naturally buoyant, it makes durable segmented
bodies. It has the disadvantage of being one color: white. The less
the quill is compressed by flattening, the more air is trapped for
flotation. Porcupine quill is also adaptable as a tube slipped over
the eye of the hook and down the shank. With scissors, snip off the
end of the quill, leaving a hole just large enough to slip over the
eye of the hook; then cut the quill the desired length, allowing
room to fasten the wings and hackle. It is best to entrap the air
within the quill by sealing both ends with winding thread and
cement. Don't attempt to wrap *over* the quill; build tiny gaskets at
each end with the winding thread, and cement them well.

Moose mane, a most versatile material, should be in every fly
tier's cabinet. It simplifies making dark- and light-banded quill-
like bodies because the width of the banding can be controlled by
the tier. Two hairs, one light and the other dark can be wound
simultaneously, or, if wider segmentation is needed, the lighter
hair can be wound on first and the darker spiraled over it to create
the proper spacing. Moose mane is durable material and serves
the tier well.

Horsehair, like moose mane, is good for segmented bodies.
The fibers are smaller in diameter, limiting the banding to the
smaller fly sizes from 12 down.

Monofilament, for its toughness and translucency, has become
accepted as good body material in recent years, particularly for
wet flies. Its density is not ideal for dry flies. Still, many good
dry flies are ribbed with monofilament, mayflies especially. For

streamers it is excellent in either clear or dyed finishes. Its trans-lucency simulates the "gutlike" appearance of small minnows. One of the best streamers for striped bass I know is dressed with 20-pound clear monofilament closely wrapped over an aluminum-foil underbody. I have seen it take stripers when no other streamer would, regardless of how fished. The consensus among several knowledgeable anglers is that the subdued but definite silver glint of the body makes the difference.

Wing Materials

It would be difficult to list all of the wing fibers, hair, and synthetic materials that have been used to make the wings on artificial flies. Time was when a pattern tied with other than the specified wing was considered an abomination. Some bird plumage once was believed to be almost sacred in the winging of a fly, but that was before the bird having such plumage neared extinction or became protected by import regulations to prevent its extinction. In time the substitution of feathers similar to the originally specified ones proved that flies winged with them are no less successful than the "real thing." Trout and salmon take the imposters, being none the wiser. The ability of the fish to be so discriminating was man's idea in the first place and probably was founded on the theory that anything exotic and hard to obtain—legally or otherwise—had to be better than an easily obtained domestic equivalent.

Ducks, geese, turkeys, crows, guineas, coots, starlings, grouse, pheasants, partridges, pigeons, chickens, and dozens of others are more or less standard sources for the wings of trout, bass, and salmon flies. The textures differ, naturally; that is, water birds such as the duck, goose, and coot have smoothly adhering feather fibers, which resist separation during tying better than others do, and they are more water resistant.

A bird has many kinds of feathers for winging flies. Some are more suitable than others. The duck has no less than 12 distinct types, pheasants more. The following are descriptions of the types most generally used. Coloration may vary from bird to bird.

Wing Quills, known as primary (pointer) and secondary (flight) feathers, are standard for great numbers of trout wet and dry flies. *Primaries* are the long feathers—six or seven of them —located from about the center of the wing to the tip; they have short, bristly fibers on one side and softer, longer fibers on the other. The short fibers are of no use for wings but are excellent

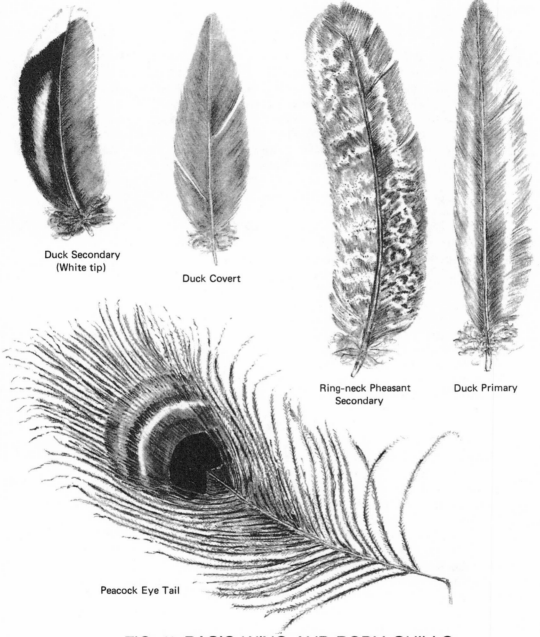

Duck Secondary
(White tip)

Duck Covert

Ring-neck Pheasant
Secondary

Duck Primary

Peacock Eye Tail

FIG. 11. BASIC WING AND BODY QUILLS

JEL

for quill bodies. The long fibers have been the criteria for dry-fly and wet-fly wings ever since the artificial fly came into being. Colors range from medium gray to near pearl. The first primary feather often is disregarded because it is too bristly, and the fibers separate easily. There are usually six remaining primaries on each wing, ideal for winging trout flies and smaller bass and salmon flies. *Secondaries* are the shorter, softer feathers, similar to the primaries, but located from about the center of the wing to its origin. In the mallard, the color is metallic blue, with white tips shading to dark gray toward the butt end.

The underside of the duck's wing is covered with white, smooth, fine-textured feathers (satinets) in multiple layers. Satinets are suitable for trout-fly wings and, when paired with the center quills remaining, make durable bass and salmon fly wings.

Flank Feathers are the soft, long, gray- and white-banded body feathers found immediately under the duck's wing. Some have fibers of equal length and texture and are used often as whole, matched feathers or cut sections, as will be described later.

Nashua (Grand Nashua) feathers are few per bird. Edging the top of the wing, they are tan to brown-barred and are said to be the most beautiful of all winging material; but for their paucity they are often set aside for winging select salmon flies. The mallard drake, the older the better, is the source of these brown-barred feathers.

Breast and Body Feathers are of many kinds, hues, and markings. Mallard throat feathers are burnished brown and represent the wings of some drake mayflies. Even the greenish feathers from the mallard's head are used to hackle wet flies. The tier could sort all the plumage from a wild duck into many groups by shape, size, color, marking, and texture. At first this might seem the logical, if not the only, way to separate and store them; but it is needless, contributing to making fly tying a chore rather than an art. Unless you are a commercial tier doing quantity work, the gathering of multitudes of bird skins is also rather pointless. Few complete skins are necessary to satisfy the needs of the angler-tier. As a matter of fact, purchased separately, the wings, capes, crests, flank plumage, and breast feathers—all packaged and graded —are not costly, and eliminate the confusion, the time, and the fumbling involved in sorting and packaging at the bench. The chances are good that the ounces of boxed miscellaneous feathers saved for "future use" simply will occupy space and collect dust and moths. Such saving often is a trap into which many beginners fall. Eventually they try to get rid of the useless collection by trading it; or they throw it away altogether.

Tail Feathers are usually coarse-fibered, and attempts to use them for winging small flies are a waste of time. They are useful for wings on flies size 6 and larger, if tied down-wing style. The turkey has short tail feathers that are dark, greenish gray and long ones that are white-tipped, dark, mottled brown. Pheasant tails are beautifully cross-barred, black on dusky tan, the tips faintly barred and touched with a pinkish overtone. If carefully handled and tied, they make fine low-water salmon fly wings and larger trout wet-fly wings.

Hackle Tips and Whisks are popular for winging all types of flies, from the tiniest midge to the full-sized salmon fly. Their popularity is natural, for they are easy to handle and tie; come in all sizes, shapes and markings of interest to the tier; take dye readily, and cost less per fly than about any other winging material. Grizzly dyed to suit is equivalent to many naturally colored and barred feathers. The light chinchilla dyed pale tan compares with natural woodduck, the darker phase (undyed) with dark teal.

Next to the duck and goose, the pheasant contributes probably more to the fly tier's wing stock than any other bird. It is clothed in an array of solid, multicolored, barred, shaded, spotted, and streaked feathers, and there is hardly one, unless too small, that is not a candidate for a wing of some sort, a tail fiber, a cheek, or a shoulder.

Golden Pheasant

The golden pheasant is most known for its crests and tippets. The crests are brilliant gold, almost metallic, and are required for wing topping (and tails) on many salmon patterns. The tippets are the orange cape feathers barred in black, fibers of which tip the end of the Royal Coachman, Queen of the Waters, and others. The deep blood-red body feathers are also good for wings and tie similar to mallard and teal flank feathers, and are just as good for tails and shoulders. The golden-yellow rump feathers are used for the same purpose, and they are fine wet-fly hackle. In the plumage of every golden pheasant there are a few long, brilliantly red spears that contain lustrous, resilient fibers, which can be tied in as topping on salmon-fly wings. The wing quills range from dun through rusty tan.

Amherst Pheasant

The Amherst pheasant also is known best for its crests and tippets, the crests being metallic red and the tippets barred black on white. The crests are ideal for topping salmon-fly wings or for tailing trout and salmon flies. The neck feathers are metallic greenish-blue, the rump feathers red and yellow. The body feathers are also greenish-blue. A few orange spears of metallic brilliance add much, as topping, to the wings of salmon flies. The tails of silver-buff are barred with deep brown. Almost every feather in an Amherst pheasant is suitable for winging, shouldering, and tailing quality flies.

Ring-Necked Pheasant

Hunters who do not tie flies generally have a standing line of friends who do, waiting to pluck feathers, which seems like a good arrangement; the plumage of the cornfield ringneck is needed for dry flies, wet flies and nymphs. The flight feathers vary in hue from light clay through light brown with irregular buff bars and have no equivalent, so far as I know. The back feathers are known as "church windows" for their light and dark blotches, so useful for simulating the thoraxes of nymphs. Bronze-brown, thinly tipped in black, and deep reddish-metallic, and barred cinnamon are the colors of the body feathers—all excellent for wings and for hackling trout dry and wet flies, although the technique for tying them is rather special, as will be described later. The rump feathers are long-fibered and coarse, ideal for "legging" nymphs and large spider-like trout flies.

Zebra Pheasant

The Zebra pheasant stands apart from other pheasants in that it is uniformly white with irregular black bars, which, as pheasants go, are relatively faint. The feathers from the Zebra pheasant are best-known for shouldering streamers—the Gray Ghost, long famous for landlocked salmon, in particular.

Natural Hair

Hair from the tails and bodies of the deer, squirrel, calf, fox, badger, goat, skunk, porcupine, raccoon, bear and other animals has been the source for steamer and wet-fly wings for years. "Bucktail," the long hair from the tail of the deer, is an old standard, although "deertail" is probably a more appropriate name: The tail from a doe is equally good, if not better. Coarse deer tail is difficult to control because it fans out from the point where it is tied and it often is brittle. The finer hair, much of which is found on the belly, is naturally softer and ties better in some respects. The natural colors are white, brown and brown-black. Deer hair dyes well.

Squirrel tail ranges in color from pale gray through brown to near black. It is barred and most effective simulating the wide banding common to some minnows. The gray squirrel is light gray at the roots, black barred and white tipped. The larger Canadian gray squirrel has the same coloration, but the hair is longer. Fox squirrel is brown and barred with black. The Canadian fox-squirrel tail also is larger. Arctic fox is ginger brown with darker brown bars. Black-squirrel is really brown-black and is harder to get.

Calf tail is marketed as Impala and Kip. Both terms are misleading, for the true Impala is an African antelope. You may actually be buying a calf tail instead of an impala tail. The difference is more technical than real. Calf tail is most often crinkled, sometimes straight, and occasionally twisted. The twisted is quite useless except for streamers designed to have a corkscrew effect. The crinkled and straight hair is excellent for both small and medium-length streamers; it ties well and is inexpensive. Regardless of the name you know it by, calf tail serves a good purpose.

Foxtail contains both fur for dubbing and long hair for streamers. Many tiers do not separate the fur from the hair; they like the soft fur for its wavy motion in the water. The length of the hair varies with the type of the fox. White fox will average about 2 inches, the red fox 2½ inches and the silver fox, with the longest hair, 3½ inches.

Badger body hair is barred black on buff to cream and is similar to squirrel tail. Long preferred for streamers for its strength and motion in the water, badger is a good choice when barring is required.

Skunk body hair is ideal for medium-length streamers. The length is 1½ to 2 inches. It ties well and has an attractive undulating motion. Colors are black or dark brown with white stripes. Hair from the European polecat, the Fitch, is of good texture for winging flies.

Skunk tail is longer than the body hair. About as black as any natural hair can be, it is unsurpassed for streamers and is resilient and tough.

Goat body hair, a long-time favorite for its weaving motion as a streamer wing, is dense but fine. It is the perfect streamer material. It is nearly translucent, has good texture, and is a pleasure to work with, despite its occasional brittleness.

Porcupine body hair is grayish and usually crinkled. It ranks high for streamers because it undulates attractively when retrieved.

Raccoon body hair is barred grayish-brown, averaging about 2-inches long, the correct length for small-to-medium streamers. The buff tail is black tipped.

Bear hair. Near translucency is the outstanding characteristic of bear hair. Polar-bear hair, long sought for its glassy consistency, is about as available as snake feet. Synthetics that are claimed to be its equal are fair substitutes, but they are far from the original in any department. *Black, cinnamon, grizzly,* and *brown* bear hair is available from most suppliers. Bear hair is similar to squirrel tail.

Many other animals have hair suitable for streamers. Practicality precludes mentioning them here, for they are numerous, and their properties are little different from those already described. The buyer must use good judgment and not be carried away with the idea of having one of everything available in his supply chest.

Hair for Dry-Fly Wings

The hair from relatively few animals is suitable for dry-fly wings. It is too coarse for the size of the hook in general and is awkward to handle. Hair from the badger, goat, squirrel, groundhog, and fox has texture fine enough for the purpose. Regardless of the choice, the hair must be tied rather sparsely, to avoid bulk on the hook shank. The guard hairs from the bodies of water-frequenting animals is excellent for smaller dry flies.

Synthetic Hair

Synthetic hair that I have used does not measure up to natural hair in texture and mobility, but its other properties—

translucency and flash—are good for simulating the flash of minnows. One of the best examples is clear-white nylon hair for topping silver-bodied streamers meant to imitate the silversides, an abundant forage of the striped bass. It is produced crinkled and uncrinkled, the crinkled being especially good for mixing with natural hair, to add just enough glint to represent the flash of a minnow. Nylon hair is very reflective at night, and I consider it better than radiant or fluorescent natural or synthetic hair, although it is prepared as such by some supply houses. Lengths vary from 2 to 6 inches, diameters from .003 to .006 inch. Colors are white, yellow, red, and black; some suppliers also list blue. Nylon hair is easy to use because it is supplied in squares quite like those cut from an animal's skin. It is rot proof, stays clean, and is cleanable. Its single disadvantage is its lack of mobility when compared with natural hair. Yet, for striped-bass streamers, particularly, it is an essential and rates a prominent place on the bench of the tier who fashions saltwater streamers. The yellow color closely resembles the crest of the golden pheasant, and I have substituted it for that purpose most successfully. Mixtures of the clear white and the yellow add much to any minnow-simulating streamer.

Shoulder Materials

Plumage from ducks, pheasants, and some exotic birds is standard for the shoulders and cheeks on hundreds of fly patterns. But the list does not end there. Any body plumage of soft texture and the needed color and markings is appropriate, and that includes feathers from the common barnyard chicken and the starling. Alone, or in combination with others, such feathers can be arranged to represent the gills and heads of minnows with surprisingly good results. A mallard breast feather tied over a white body feather dyed red so that just the edge of the red shows and represents an open gill; and a body feather with an enameled eye represents a head. A little imagination on the part of the tier can perform wonders.

Jungle Cock

The jungle cock, an Indian fowl, has been the tier's champion source of "eyed" feathers for shouldering wet flies and streamers. Trading regulations have prohibited the use of it, and stock already on hand is expensive and limited. The feathers are rather long and narrow with wax-like cream-to-tan spots, the "eyes" of the streamer and salmon fly. There is no question about their effectiveness, and years ago tiers were quick to see the advantage in using them. Plastic substitutes have been developed in colored, precut form in the approximate shapes and sizes of the natural feathers. Some are excellent and even have the feel of jungle-cock feathers.

Lacquered Feather Substitutes

The protection of the jungle cock has caused fly tiers to seek substitutes from the plumage of other birds. The *starling,* for one, is covered with "eyed" feathers that, when properly tied in place, resemble those of the jungle cock. Starling feathers are smaller, and allowances for the difference should be made.

Mandarin black-and-white barred feathers are also good substitutes for those of the jungle cock. One large flank feather contains enough fibers for several strips of "eyed" shoulders.

Amherst-pheasant tippets are white with black tips. The larger tippets have a narrow black bar midway in the feather. Several strips can be snipped from one tippet. The center wedge is the best.

Ring-necked pheasant plumage contains an abundance of barred feathers every bit as good as jungle cock. Although the coloration is rusty or brownish, the barred effect is prominent. The center wedges are black tipped.

Turkey tails (white-tipped) also are suitable substitutes for jungle-cock feathers.

Guinea feathers have an abundance of white polka dots on gray or black backgrounds. Each feather can be trimmed as needed.

These are only some of the useful natural substitutes for jungle-cock feathers. There are many others. Even the breast feathers generally reserved for fan wings can be used, particularly those with single spots in the center. The list is endless.

Lacquering the feather is essential, for it gives the tier the opportunity to shape the fibers by stroking them between the fingers while the lacquer is wet.

Spot-lacquering the eyes on plain feathers is another wrinkle that works well. A nail, toothpick, or the tip of the dubbing needle dipped into the lacquer is the only required tool. Controlling the size of the drop comes with a little experience. Ball-point applicators are on the market and do an excellent job. Apply the tip to the place where the eye should be after the lacquer has dried.

Tail Materials

Selecting feather fibers or hair whisks for tails involves more than choosing a material for its hue, speckles or barring. Texture, thickness, absorbency, and stiffness enter into the selection. Soft, absorbent fibers are next to worthless for dry-fly tails but are ideal for wet flies. Conversely, stiff, resilient fibers that are water resistant are best suited to dry flies; they help to float the fly and to balance it for a proper attitude during its downstream journey.

Animal hair, wing fibers, breast and side plumage, tail feathers, shredded wool, crests and tippets from pheasants and exotic birds, hackle fibers from the cock and hen chicken—in fact, nearly everything found on the tier's bench—have been at one time or another tied to the end of a fly. Combinations of two or more kinds and colors and even of materials of unequal lengths produce interesting effects. The McGinty in the steelhead pattern is an example of such a combination: dark-barred teal and scarlet Amherst-spear fibers or glossy-red hackle fibers. Whether dyeing the teal fibers red would modify the effectiveness of the McGinty is moot. I have never been so disposed to find out. I do know that the McGinty without tails and just stripped by the vigor of a big fish has continued to take fish despite its dismemberment and with surprising regularity; but that is another story. However, I would never tie a McGinty without its proper tail fibers.

The list that follows includes the materials generally accepted for tailing flies. Some are not included for the simple reason that more than a few birds and animals are now protected from the milliner and the fly tier. This list is practical, including those materials available from both the supply houses and the hunter's game bag.

Wing-Quill Fibers

Fibers from the wings of the duck, goose, turkey, grouse, partridge, the pheasants, the crow, coot, starling, chicken, and a whole host of others are standard, dyed or undyed.

Body Plumage

Body feathers from most birds are an endless source for tail fibers. The mandarin, teal, mallard, pintail, widgeon, coot, and most other wild ducks; the guinea; the Amherst, golden, and ring-necked pheasants; again, the common chicken; quail, grouse, turkey, and about everything that flies has its use.

Tails

The same can be said about tails. Fibers from the tails of all birds are good for tailing flies, although they are generally coarser, which is an advantage in tailing nymphs and large drakes. White-tipped turkey is an old standard, as is the beautifully mottled ring-necked pheasant.

Hair

The emphasis has shifted to hair for tailing flies in recent years. In some respects hair is more durable, but it may lack the barrings of certain feathers. Depending upon the size of the fly, the following types of hair are used generally: rabbit mask, porcupine (fine), moose mane, bucktail, goat, caribou, bear, mink (for dry flies), squirrel, calf, fox, badger, skunk, raccoon, groundhog, as well as synthetics and monofilament.

Hackle

Hackle fibers will probably remain a favorite for tails so long as there is a fly to be tied. Hackle is so readily available, has the right properties, is naturally arranged to size on the quill, dyes and ties well, and is, in my opinion, the most versatile material the fly maker can have. Although there has been a flurry of interest in mink tail, of late, I still believe a tail of prime hackle fibers is hard to equal.

Mylar

Two or three strands unraveled from Mylar tubing add flash and flutter to the tails of streamer flies. For that matter, a few strands blended in with the fibers of a bucktail wing have been known to turn a dud into a top performer for striped bass.

Monofilament

Monofilament has several important uses. The extra-fine size is superb for counterwinding peacock and ostrich herl. Herl is naturally subject to fraying and breaking, and the transparent monofilament wound a few turns around a herl body prolongs its life. Monofilament also makes an almost indestructible body, for it is tough and rot proof. Its specific gravity makes it better material for wet flies than for dry flies; and it is in the streamer that monofilament shows to best advantage. One of the best, if not the very best, imitations of the silver streak in minnows is monofilament wound tightly over aluminum foil. "Mono" has also replaced light wire for the trailer hook in salmon flies and the like. It does not kink like wire—although it will curl if crammed into the tight places of a fly box—and it ties well. Available in clear, pink, amber, blue and green, monofilament has a wider range of body colors than many tiers may suspect.

Glass Eyes

Glass eyes attached to soft wire stems for easy winding to the hook shank have been used successfully for years. They add much to the appeal of surface bugs, streamers and large nymphs. The wire on which the glass eye is molded is conveniently long and is cut to suit the method of attaching it to the hook shank. For example, it may be cut short, and bent to form a right angle and tied in place, or the wires may be left uncut and wound up the shank to the place where the glass eye should appear. Glass eyes are seen more often in hair surface bugs than in any other type of lure and have the beneficial side effect of adding a little ballast when tied below the center line. Usually clear with a dark pupil, the eye can be made more attractive and lifelike by coating the inner surface with white or yellow lacquer.

No material list could include everything a tier *might* use; what would be the point? But the items listed here are more than enough to stock your materials chest. Just be sure that you buy, trade, or leech only the feathers and hair you really need. Otherwise, you are apt to end up with shoe boxes full of "stuff" in such amounts that you'll have little if any room for the vise and tools; then you may take up golf, instead of fly tying—a mistake, indeed!

FUNDAMENTALS

As in any other craft, organization of the work area and orderliness of both the tools and materials simplify performance. I have known a few tiers whose tying corners looked like rats' nests, yet they still tied magnificent flies; but they are the exception. It pays to lay out tools and materials systematically. Place the scissors, dubbing needle, cement, razor blade and other tools conveniently to the right, but not so close as to be knocked off the table or lost among hackle capes, a bucktail, or perhaps plastic bags of this and that, which should not be there in the first place. Materials are best kept to the left. Discipline yourself to keep them there and the tools to the right.

Locate the vise directly to your front and attach it securely to the table top, the jaws pointing to the right. Place a white cardboard sheet, dull side up to minimize glare, over the work area. Strip the edges with masking tape, which peels easily when it is time to replace the cardboard. Adjust the lamp to illuminate the work area to best advantage but at an angle comfortable for your eyes.

With the exception of some dry-fly types, tying begins at the tail of the fly and progresses to the head, from left to right. After each step, the thread is wound two or three turns toward the eye of the hook, to clear the material just wound and to leave enough space for spotting the work with a touch of cement. The weight of the bobbin keeps sufficient tension on the thread to prevent unwinding.

Select a size-8 or -10 turn-down eye wet-fly hook which is large enough for first efforts yet small enough for you to "get the feel" for tying a fly. If you are new at the game, a hook smaller than size 10 will compound the normal difficulties that you must expect.

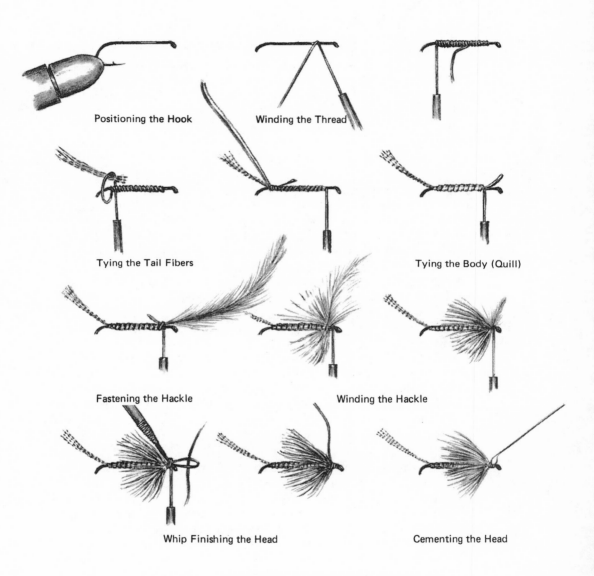

Positioning the Hook

Winding the Thread

Tying the Tail Fibers

Tying the Body (Quill)

Fastening the Hackle

Winding the Hackle

Whip Finishing the Head

Cementing the Head

FIG. 12. TYING A SIMPLE FLY

JEL

Positioning the Hook Place the lower part of the hook in the vise jaws, as shown in Figure 12, with the shank parallel to the table top. At first you may insert the hook too far, believing it wise to cover the barb and the point. Don't do it! Too much of the hook will be obscured by the vise and valuable working space lost; more important, the barb, the point or the wire of the hook itself may be fractured without your noticing, and the fracture may be detected only later, when it is too late. As for the projection of the hook point: Yes, you may stick your finger once or twice during your first efforts, but you will overcome that natural failing in short order. Be sure that the jaws hold the hook tightly. If the hook is not rigid, tighten the vise. A tightly held hook will "ping" when pulled and released by the fingernail.

Fastening the Thread The tendency at the beginning is to overwind the tying thread, which results in a misshapen body that does not hold together. Pull about six inches from the tip of the bobbin. Hold the tip of the thread between the left thumb and forefinger and place it diagonally against the hook shank. Holding the bobbin in the right hand, wind the thread over itself a few turns. Now is a good time to check the tension of the bobbin; it should be set to release the thread yet not to slip from its own weight. Leave a slight space between the turns, and wind to the left until the last turn at the end of the shank. Clip the tail of the thread where the winding began.

Preparing and Tying the Tails From a well-marked mallard flank feather, clip five or six fibers close to the quill. The tail fibers should be a little longer than the length of the hook shank. Holding them between the left thumb and forefinger, with the butts toward the hook eye, place the fibers on top of the shank. With the bobbin in the right hand, wind two or three turns around the fibers—enough to hold them while you check their position and length. If they are too long, grasp the butts and pull them forward; if too short, grasp the tips and pull them backward. Sometimes the fibers may incline to the right or left. A slight rolling motion of the fibers between the thumb and forefinger will align them. If the fibers look right, continue winding toward the hook eye, stopping about two thirds up the shank. Clip the butts of the tail fibers, and lightly cement the windings. While the cement is tacky, wind back toward the tails to the point where the body material will be fastened.

Tails can be made to project upward or downward, and they can be divided. To make them project upward, wrap several turns

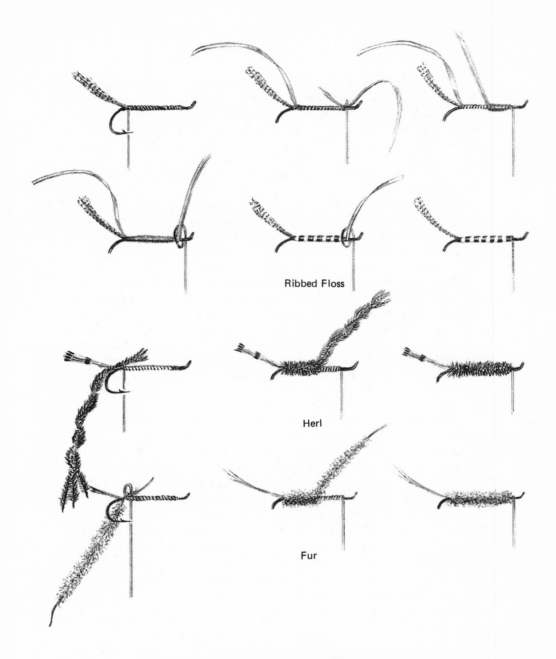

Ribbed Floss

Herl

Fur

FIG. 13. THREE TYPES OF BODIES

of thread to the left of where the tails will be tied, forming a slight ball, to wedge the fibers upward when they are tied in place. To make them project downward, omit the ball, and wind the fibers a short distance down the curvature of the hook bend. Don't overdo either; a little inclination up or down is sufficient. To divide them, place half of the fibers on each side of the shank. Another way is to tie the small ball first before fastening the fibers on each side.

Preparing and Winding the Body Many flies, otherwise good, are poor because their bodies are irregular or not tapered when tapering is called for. The extra care needed to form a good body is well worth the effort, whether the body is quill, fur, herl or floss with a tinsel ribbing. Such bodies of one material are simply fastened on at the end of the shank and carefully wound toward the eye of the hook. Bodies of two or more materials are wound in successive steps; that is, the ribbing material is tied on first and the basic material last. The basic material is always wound first, but tinsel for ribbing is *tied on* first and the fur or floss next; the tinsel is kept to the left, out of the way, while the fur or floss is wound to form the body. The tinsel is then spiraled up the body, evenly spaced.

Fur Bodies

Of many textures and colors, fur is most versatile. It can be bleached, dyed and mixed to meet any color requirement, and it can be rolled on tying thread, twisted into a skein, or spun to form smooth or segmented bodies. The easiest method is rolling. Clip from close to the skin several small sections of fur from, say, a foxtail, removing the long hairs until only the soft fur remains. Separate the fur with the fingertips until it is a ball of fluff. Thoroughly wax a section of tying thread, and cut off a 6-inch length. Scatter the fur over a small area of the work table, and, with the fingertips, roll the waxed thread across the fur until it resembles a skein of yarn.

Tie the tip of the dubbed thread to the end of the shank. Start the body taper by catching a shred of fur from the tip of the rolled section under the winding thread. Wind the dubbing to the right, developing a slight taper by avoiding overlaps and bald spots. Repeated rollings compact the fur, which is useful for segmented bodies. The segments are formed by twisting the dubbed thread with each body winding.

Some tiers do not use separate thread for dubbing the fur, preferring to attach the fur directly to the tying thread. My objection to this is the fur does not adhere well to the fine tying thread. Heavier thread is better for the purpose and has the advantage of showing its color through the fur on finely dubbed bodies. An excellent example is the blue-gray fur from the muskrat dubbed on dark-red tying thread.

Mixing fur of two or more colors—natural, bleached or dyed—is effective for matching hues of some insect bodies, although the blending is hard to repeat. Fur with some of the guard hairs remaining is required for patterns such as the Hare's Ear and a number of fur-bodied salmon flies. Simply leaving the guard hairs in with the under fur is all that is needed. If the guard hairs are longer than one-half inch, cut them with scissors. A good reinforcement is fine monofilament counterwound through the dubbing. Stroking the fur body lengthwise with a razor blade will roughen it.

Much has been written about tying fur bodies. One tier will develop a certain touch for winding it and a second tier another. As long as the effect produced is successful, one way is as good as another. The fact remains that, as a tier, you will develop your own techniques. Those offered here are simply guidelines that have been proved over the years.

Quill Bodies

As explained in the section on materials, there are many kinds of quill that make good trout-fly bodies, although the fibers from the peacock-tail eye are best known, for their distinct banding effect. Unfortunately, the usable part of the fiber is short, limiting the best peacock-eye quill to a size 8 hook.

Peacock-eye quill (see Figure 11), like the herl, is brittle but well worth the effort of learning how to use it, for it gives the fly body a segmented appearance hard to duplicate. The quill is edged with dark metallic flues which are usually removed for segmented bodies, by pulling the quill between a razor blade and the table top; by stroking the quill with a rubber eraser; or by soaking the quill in warm water, then pulling it between the thumb and forefinger. Some tiers soak the quill in Clorox or hydrogen peroxide to dissolve the flues.

These quills are shorter than ideal and are best wound with hackle pliers. De-flue the quill carefully, concentrating on the lower part; the upper is too fragile for a good body winding. Two inches of fiber are sufficient for flies to size 10, including enough to spare for the jaws of the hackle pliers.

Tie the narrow end to the end of the shank and over the point where the tail fibers are fastened. Two or three turns with the tying thread will hold it; more will form a lump, the nemesis of the quill body. Wind the first few turns of the quill with the fingertips; then, holding the windings in place with the left forefinger, fasten the hackle pliers to the butt end, and carefully wind the remainder of the quill up the shank. In nearly all cases the last turn of quill on a size 10 hook will end short of the hook eye, which is good, for it does not bulk the area where the wings and hackle are to be tied. Half-hitch the winding thread a time or two after completing the body. Stroke the body with a thin coat of cement. I mix three parts of thinner to one part of cement just for that purpose.

Floss Bodies

It is best to wind floss in two layers. The doubling makes for better color retention and body taper. Tie the floss a short distance behind the eye of the hook, and wind it to the left, then back again. Keep the tying thread to the right, near the hook eye. If tinsel ribbing is required, tie the tinsel immediately after fastening on the tail fibers. Keep the tinsel to the left and out of the way, while winding the two layers of floss. The material clip is useful for this purpose.

Preparing and Winding the Hackle Strip the down from both sides of a hackle feather, pulling toward the butt. Place the butt of the hackle on top of the hook and immediately in front of the end of the body as shown in Figure 12. Press the hackle firmly with the thumbnail of the left hand, while securing the butt with several turns of thread. The hackle feather now should be positioned with its dull side up, projecting beyond the eye of the hook. Apply a touch of cement to the windings.

Fasten the hackle pliers perpendicular to the tip of the hackle—their weight will prevent the hackle from unwrapping halfway through the winding process, if you have to use both hands for another operation—and slowly wind the hackle, starting where the windings cover the butt of the hackle. Pass the hackle pliers from right hand to left hand and back with each turn. With the left thumb and forefinger, stroke the hackle barbules slightly to the left, while winding each turn. The hackle feather naturally will shorten as it is wound. Allow sufficient length for tying the tip, and secure it with two or three turns of tying thread.

Clip the remainder of the tip close to the last windings. Pull the wound hackle slightly to the left, and wind two or three turns with the tying thread in front of the last hackle winding. Touch the windings with cement, and finish with a couple of half hitches or the whip finish. Apply another drop of cement to the head just formed, clip the tying thread and remove the fly from the vise.

The fly just tied is a simple hackle fly, having no wings. Each of the operations discussed will prove useful in the sections to follow, however, and in tying any type of fly; it will pay to tie at least a dozen or more flies of the same pattern and size, if for no other reason than to demonstrate the improvement that naturally follows with the tying of each successive example.

Techniques for preparing and tying wings are described in the following sections on the many types.

TROUT FLIES

The Wet Fly

Wet flies represent the underwater stages of countless insects, which comprise a fascinating world too few anglers explore. Technically, the *true* winged wet fly is man's facsimile of the mayflies and caddisflies and some drowned terrestrials that trout have learned to look for. The March Brown, *Stenonema vicarium,* which habitually molts just beneath the surface, and the Gordon Quill, *Epeorus pleuralis,* which shucks its nymphal case, often close to the stream bottom, to become a vigorous, surface-seeking dun, are the best archetypes of the winged mayfly for copying. The pupal stage of the caddis clan is also winged, as are some of the female adults, which dive underwater in search of aquatic flora for ovipositing.

Because they withstand pollution better than do mayflies, caddisflies have increased in abundance in recent years, in waters previously occupied almost wholly by the myriad mayflies anglers know so well. Consequently, the caddisfly is getting more attention from anglers than it once did. Its simulation by the fly tier is a wise investment of time and study.

Insects in their underwater phases possess strong means of locomotion; they are most agile and capable of maintaining headway against fast current. Their legs, tails, and fringed gills, and in some cases their antennae, give them surprising mobility. The aspiring fly tier will do well to keep this in mind when he selects hackle, wing and tail fibers. For the slim, alive appearance we all like to see in a wet fly results from the combination of wings that quiver and legs (hackle) and tails that seem to pulse when the fly is twitched through the water. Few are the wet flies that possess such mobility; rather, they are overdressed and clumsy: The

85

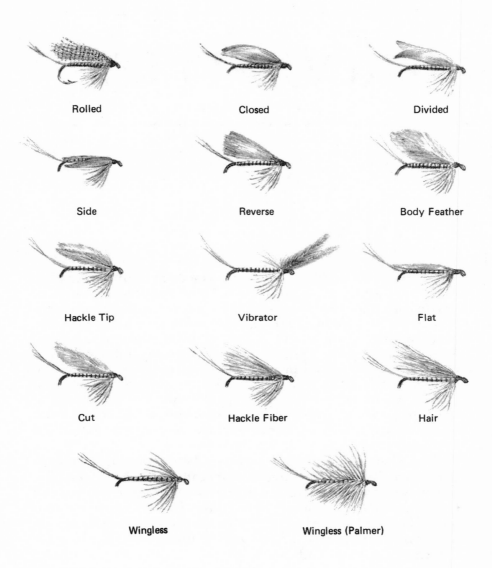

Rolled Closed Divided

Side Reverse Body Feather

Hackle Tip Vibrator Flat

Cut Hackle Fiber Hair

Wingless Wingless (Palmer)

FIG. 14. WET-FLY STYLES

JEL

hackle is crowded or applied "beard fashion" with little if any movement, the tails are bunched together in a stiff, lifeless mass, and the wings undulate about as much as a house key.

Tradition has had strong influence on the wet fly. The profile of a typical wet fly represents only the *end* of a swimming pulse; that is, the legs are drawn up under the body, and the tails are pressed together. As for the wings, they are normally sloped to the rear under nearly all conditions. Little pulsing action occurs in a wet fly so tied. A more effective way to simulate leg and tail movement is to tie the tail whisks well apart and the legs (hackle) so that they project perpendicular to the hook or even forward, like dry fly hackle. When the fly is twitched, the whisks move rearward, then open again, and the tails "swim" realistically. Partridge, mallard, woodduck and guinea fibers are especially good for this purpose because their fibers are soft and flexible.

The dimensions for the wet fly—the relationships of wing length to body length to leg length—vary, according to the order of insects, the genera and the species being simulated. The proportions of the mayfly, for example, differ from those of the caddisfly; and even the proportions of the mayfly dun differ from those of its final form, the spinner, which, drowning at times, becomes a wet fly.

Some years ago, the body length of the fly determined the hook size, and the wings and tails were proportioned accordingly. The body and tails were the same length, and the hackle was tied beard fashion below the body. The wing was usually specified as the length of the hook, less the eye and fly head. These proportions were "man made" and patterned after the mayfly, the predominant and then most-copied aquatic insect. For that reason, they seemed logical, and just about every fly in the book was tied accordingly. But they are far from correct for simulating the caddisfly which, as stated, is one of the underwater insects most sought by the trout.

Wet flies, exclusive of the nymphs and pupae, divide into two main categories: those that, in one way or another, represent insects, and those that attract by color and flash. The former are more popular for their challenge to the fly tier. The latter, which include patterns as old as the English "winch" have become less popular through the years, although the Silver Doctor, the Alexandra, the Royal Coachman, and the like, still have their place in the sun in plenty of areas. The chances are good they will remain in many fly boxes and fly books so long as there is a trout to catch.

The depth the wet fly is fished is largely governed by the weight of the hook. (Overdressing does not make a fly sink.) Too little thought is given to the wet-fly hook, and a large percentage of unproductive wet flies is the natural result. The longer 2X- and 3X-long shank hooks are more adaptable to wet flies, and I prefer them to hooks of regular length. The 2X-stout gauge is ideal in either ball eye or taper eye for mid-deep and deep swimmers. The eye is strictly a matter of choice.

When the Gordon Quill *Epeorus pleuralis* is experiencing its transition from nymph to dun well below the surface, a deep-traveling fly simulating that transition is almost always solid reason for expecting strikes!

Sparse but spraddle-legged wet flies tied on light-weight hooks are excellent foolers of trout when caddis pupae and the March Brown duns are emerging. They ride high in the surface film, where the March Brown puts on its enticing performance, and the caddis struggles to maturity. Still, all productive wet flies need not be winged. The plain "hackle fly" is always effective, particularly if tied with long, sparse hackle, like the fibers from the breast and flank plumage of the woodduck, partridge, teal, grouse, and others of similar texture and mottling. The old, reliable "hackle fly" has accounted for prize trout and salmon in all quarters, and I sometimes wonder about the need for wings at all! There are times when a Gray Hackle with a yellow body, or a Brown Hackle with a peacock-herl body will outfish the best of meticulously crafted winged flies—even the live minnow and worm. For decades anglers have pondered the reason. Once I thought I knew a good one, but in recent years I have forgotten about it; simply remembering when to use those two old patterns proved far more important.

Most authors on fly tying choose the wet fly as the beginner's model because, so they claim, it is the easiest of the many types to tie. I have always questioned that premise and counter with the contention that a wet fly, if properly tied, takes every whit as much time as a dry fly. In fact, many a fly tier can produce a helluva dry fly at a merry clip, but his wet flies can be as awful as his dries are good. A wet fly is subjected to more scrutiny by the trout than is a dry fly. Below the surface the aspects of realism are the first order, and an ungainly glob of whiskers, with or without fancy treatment, is usually passed by a mature fish.

A well-tied wet fly is a gem in the hands of a skillful angler. It caught trout for centuries before the dry fly existed, and, among anglers who really know how to tie it and use it, the wet fly remains the trout's filet mignon.

Tying the Wet Fly

There are nearly as many ways to tie a wet fly as there are types. Any one is right, whether tied to traditional standards or not, if it gets the trout's attention. Standards are always temporary until replaced by new and better ones. More than 20 years ago I abandoned tying wet flies with the then standard hackle treatment: a pinch of hackle whisks tied beard fashion under the body or a few turns of hen hackle tied back around the body. Neither had enough movement to simulate the "pulse" of an insect's legs effectively. When wet, the hackle was merely closer to the body than when dry. Tying hen and partridge hackle perpendicular to the body and winding the tying thread through the fibers made the fly perform better than any arrangement I had tried. The desired pulsing leg action was obvious, and as a side benefit, more of the body was exposed.

Wet flies are best classified according to their wing types, which may be a bit superficial, because the hackle and body treatments are left out of account, but for recognition it is a good start. Figure 14 illustrates the wing types. With the exception of the vibrator type, in which the wings (hackle tips) point forward to flutter when the fly is retrieved, wet flies have *down* wings, that slope over the body.

Rolled Wing

Materials One medium mallard or teal flank feather, one ginger hen hackle and one large fiber from the eye of a peacock tail feather. As explained in Fundamentals, remove the fluff from the base of the flank feather and the hen hackle, and stroke the flues from the peacock-quill fiber. Select a down-eye size 10 hook.

Tying Tie on the winding thread a short distance behind the hook eye, and proceed to wind to the left. Tie on four or five whisks from the hen hackle for tails. Apply a touch of cement to the windings. Next snip off the fine tip of the peacock quill to the point where the light and dark edges are distinct, and tie the narrower end of the remaining quill to the top of the shank with the narrow end pointing toward the hook eye (see Figure 12).

Avoiding the formation of lumps or spaces, wind the quill up the shank, stopping short of the hook eye. The chances are the windings will not reach the eye anyhow. Leave space behind the eye for tying on the hackle and wings. It may help to fasten the hackle pliers to the other end of the quill before attempting to wind the body. If so, grasp the hackle pliers with the right hand, and wind up and over, and with the left hand, down and up. After tying a few quill bodies, you will be able to overlap each preceding winding. If done carefully, the slight overlapping reinforces the quill without losing any of the segmented effect. Secure the end of the quill with two or three turns of the thread, but do not half-hitch. Examine the quill for uneven windings. If there are any, unwind the thread to release the quill, and repeat the winding. Tie down the butt with a pair of half hitches, and touch the knots with cement. Some tiers like to cement the entire body.

Strip the hen hackle down one side by holding the feather between the thumb and forefinger of the left hand and pulling the barbules from the other side toward the butt with the right. The stripped or "half hackle" is more easily controlled while it is being wound, and the barbules will project outward from the body better than will those of a whole hackle, the inner, un-stripped barbules of which cling to the body and are wrapped under by the feather quill.

Clip out a few barbules from the tip of the hackle. The tip is to be fastened to the body, and trimming the surplus barbules reduces the bulk that too often accumulates at the head end of the fly—the very place where bulk is undesirable. Tie the hackle with the inner side up, the tip pointing to the left. Do not crowd the winding toward the hook eye; the wing has yet to be tied on. At this point a wet fly becomes a good one or a poor one, depending on how the hackle and then the wings are positioned and tied.

Fasten the hackle pliers to the butt of the hackle, and wind carefully, keeping the stripped side to the inside, next to the body. Two turns are adequate for hackling most flies—lifelike ones, that is—but, if you prefer, take another turn with the hackle. For best results, do not overlap the turns; let the fibers project as they will. Bind the butt of the hackle with three turns of tying thread, clip the remainder, secure it with a half hitch and touch the knot with cement.

If all has gone as it should have, your wingless wet fly now should be ready for winging, provided there is sufficient space between the hackle and the hook eye. But if there isn't, and the

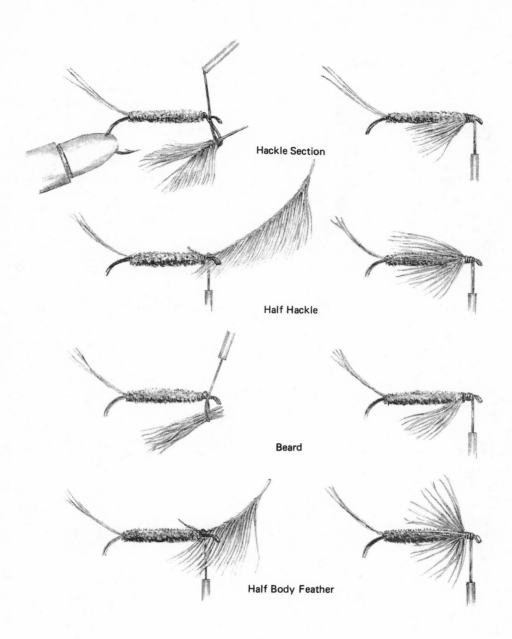

Hackle Section

Half Hackle

Beard

Half Body Feather

FIG. 15. FOUR WAYS TO HACKLE A WET FLY   JEL

Cut equal sections
from paired quills.

Edge the wing windings
with the thumbnail.

A double-width section folded
lengthwise ties easily.

Cut tip from stem.

Strip short fibers and
down from butt.

Remaining fibers after being
rolled resemble hair.

FIG. 16. TYPICAL WAYS TO WING A WET FLY

JEL

whole affair looks too crowded toward the eye, don't despair. You have just joined the club! All too often wet flies—and most others, for that matter—are hackled and winged too close to the eye, even by experienced tiers.

Now open the barbules of the mallard or teal flank feather to be used for the wings by gently stroking them toward the butt. The object here is to locate the stiffer barbules of the tip, which roughly forms a triangle. Remove them by cutting the quill—not the fibers. Save the fibers for tails. The flank feather now will resemble a V. Medium flank feathers have slight curvature that is best removed. Do it this way: Stroke the barbules back to their original positions and roll the feather between the palms of both hands; if you do it well, the curvature will be gone and the flank feather will resemble hair.

Estimate the distance between the tips and the point where the base of the wing will be tied to extend to the end of the hook. Grasp the feather firmly between the left thumb and forefinger, edging with the thumbnail the point where the fibers will be tied. With the right hand, wind two or three turns of tying thread around the fibers at that point. If the wing looks right, wind several more turns, and trim the projecting butts diagonally with the scissors. Wind a few more turns to the eye of the hook and touch them with cement. Whip-finish the head and seal it with another coat of cement.

The wet fly just described represents one of many mayflies having segmented bodies, barred wings and tannish legs and tails. Once having acquired the feel for tying the rolled wing, you likely will develop many successful patterns around it. It is a good and useful tie in any fisherman's bag of tricks.

The descriptions of the wet-fly types that follow, deal only with the preparation and tying of the wings themselves and their differences. Repeating the same body, hackle, and tails of the rolled wing, the type just tied, is advisable as the best means of emphasizing the characteristics of the wings; so, for the moment, do not experiment with other bodies. Instead, tie a dozen quill-bodied flies without wings, then wing each one according to the following procedures.

Closed Wing

Closed wings are paired sections cut from the left and right flight feathers of duck and goose wings and the like. They are found on the Blue Dun, Ginger Quill, Royal Coachman, Wickham's Fancy,

Slate-Wing Coachman, Black Gnat and a host of others, some almost as old as the fishing rod itself. Tying is relatively easy, although positioning and keeping the wing sections aligned require a little patience.

Tying There are two ways to prepare the wing. Each has its advantages and only the tier-user can judge which better serves his purpose. The first takes a little longer with the gain of having nearly perfectly matched, untrimmed wings. About one third the distance from the butt of one flight feather, separate the fibers with the dubbing needle, as shown in Figure 16. The natural curvature of the fibers is usually slight in this area. With the dubbing needle, again separate the fibers the width of the wing, which, for a size 10 hook, is about $5/32$ inch. Snip this section close to the quill. Remove an equivalent section from the other flight feather in the same manner. These two sections are longer than necessary, but the extra length is helpful when they are tied to the hook. The barbules naturally cohere to one another and allow for slight shifting during the tying process without splaying.

With the dubbing needle place a small drop of cement behind the eye of the hook, and stroke a tiny bit toward the top of the hackle. Place the wing sections together, the slightly curved sides together, and adjust them, if necessary, until they are matched at the tips, which now should follow the natural slope of the feather. Holding the tips between the left thumb and forefinger, the thumbnail edging the place that will become the front of the wing, lay the paired wings on top of the body, the butts projecting to the right. Continue holding the wings firmly and wind two loose turns around the wing butts. Slowly draw the tying thread tight against the edge of the thumbnail; then wind two more turns to snug the wings in place.

Remove the left hand to check the position of the wings. If they have remained in position and slope neatly to the rear, you have done well. Trim the surplus butts extending over the hook eye with your fine scissors, cutting the fibers at an angle, to avoid leaving a blunt end that will be difficult to tie down. Finish the head with the whip finish, and touch the knot with cement. If any hackle barbules are wrapped under or out of position, put them aright with the dubbing needle.

One way of making a neat head is to knot the tying thread with a half hitch, cutting the thread with the razor blade, then finishing the head winding with finer thread. The reduced breaking strength of the finer thread must be considered, however; otherwise, the finer thread is superb for finishing the head. In the minds of some tiers, a second and easier way to prepare the closed wing eliminates matching the sections from paired right and left feathers. Instead of clipping a section from each feather, clip only one from either feather—but twice as wide—⁵/₁₆ inch. Fold the feather lengthwise on itself with the fold at the top, as shown in Figure 16, and tie it ahead of the hackle in the described manner. When there is only one feather left of a particular kind or quality, you can still wing a fly by following this method. I have, more than a few times.

The single objection to folding the wing is the resulting dissimilar curvature of the tips, which can be adjusted by gently pulling the fibers lengthwise on one side of the fold to equal those on the other.

Most large wing and tail feathers are ideally mottled, simulating the markings of some insects' wings. Unfortunately, their fibers are too coarse for cut matched sections, and they splay at the tips when tied down. The folding method makes the use of such feathers possible, although the tips may have to be touched up with scissors after the fly is finished.

Flank feathers can be tied closed-wing style, but the fibers tend to separate, which accounts for my preference for the rolled wing.

Divided Wing

The divided wing differs from the closed wing only in the placement of the wing sections. In the divided wing the outer surfaces of the sections are placed back to back so that the tips flare outward.

Side Wing

The side-wing fly has narrow, short wings representing those of the caddis pupa. Instead of being tied on the top of the fly, they are tied on the sides, their length about half the length of the body.

Reverse Wing

The reverse wing is tied on by the tips, with the butt ends of the feather sections over the body. Coarse-fibered wings and tails tie well this way, and fastening them by the tips makes small, neat heads. Although the butts may open up during casting, they will return to shape underwater. Wings so tied may not have the eye appeal of others, but they are effective nevertheless.

Body-Feather Wing

Body-feather wet-fly wings feature paired small body feathers with center quills found on most birds. Hen hackle, breast and side plumage and the narrow tips of small flight feathers are examples. Such feathers tie beautifully, but the quills are delicate and feathers small enough for trout flies require a gentle touch when being tied. The lower half of the feather can be stripped clean or trimmed off to reduce width, leaving some feathers more winglike.

Tying Remove the down from the paired feathers. Hold one feather over the body of the fly, the end of the feather reaching to the end of the hook. With the dubbing needle, separate the fibers at the point immediately above the hackle binding. Trim the fibers beyond that point from each side of the feather. If the feather appears too wide, remove the fibers from the lower half by trimming with scissors; stripping fine quills will reduce their strength, which isn't much to start with. Pattern the second feather after the first, and place both together, with the curvature, if there is any, facing inward. Crimp the quills slightly with the thumbnail, and place them over the hackle binding. Wind around the crimp two or three turns; then check the wings for alignment and the proper slope over the body. Touch the windings with cement, and finish the head.

Body-feather wings fulfill the need for richly mottled fly wings, which are often hard to find among the usual wing and tail feathers that tiers keep on hand. Some have a full and a shallow side, others are nearly equal on both sides of the center quills. The latter are more troublesome, the fibers on the lower side causing the wings to remain objectionably upright. As mentioned, trimming the fibers from the lower side will position the wings properly.

Hackle-Tip Wing

Hackle is a favorite material for wet-fly wings. It is versatile, easily tied, and is about as dynamic in the water as any material can be. Hackle tips make easily tied wings, whether single or paired, and the fibers, when stripped and bunched, are like hair. Hackle tips from gamecock necks are lustrous and resilient, adding desirable activity to any wet fly.

Tying Measure one hackle for length by holding it over the body, with the tip extending to the end of the hook. Trim (do not strip) the barbules from the butt ends to the point immediately above where the hackle is tied down. Do the same to the second hackle tip. Hold both hackle tips between the left thumb and forefinger, and place them on top of the body, with the stems extending to the right. Because the stems are so resilient, it is advisable to crimp them with the thumbnail in most cases, to help keep them aligned. Wind the tying thread two or three turns around the crimp, then check the lay of the wings. If satisfied with their slope and position, make them fast with the head windings. Finish by touching the head knot with cement.

A second method for applying the wings is to straddle them *over* the body, one wing on each side. This separates the wings, adding more flutter when the fly is retrieved.

A third method is to cock the hackle tips forward beyond the eye of the hook. The forward wing has been known for years as the *vibrator,* for its jerking, swimming motion, so deadly at times to large, reluctant brown trout.

Flat Wing

Flat wings resemble the wings of the female stonefly, which submerges to oviposit. They may be sections from flight or flank feathers or they may be paired hackle tips.

Tying The stonefly is a long-winged, awkward flier, and its wings at rest, project well beyond the tip of the abdomen. Accordingly, prepare the wings, whether sections from wing quills or paired hackle tips, so that they are about one fourth longer than the body. Folded wings work well for this type. Keeping the wings close to the body presents some difficulty. Forming a small knob behind the hook eye is the solution. Before fastening the wings, simply wind the thread behind the eye until the knob is large enough to serve as a wedge, tilting the wings down over the body. Ideally, the left edge of the knob will abut the edge of the hackle binding.

Cut Wing

The cut wing is simply a hackle feather, often from a hen, or is any fine-stemmed body feather cut to shape. Shaping the feather at the start is a challenge. Several "wing cutters" have been marketed, but scissors and toenail clippers do as well. Always cut from the tip toward the butt of the feather with sharp, straight scissors. Toenail clippers are excellent for shaping the tips, the natural curvature of the blades being right for blending the straight scissor cuts.

The cut wing derives its strength only from the center quill. Avoid feathers with weak quills; conversely, do not use any with coarse, stalky center quills.

Tying Like the hackle-tip wing, the cut wing can be tied as a closed, divided, or flat wing, as previously described.

Hackle-Fiber Wing

The fibers (barbules) from one or more hackle feathers make an excellent wing. Mottling, barring, and edging are more possible than with any other feathers. Moreover, the bunched fibers are tough, tie well, and occupy relatively little space at the head of the fly. Fibers stripped from hackle dyed blue-dun, gray, olive, and rust are effective; and a few whisks of brown intermixed with light gray lend the effect of veins in the wings of a natural insect.

Tying From a glossy hackle, strip the fibers that can be gathered and held between the left thumb and forefinger, and place them lengthwise over the fly body. Secure the butt ends in place with the tying thread, and finish winding and cementing the head.

Hair Wing

Hair from the tails of the gray and red squirrels, and the fox, and guard hair from the badger, raccoon, and groundhog, among many others, makes the best of wet-fly wings. It has the fine texture needed for working and weaving underwater.

Tying Clip a tuft of hair while holding the tips between the left thumb and forefinger. Some of the under fur will be included, but do not throw it away. Continue to hold the hair by the tips while you pull the fur from the butt end of the cutting. Save this fur for dubbing. Before tying the butts in place, spot the space behind the hook eye with cement. When the cement is tacky, secure the hair wing with several turns of tying thread; then check that the wing has not rotated out of position. If it has, grasp it between the thumb and forefinger, rocking it slightly until all the hair is properly on top of the hook. Apply another coat of cement to the head windings after trimming the butts and finishing the tie with the whip knot.

Wingless Wet Flies

A wingless wet fly, otherwise a hackle fly, is hackled at the front behind the eye of the hook, or hackled spirally up the body and termed, "palmer hackled." Both represent a large cross section of nymphs and pupae and have caught more than their share of trout. Doubtless they will continue to do so, despite the innovations that occur each season.

The common hackle fly, tied in the proper size—even in sizes as small as 24—is as good a trout getter as anything in the book. It serves admirably down deep, at mid-depth, or in the surface film. The same applies to the palmer-hackled fly; but tie it sparse, so the body effects are not obscured from overhackling. The lay of the hackle should face the tail, not the head.

Tying Tie the tip of the hackle at the end of the shank immediately over the tail windings; then wind the body. As you spiral the hackle, stroke each turn of the barbules to the left, allowing at least two body diameters of space between each spiral, which are sufficient for the body to show through. Remember, you are tying a wet fly, and bulk serves no purpose.

Many palmer-hackled patterns feature tinsel bodies or tinsel ribbing. The tinsel is tied at the end of the shank before the tip of the hackle is tied. After winding the tinsel, I like to counterwind the hackle, that is, to wind it in the opposite direction.

The Dry Fly

Much of the joy the fly man experiences from fishing the dry fly comes with the strike. *Seeing* the trout rise to the fly, to take it subtly or viciously, depending upon the hour, the fly, or the season, then dart for parts unknown is nothing short of electrifying and ample reason for raising the hackles on the neck of the most blasé angler. The devotee of the dry fly knows this only too well, and because of it he may be too persistent about fishing "on top" at times, when drifting a wet fly would be more logical; for, to him, one rise to the dry fly is worth any number of strikes on the wet.

The dry fly simulates—at least it should, if tied well—the

insects and some arachnids that have come to the stream surface, voluntarily or involuntarily. Nymphal and pupal phases of aquatic insects rise to the surface to shuck their skins and may rest there only for a second or two, or they may mull about for a minute or longer, punctuating their efforts to escape the confinements of the water film with moments of quiescent drifting. Those fortunate enough to escape the questing trout fly away for hours or even a day or two, after which they return to the stream to perform their last act—procreation of their kind—ovipositing over, on, or beneath the surface. They come to the stream voluntarily and are the models for so many of the dry flies that fly from the tier's vise.

Those reaching the stream surface involuntarily are the terrestrials, the caterpillars, bugs, and myriad other land-inhabiting insects that fall upon the water to kick up a fuss or glide along until sucked down by a trout. One need witness only once the commotion of trout feeding on the fallen residents of a rain-battered bush to realize how avidly trout take terrestrials. Many of them are almost infinitesimal, but sought by trout nevertheless, particularly during hot summer days, when the swarms of rising mayflies have all but ceased for the season, and the emergence of the fluttering caddisflies has become completely nocturnal. So enter the midge fly—the tiny size-24 and -28 miniature that in recent years has been responsible for a whole new logic in dry-fly technique and has a breed of votaries who speaks in an almost exclusive vocabulary with emphasis on the prefixes "micro" and "mini."

By popular definition, the dry fly rides high on the surface, because it is supported by many barbules of resilient hackle. Hosts of dry-fly men will not look twice at a fly that is not packed with hackle from midway down the body to the very ring of the hook eye! There are others who practically count the fibers in search of a fly with six legs, like the natural insect. A small percentage wants a fly with the least amount of hackle that will keep the fly on top, a rather intelligent choice.

There is much to be said about the amount of hackle wound on a dry fly, just as there is much to be said about quality, spread, the spacing between winds, and the design, size, and weight of the hook. There is no single formula, although anglers and tiers have tried to conjure one for decades.

Trout dry flies divide into three major styles: winged, wingless, and hackleless. All are patterned after mayfly duns and spinners, caddisflies, stoneflies, terrestrials and the like. There are many subdivisions, for dry flies vary almost as much in hackle spread as in their wing characteristics. The hackle has much to do with the total image of a fly as it rides poised on the stream surface. Winged dry flies have followed traditional standards for years and have changed relatively little. Except for substituting materials, there is little the tier can do to deviate, but he *can* concentrate on proportioning and tying the fly to *act* like a natural insect.

The winged dry fly subdivides into five classes: (1) upright wing, (2) spent wing, (3) fan wing, (4) down wing, and (5) flat wing. The *material* in the wings does not determine the class. The material may be the same in each, although there are preferences, which later descriptions will show. The terms "upright," "spent," etc. denote the position and shape of the wings. Each class, however, subdivides into types determined by the wing material and its arrangement. For example, the upright hair wing is tied closed or split, and the upright fiber wing is tied closed, divided, or sometimes with double layers.

Tying the Dry Fly

Tying the dry fly usually begins at the right. The wings are tied on first. There are two reasons. The butts of the fibers must be wound over and tapered before the tails are tied and the body formed. The hackle must be wound last. There are some exceptions, but tying the wings on first is easier and makes for a neater, better-balanced fly.

Upright Wings

The easiest of the upright-winged dry flies to tie is the rolled split wings made from the fibers of a flank or breast feather from the mandarin, mallard, teal, widgeon, or similar duck. Winging is fast, the fly is not bulky, and the wings retain their shape after frequent mouthings by the trout. As originally tied, the rolled split wing cocked too far forward to satisfy some critical trouters, who insisted that the profile was wrong. Yet, tied in the Cahill, Hendrickson and Gordon-Quill patterns, the rolled split wing was, and is, a productive floater.

Nearly 40 years ago Ray Bergman showed me how to tie and split the wing, and I could not begin to guess how many hundreds of dozens of flies I have patterned after his superb examples.

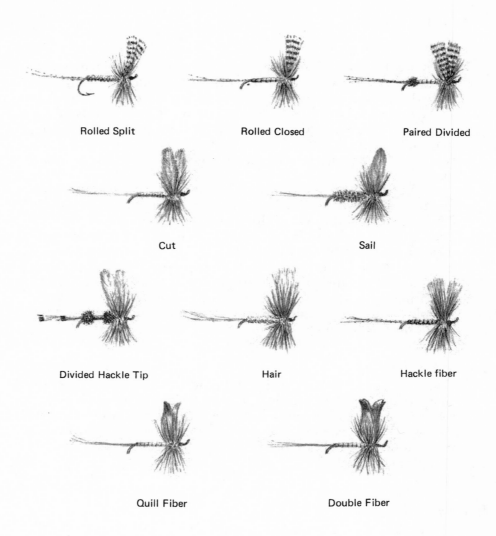

Rolled Split   Rolled Closed   Paired Divided

Cut   Sail

Divided Hackle Tip   Hair   Hackle fiber

Quill Fiber   Double Fiber

FIG. 17. DRY-FLY STYLES—UPRIGHT WINGS

JEL

In addition to those patterns having speckled flank- and breast-feather wings, others with wings of comparable texture in solid gray, brown, and white appeared in later years, replacing the classic flight wing with fiber wings that are more difficult to tie.

Rolled Split Wing

Materials A regular-weight No. 12 hook; a medium flank or large breast feather from a mandarin duck; a de-flued, bleached quill from a peacock-eye tail, and one blue-dun cock hackle. These are the materials for making the Gordon Quill, an excellent dry-fly pattern.

Tying Fasten the tying thread about one third the shank length from the hook eye. Wind the thread in criss-cross fashion for several turns to form a secure base for the wing butts. Remove the down from the butt of the mandarin feather; then stroke the fibers toward the butt, to locate the center wedge of fibers. Clip the wedge, but save it. Stroke the fibers back to their normal position; then rub the feather between the palm of one hand and the fingers of the other, to straighten the naturally curved lay of the fibers.

Hold the butt of the feather between the left thumb and forefinger so that the fiber tips extend about one shank length beyond the hook eye, and fasten the feather with three or four windings about one third the shank length from the eye (see Figure 20). Remove the thumb and forefinger, and evaluate the height of the wing by pulling back on the tips. If they appear about equal to the length of the hook shank, cement them in place. Splitting or dividing the wing fibers is the next operation. Divide them equally with the dubbing needle, and criss-cross the winding thread between the divisions. Viewed from the front, the separation should resemble a slight V. Secure the thread with a pair of half hitches. At this point the fibers may project too far forward; if so, they can be pulled to the left to the desired angle and fastened with several turns of thread wound tight against them.

The hackle is fastened butt first, the inside surface up, the tip projecting to the right beyond the hook eye. Do not half-hitch yet; hackle sometimes breaks, especially if it has been bleached, and it may have to be replaced. So test it by making a trial turn or two. Snip the hackle stem to the rear of the windings, and, with the winding thread to the right, trim the butts of the wing toward the left, leaving a few fibers to add taper to the body. The amount is determined only by trial and error, the hook size, and the characteristics of the body yet to be wound. Quill, for example, tapers very well, giving the body a most natural appearance. Dubbed fur, on the other hand, can be tapered as it is wound, without need for any undertaper.

Winding to the left, cover the remaining wing-butt fibers, and stop just short of where the tail fibers will be tied. From a stiff-fibered hackle feather plucked from the side of a blue-dun cape, select five or six barbules that are glassy clear and at least the length of the tail section, which, as a rule of thumb, should be equal to the overall length of the hook, less the eye. Secure them in place with three or four turns of thread, and snip off the butts; then wind to the left, where the peacock-quill fiber will be fastened. Ideally, the addition of the tail fibers will complete the taper started with wound-down wing butts.

Tie the peacock-quill fiber at the tip but at the point where the dark and light banding is distinct and the fiber is long enough to be spiraled up the body. This is, at first, also a matter of trial and error. On the average, peacock-eye fibers are well banded and long enough for size-10 hooks. The quill winding need not extend all the way to the base of the wings, however; the hackle is wound a few turns behind them and will cover any short unbanded space.

Always wind the quill carefully and evenly. If it is wide enough, wind it over the edge of each previous wind, to prevent unraveling; if not, counterwind with fine monofilament or gold wire fastened on before the quill. Some tiers like to apply lacquer or cement to the finished body. I consider it a matter of choice, for I counterwind all peacock-quill bodies with invisible monofilament.

Now back to the hackle. Fasten the pliers to the tip, and wind clockwise, starting immediately behind the wings. Some tiers favor compacting the windings, claiming that such dense hackle floats a fly better. My own experience is to the contrary: The same amount of hackle distributed over a greater part of the shank affords better support and, to boot, permits the light to penetrate the fibers and reveal more of the body. A hackle, so tied, often will float the fly with the hook and the tail fibers out of the water!

Wind two or three turns behind the wings; then proceed through the space between them, and complete with several turns in front of them, but a short distance behind the hook eye. Check the lay of the fibers. If they are not perpendicular to the hook, something is awry. Simply unwind the hackle to where the problem is, and rewind it.

Tie down the hackle tip carefully, keeping the head knot behind the hook eye—not on it—and finish with a touch of cement. If the finishing knot crowds and slants the hackle rearward, the fly will "fall on its face" instead of floating parallel to the water surface. I prefer the whip finish. It is permanent and simple to tie, as is the "head knot." Both are described earlier in the book. In the beginning a couple of half hitches will do, until you have acquired the feel for tying the dry fly; but learn to whip-finish early.

Rolled Closed Wing

The obvious single difference between the closed- and split-wing versions is the wing fibers in the former are not divided. Otherwise, the tying is exactly the same. The closed is ideal for winging extra-sparse flies in size 16 and smaller.

Paired Divided Wing

Paired flank or breast feathers comprise the wings on this type. Smaller sizes are best winged with sections of feathers, rather than the whole feather. The wedge-shaped tips clipped from the feathers used to make the rolled wing are favorites. The fibers are firm and make a neat wing.

Tying Hold the paired sections between the left thumb and forefinger. Straddle the ends over the hook, and fasten with three of four winds. Pull the ends extending below the hook toward the rear, cocking the wings slightly forward. Taper-cut the fiber butts to avoid bulk, and wind several turns around them to the left. Wind back to the right to tie in the hackle.

Finish the fly in the same manner already described.

Cut Wing

The cut wing features paired whole feathers that have been cut to the shape of an insect's wings. Many feathers formerly considered unfit for winging dry flies now are recognized as ideal for the cut-wing technique.

Cutting the wings to shape is not difficult, although too much has been made of it. There are cutters manufactured for the purpose, and they are useful, but a pair of sharp, straight-blade scissors will do nicely. Toenail clippers are better than curved scissors for cutting the ends of coarse-stemmed feathers, provided they are sharp and the cutting edges are well matched. For the typical dry fly, only feathers with relatively fine but resilient stems are desirable.

Tying Select matched feathers, a right and a left, if possible, the quill stems of which are equal and resilient. Avoid feathers with pulpy stems because they occupy too much space, bend, and make the fly wing heavy. Trim the down from the base of the feather, and cut the tip perpendicular to the stem, leaving a triangle the required length of the wing.

Shape the wings by cutting from the tip toward the butt, against the natural angle of the fibers. It is best to have a pattern to follow, and there is none better than the natural insect. Lacking that, refer to a good text on entomology. Mayfly wings, for example, are approximately right-angled with a parabolic trailing edge; and, being the most copied, at least as the models for cut wings, they are good for starters. The front half is cut close to the center stem, the tip slightly rounded into the curvature of the rear half which blends into the trailing edge of the wing.

As only the quill stems are fastened to the hook, the wings must be positioned carefully. Straddle the hook with the trimmed stems, and snug them with three turns of tying thread. Check their position, and, if they are equal and aligned, tighten the thread slowly, pulling the stems to the left and securing them with several windings. Finish the remainder of the fly as described in this section and in the section on Fundamentals.

Sail Wing

The sail wing is well adapted to sparse, slim-bodied flies tied on light-weight hooks. The wing is a single hackle tip without curvature. Most good dry-fly capes contain small, straight hackles near the top, many with spreads too small for hackling all but the tiniest midges. They are perfect for the sail wing. The wing is often white, serving as a flag to indicate the wherabouts of a dark-bodied, dark-hackled fly.

Tying Because the butt of the single hackle feather occupies so little space, the sail wing can be tied on after the hackle has been wound, a method preferred by a good many tiers. Fact is, I have put a white sail wing on several dark-hackled patterns two or three seasons old for fishing in darkened areas.

Divided Hackle-Tip Wing

The upright hackle-tip wing has been a favorite for decades. It is not bulky, ties easily, and is adaptable to light-weight hooks, because it is not wing heavy. The spectrum of natural and dyed hackle is almost limitless, giving the hackle-tip unparalleled latitude as an effective substitute—if "substitute" is an appropriate term—for mandarin, teal, brown mallard, widgeon and the like.

The light-grizzly (chinchilla) hackle makes extra-fine wings for the Light Cahill, Gordon Quill, Hendrickson, and others.

Tying There are two usual methods for fastening hackle-tip wings: straddling the butts over the hook shank, the feathers back to back, or placing the feathers lengthwise on the hook and pulling them upright after fastening the butts. The second method is better for tying double-layer wings, because the two hackle tips on each side will not rotate so easily. Criss-cross winding often will correct the lay of a single tip that has gone askew.

Hair Wing

Hair for dry-fly wings must have fine texture, and few animal skins provide it. Among the best that do are the groundhog, badger, goat, squirrel, polar bear, and lynx. The finer belly hair of a deer is good for winging larger flies, sizes 10, 8 and 6.

The tendency is to crowd too much hair into the wing area, making the fly awkward to tie and unstable on the water surface. The fine-textured hair just mentioned does not compress well, despite its other excellent properties, and it enlarges the body if tied too fully.

The upright hair wing is generally tied split-wing style, although it need not be.

Tying Fine-textured hair ties quite like the fibers of flank and breast feathers. Clip a section close to the skin, and remove the fur from the base. A toothbrush is handy for the purpose. Place the tuft of hair as you would a rolled flank feather on top of the hook, the tips extending over the hook eye. Secure the hair in place with several turns of the tying thread, and apply cement to the windings. Let the cement harden before attempting to divide the hair (if you want a split wing) or trying to position it upright. Taper-cut the butts, but do not blunt them; try snipping a few hairs of different lengths at a time. Wind a few turns down the body to cover the trimmed butts; then wind back to the wings. With the dubbing needle divide the hair, criss-cross winding between the divisions while pulling the wings by the tips to the left. Two or three winds tight against the base of the wings will wedge them upright. A drop of cement placed between them will hold the wings in position permanently.

Hackle-Fiber Wing

Hackle fibers are resilient, nearly translucent, and tie well, resembling fine animal hair. They are superb for winging sparse flies on light-weight hooks and offer the side benefit of being surprisingly durable. Few flies call for hackle-fiber wings—why, I do not know. I have found them most effective in dun, ginger, cream, and pure white as wings for quill-bodied 16s and 18s. For winging delicate patterns they are unsurpassed.

Tying There are two methods of tying hackle-fiber wings. The first is cutting the fibers from the feather and tying them like hair or flank feathers to the hook. The second is winding the hackle closely, as when hackling a fly, then trimming a notch in the top and shearing the barbules from the bottom and as many from the sides as necessary to form divided wings.

Refraction of light at the stream surface is the undoing of many dry flies having dense, opaque wings. Because the wings of aquatic insects, mayflies in particular, are translucent, every effort to effect translucency in imiations will be rewarded. The hackle-fiber wing is a sure choice. Whichever method you prefer for tying it will prove the point. A Gordon Quill or a Light Cahill having upright wings made from the glossy fibers of a chinchilla (light-grizzly) hackle is a delight to use. Each is a perfect companion for the extra-light dry-fly hook and the 6X-leader tippet.

Quill-Fiber Wing

More patterns of trout flies have been developed around the upright quill-fiber wing than around any other type. For at least three centuries it remained the standard, and only the difference in pattern—the color, size and body treatment—made one fly different from another. Nearly every trout fly was fashioned after the mayfly, it seems. Double-fiber wings, two layers of fibers in each wing, were the ultimate in the craft of winging flies. Even the sedges, the adult caddisflies, were tied that way; but in recent years the popularity of the double-fiber wing has declined, doubtless because it is wing-heavy when dressed on light-weight hooks. Yet, the old Wickham's Fancy, Iron-Blue Dun, Whirling Dun, Silver and Cinnamon Sedges, Royal Coachman, the quills and many others served well and still do for those who hanker to turn back the pages to earlier times.

The wing and tail feathers of the grouse, goose, duck, turkey, starling, pheasant, guinea, pigeon, woodcock, and a host of others were selected with care for the "perfect" wing, the fibers meticulously paired, the right wing exactly matching the left.

Tying Primary and secondary duck wing quills are the most used. The fibers handle and tie well, are resilient, and the barbuled edges cling to each other better than do others. The best fibers are located in the middle two thirds of the feather.

Strip the down from the base of a pair of matched wing quills. With the dubbing needle, test the fibers on the wide side of the feather for good quality, by separating them at the tips in ⅛- to ³/₁₆-inch widths. Fibers nearer the base are usually paler and separate into weak, sickle-shaped sections; they are useless. Fibers near the tips are coarse and darker but distinctly marked on the edges; they make good body quills for small flies.

From one feather separate and cut close to the quill a section the width of the wing. Here *width* is relative. Wings too wide (and it's the tendency at first to make them too wide) fold, split or twist awry during the building of the fly. Narrow wings are easier to tie; if too narrow, they lack proportion. There is no hard-and-fast rule for gauging the width. But, as a rule of thumb, wing sections ⅛-inch wide are about right for size-12 and -14 flies and sections ³/₁₆-inch wide right for sizes 8 and 10.

Prepare in the same way a section from the other feather. Place the two sections back to back so that the natural curvature bends outward. The curvature decreases among the fibers nearer the tip of the feather. Placed face to face or with their inner surfaces together, the sections will form a closed wing. Either the divided or closed wing make a good fly, and the choice is the tier's.

The wings can be fastened to the hook in several ways, any one of which is as good as any other, so long as the wings are well shaped, in proportion, and located properly. Two methods are discussed here because they are simple and leave the area between the wing and the hook eye clear for winding the last turn or two of hackle and finishing the head.

In the first method, the wing sections are straddled over the hook. Hold the matched sections firmly between the left thumb and forefinger, with the butts protruding beyond the thumbnail. The length of the wing should be the length of the shank. The natural curvature of the fibers should incline to the left, to reduce their tendency to separate later during casting, although some tiers like the curvature inclined to the right, on the premise that it follows more closely the shape of the natural insect's wing. I do not, preferring the slight rearward slope.

Snug the wings in place with two or three turns of winding thread directly against the thumbnail. Grasp the butts, and pull them under the shank to the left, meanwhile watching the movement of the projecting wings, which, at this point, should incline vertically, sometimes even forward a little. Holding the butts firmly with the left hand, with the right wind a few turns to the left around them until the wings are stable. Place a drop of cement at the base of the wings, and let it become tacky. Trim the butts progressively toward the left, carefully tapering the cuts to avoid steps that will be repeated in the outline of slender bodies—quill, floss, and the like.

Wind back to the wings, and fasten the butt of the hackle, the stem to the left. Trim the stem close to the wings, then wind back to the end of the shank to fasten the tail fibers.

In the second method, the wing sections are not straddled over the hook but are tied on *top* of it (see Figure 20). There are some advantages. If tied well, the wings will have less V, and shorter sections from smaller feathers can be used. Hold the sections by the butts between the left thumb and forefinger, the tips projecting beyond the hook eye, the butts resting on *top* of the shank. Wind three turns of thread around the butts immediately in front of the thumbnail. Apply a drop of cement to the windings, and let the cement become tacky. With the left thumb and forefinger, pull the wings upward, and wind several turns against their front. It is characteristic for wings so tied to cock forward, so do not attempt to make them exactly vertical. Taper the butts with scissors, and wind over them to the left, then back to the rear of the wings where the hackle will be tied.

Double-Fiber Wing

As mentioned, double-fiber wings consist of two identical layers of fibers in each wing. Tying can be by either of the described methods, much depending upon the skills of each individual tier.

Spent Wings

There are times when the spent wing that simulates the mayfly spinner, exhausted from oviposition, is needed. The mayfly spinner is a delicate, transparent insect that comes to rest on the water surface, its wings outstretched. To be a good copy, the artificial must be sparse and slim and must have translucent wings. This is quite an order, taking more than a little practice with feathers and quill. Seldom is the spent wing required to float over brawly water, for most of the natural insects seek the quiet surface of pools for their final act. Therefore, two or three turns of hackle are sufficient; overhackling the spent wing puts it on stilts, placing the wings above the surface in an unnatural manner. The trout, highly sensitive to any break in pattern, surely views such a representation as a maverick and will likely pass it up for another that

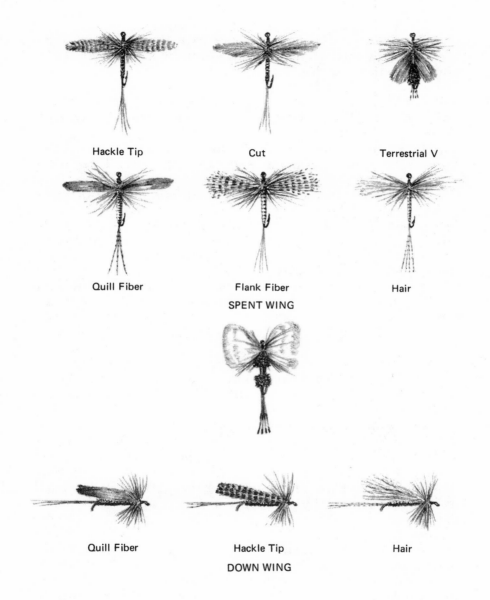

Hackle Tip   Cut   Terrestrial V

Quill Fiber   Flank Fiber   Hair

SPENT WING

Quill Fiber   Hackle Tip   Hair

DOWN WING

JEL

FIG. 18. DRY-FLY STYLES—SPENT, FAN AND DOWN WING

drifts low on the surface film. So learn to tie the spent wing a little too sparse, by some standards, and profit by it. Naturally, light-gauge hooks are essential.

Hackle-Tip Wing

Small cock hackles are ideal for the spent wing, being permeable to light and resilient. Chinchilla, glassy-cream, badger, and ginger variations are high on the list. The double wing—with two hackle tips in each wing—is popular in some regions and is best tied on regular-weight hooks to reduce the tendency to be upset.

Tying There are several methods for tying hackle-tip spent wings. Again, one's own dexterity rules, and it becomes a matter of choice. The first method, much preferred for size 14 and larger hooks, features tying the paired wings, their glossy sides back to back, straddled over the hook, then securing them in the prone position with criss-cross windings.

The second method differs in that the wings are tied over the shank of the hook, one on top of the other, their glossy sides up. The wings then are pulled forward and fastened with criss-cross windings. This method is better for small-sized flies, say from 16 through 20.

The third method is opposite to the second: The hackle tips are fastened on top of the hook but project over the eye, then are bent back into the prone position and held in place with criss-cross windings.

Tying the spent wing with the glossy sides of the hackle tips down instead of up, according to some authorities, lets the fly drift to the water surface more naturally because the curvature of the hackle tips is reversed and does not cup the air during descent. This claim may be straining a bit; nevertheless, many believe it. If anything, the glossy side may seem more lifelike to the trout only for its more distinct markings. I doubt the other part of the theory.

The tandem hackle-tip is another variation of the spent wing and is considered the ultimate in representing the spent mayfly, even to the long front and short rear wings. When the natural insect drifts on the surface before dying, its four wings are folded together vertically and slant slightly rearward over the body. Not until the female mayfly is exhausted after ovipositing are those four wings visible and then only in the outstretched, prone position. The tandem hackle-tip supposedly represents that phase better than does the single pair of spent wings.

Tying The shorter rear wings are tied in first, a slight distance behind where the longer front wings will be tied. The rear wings of mayflies vary in length according to genus; some are almost aborted, others one third to (seldom) as long as two thirds the length of the front wings. For practical tying purposes, making the rear pair of wings half the length of the front pair is adequate. Wind the hackle sparsely from behind the rear wings to forward of the front wings. Some tiers tie in the short wings first, as if making an ordinary spent wing, hackle it, then fasten the longer front wings in front of the hackle and behind the hook eye.

Cut Wing

The popularity of the cut wing comes from its silhouette, the product of cutting paired feathers to simulate the wings of an insect. There is a trade-off between selecting ideally marked, oversized feathers and smaller ones, not so ideally marked. Large body feathers have coarse, pithy quills. Remember, the wings of the spent wing should be resilient, and the fine-fibered cock hackle is doubtless the best choice for spent wings, cut or uncut.

Properly made, the cut wing has its place; improperly, it is an abomination and will corkscrew 6X- and 7X-leader tippets as if it were self-propelled.

Breast and side feathers from the mallard, teal, widgeon, and mandarin; hen hackles, and fine-textured body feathers from most bird skins in the tier's cabinet are the sources for cut wings. Some may have considerable curvature, which is objectionable. Select the tip portions; the quills are finer, and the fibers are long enough for the required trimming.

Tying Follow the same procedure as for tying the upright cut wing. The single difference between the upright and the spent is the attitude of the wings. Match the wings carefully, however, to minimize twisting the fly during casting. Owing to the needed sparseness in all spent wings, the hackle is sometimes trimmed on the bottom to let the wings rest flat upon the surface. Notching a V in the lower half of the wound hackle is one way to lower the fly. Another and, I believe, better way is to cut off the lower half of the hackle squarely, leaving just a stubble.

Terrestrial V-Wing

The V-wing is another form of spent wing typical of the terrestrials, the two-wing flies, bees, wasps and the like. It differs from other spent wings in being cut from a single, covert feather, located along the base of the flight feathers on a duck's wing. The covert is symmetrical, the quill being exactly in the center, and the fibers are the same length on each side.

Tying With the dubbing needle, separate the fibers into sections the width of the wing. Snip out the fibers close to the center quill about ¼ inch in front of and behind the sections. The resulting cuts will leave a V-section, the cut quill ends of which will be tied to the hook shank. The tying procedure otherwise is the same as for other spent wings, although some tiers clip off the rear part of the quill and tie down only the front part *after* the body has been wound. I prefer to tie down both ends.

The bluebottle, bee, wasp, and the like, have rather pulpy bodies. Kapok, over which peacock herl, for example, has been wound, builds the body and adds flotation, reducing the need for bushy hackle. Therefore, two or three turns of hackle are sufficient. Most of the naturals copied by this method have no tails, and, the flatter the fly rests on the surface, the more natural its appearance will be. Chenille is a favorite for segmented bodies, the yellow and black bands of the McGinty being a good example.

Quill-Fiber Wing

The Quill-fiber spent wing differs from the upright fiber wing only in the plane in which the wings are set. The fibers are tied upright, as already explained, then set in the prone position with criss-cross windings.

Flank- and Breast-Fiber Wing

Flank- and breast-feather wings are well suited for tying as spent wings. The fibers are not dense and have the faint mottling or barring so difficult to find in any but a few hackle-tip wings, like the chinchilla. Tying is the same as for the rolled split wing except that the fibers are set in the prone position with the winding thread.

Hair Wing

The near translucency of some animal hair is ideal for spent wings. The hair of the common groundhog, barred grayish-buff; badger hair, which also is barred; the hair of the many squirrels of light or dark cast, and gray-fox guard hairs head the list. Again, tying follows the same procedure as for the upright wing, but the wings are set in the prone position.

Wound Hackle-Fiber Wing

The wound hackle-fiber wing is probably the least known of the wing forms. It is superb for small, delicate spent-wings in sizes 16, 18, and 20. The fine barring of chinchilla and the faint mottling of some of the ginger-variant hackles are inimitable for this type of wing. This really is a *hackleless* fly, by strict definition, because it has no hackle (legs) to support it on the surface, and it rests flat, supported only by the hackle fibers of its wings. Tied with long, glossy hackle-fiber tails and finely banded quill for the body, this wisp of a fly simulates the flat, fragile spinner, which coasts by and is so often seen only by the subtly feeding brown trout. It is not a fly for rough water but is intended to be drifted ever so lightly over slick, glassy pools shortly after a fall of spinners.

Tying Select a glossy feather having fibers the length of the intended wing. Wind it as if tying a plain hackle fly. After cementing the head knot and letting the cement dry, carefully trim the fibers from the top and the bottom until those remaining are wing-like. This is not difficult, but it will take a few attempts for the wings to turn out as you would like.

Fan Wings

The fan wing is said to represent the large mayfly. Many anglers tie and use them regularly for that reason and catch fish with them. Because the large mayfly rests on the water with its wings folded back over its body, or outstretched in the prone position, I find it difficult to see that the fan wing, with its lop-eared wings, in any way represents a mayfly. But a fan wing Royal Coachman, size 12, is a good hunter! I have fished it occasionally over seemingly barren water with curious results—curious for the smashing rises of trout that came from nowhere to take it. It is good tie for dusk, late in the season.

Fan wings tied on fine-wire hooks are notorious for twisting light leaders, the reason being that the cupped wings rotate propellor-like during casting. Regular-weight hooks reduce the twisting considerably. One tier I know insists on tying fan wings on 2X-stout hooks simply for ballast. Of course, he winds two hackles on fan wings, to compensate for the slight extra weight of the heavier hook.

Breast feathers from the many ducks, shoulder hackles from

roosters, and the first-joint feathers from the wings of ducks, pheasants, geese, and others are the sources of fan wings.

Tying Because they flare widely, fan wings can be difficult to tie, especially if the down at the base of the feathers is *stripped* instead of *cut* from the quill. Stripping leaves the quill smooth, and it tends to rotate out of position when tied. The short stubble remaining after the down is cut away holds the wings in place.

Wind several X-windings on the hook shank, and cement them. Grasp the tips of a matched pair of fan wings, with feathers back to back, between the left thumb and forefinger, and place them so the quills straddle the hook. Wind three turns around the base of the wing quills, and tighten the turns slowly. Remove the fingers, and check the position of the wings. If they flare equally, grasp them again, wind two more turns around the base and half-hitch the winding thread. Next, pull the stems to the left under the shank, and wind at least three turns around them. Trim off the remainder of the stems, and cement the windings. Finish the fly in the customary manner.

Variations for tying fan wings are many. For example, each wing may be tied separately, but this adds some extra windings. The stems may be tied lengthwise to the hook, the fan wings projecting over the hook eye and bent back into vertical position. Or the stems can be held below the hook until the wings are tied in place.

Any method that leaves the fan wing equally curved, and divided, and well secured to the hook, can be considered right.

Down Wings

Down wings effectively represent the wings of caddisflies (sedges) and alderflies. For that matter, when tied with a quill body and lightly winged and hackled, down wings are better representations of the folded-wing mayfly than most uprights. Years ago I learned that, and confess to having fallen into the habit of using the same down wings for fishing both wet and dry, as befitted the occasion. If I were forced to choose a single *type*—not pattern—of dry fly, I'd likely take the down wing, tied with mandarin or mallard fibers. The down wing casts well without whirling, offers a good profile to the trout, and is about as versatile as a fly can be.

Tying Start the work at the tip of the body, tying on the tail fibers (alderflies and caddisflies have none), and continue to the right to the point where the hackle is to be tied, about two thirds up the shank. Wind the hackle back and forth between mid-body and slightly behind the hook eye, leaving enough space for tying on the wings and finishing with the head knot.

The wings are paired and closed, to sweep back over the body in the vertical plane. The closed-fiber wing does this well, but flank feathers, rolled or matched, hair, and paired hackle feathers are equally good. Hold the wings parallel to the shank between the left thumb and forefinger, as when setting a wet-fly wing, and slide the butts between the hackle fibers. Wind two or three turns around the butts. Remove the fingers, and check that the wings are properly set; if so, hold the wings firmly, and wind three more turns around the butts. Trim the butts cleanly, and complete the fly with the head knot.

Down wings sometimes elevate at the rear in an ungainly fashion. One way to overcome that tendency is to form a slight knob behind the hook eye with the winding thread, leaving a slight space between the hackle binding and the knob. About six turns of thread will do. Catch the wing fibers with the winding thread in the slight space, and the resulting wedging action from the knob will incline the wings down. This takes a few attempts to do it correctly.

Cut wings are favored by many tiers for winging alders and sedges. Trimmed to size, the larger hackle feathers with dark, brownish blotches are good. In down wings, the coarse center quill is an advantage: it can be crimped with the thumbnail to form a shallow Z, the lower leg tied in front of the hackle.

Hair and bunched hackle fibers tie well, although they are inclined to spread at the tips. The tips of paired flank feathers are well marked and hold their shape. Folded fiber sections from wing and tail feathers make good down wings.

Both sedges and alders have long antennae. For realism, try two moose-mane fibers or two dark-grizzly hackle barbules tied over the hook eye before applying the whip finish.

Flat Wings

The stonefly, which folds all four of its wings horizontally over its back when at rest, is the best example of the flat wing. The willowfly is another.

Tying Start at the rear of the hook, tying on two tail fibers about one half the length of the body. Tie the body, and half-hitch the winding thread. Match a pair of glossy grizzly hackles, and

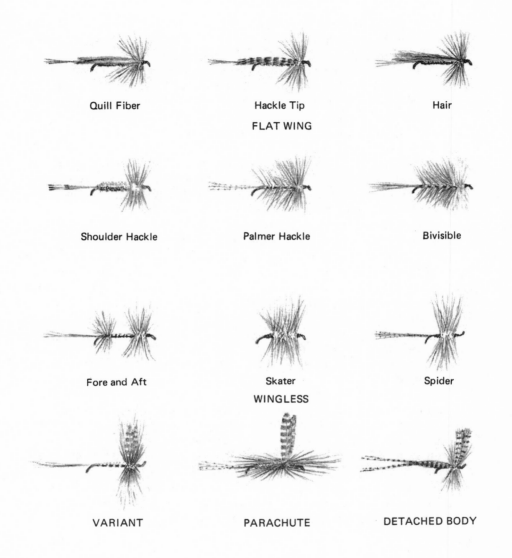

Quill Fiber

Hackle Tip

FLAT WING

Hair

Shoulder Hackle

Palmer Hackle

Bivisible

Fore and Aft

Skater

WINGLESS

Spider

VARIANT

PARACHUTE

DETACHED BODY

JEL

FIG. 19. DRY-FLY STYLES—FLAT WING, WINGLESS, VARIANT, PARACHUTE AND DETACHED BODY

place one on top of the other, the dull sides down, over the body. Stonefly wings are long and project well beyond the body as much as two fifths the body length, which accounts for their clumsy flight. Fasten the hackle wings with three turns of winding thread, leaving sufficient space for winding the hackle, the last operation. Do not half-hitch the thread until you are satisfied that the wings lie flat over the body. If they persist in elevating at the rear, unwind the three turns of thread, and crimp the butts of the quills into a shallow Z with the thumbnail. Then retie the wings by winding over the lower leg of the Z. Wind the hackle in front of the wings. Two antennae belong on the flat wing. A pair of moose-mane fibers or cock-grizzly fibers is ideal. Fasten them after securing the hackle and before tying the head knot.

The same procedure applies to tying cut wings, slender, uncut whole wings, and sections from turkey, goose, duck, and chicken wing quills. Regardless of the kind, the wings must be well aligned, if the finished fly is to represent the natural insect.

Wingless Flies

The wingless fly is usually called a "hackle fly." One of the oldest of all fly designs, "the hackle fly" has a well-deserved place in the flyrodder's fly box. Of many forms, from the tiny, infinitesimal spider to the bushy salmon "fore and aft," it often outfishes the winged flies. Some anglers use the hackle fly exclusively throughout the season, catching their share of fish with a regularity sometimes annoying to those who go to such great pains to fashion winged flies imitating the natural.

There are six types of "hackle" flies. Each differs from the others, largely in the position, spread, or characteristics of the hackle.

Shoulder Hackle

The shoulder-hackle fly is the most common of the hackle flies. It is easy and fast to tie. The work is started at the left, the tail fibers tied, the body wound, and the hackle tied and wound last. Vintage patterns like the Gray-Hackle Yellow, Brown-Hackle Peacock, Tup's Indispensable, April Gray and dozens of others are as effective today as when first contrived.

Tying The tying procedure should be quite apparent at this stage. After finishing the body, fasten the butt of the hackle, the dull side to the left, and wind it around the forward part of the body to the hook eye, and complete the fly with the head knot.

Palmer Hackle

The palmer-hackle fly features hackle spirally wound around the body; if tied well, it makes for effective high riding. All dry flies can be hackled palmer style without changing their specified patterns. The secret is hackling sparsely, to let the values of the body show through the hackle fibers. Many are the trout that have found a sparsely palmer-hackled Cahill to their liking, as it bounced atop the bubbly. I mention the Cahill because ordinarily it is not palmer-hackled; but the Beaverkill, Wickham's Fancy, the Queen of the Waters, Flying Caddis, and a host of others—all with histories a mile long—are.

Because dry-fly hackle frequently varies in quality and width, the best hackle feather may be more tapered than straight and the fibers progressively longer toward the butt. It is advisable, then, after fastening the tail fibers, to tie the body hackle by the tip where the body will be started. Always clip the fibers from the tip before tying it in place, to reduce bulk at the tip of the body.

Gold-ribbed bodies are popular for this type. With scissors, taper the tip of the tinsel, and tie it over the tail-fiber windings; then tie on the body material, winding it to the right. Next, wind the tinsel rib and tie it off; then, spacing the hackle winds so that the effect of the body is not obscured, counterwind the hackle to the right, winding under and over, rather than over and under. If all materials are in proportion, tinsel-ribbed and even quill bodies will retain their original values when so hackled. A second hackle tied behind the eye of the hook completes the fly.

Mixed hackles are sometimes better than those of one hue. Grizzly and brown and dun and brown are good combinations, the contrasting hues of the hackles seeming to alternate in the sunlight in a most lifelike way. Wind one hackle over and under, the other under and over. Again, sparseness is the key word. The object here is to simulate the legs of an insect (there are only six), and packing the fly with hackle until it looks like a thistle serves no purpose.

Imitations of caterpillars are palmer hackled. The bodies are chenille, herl, or picked-out fur, spiralled with a hackle that has been trimmed before being wound.

Clip center tip from
quill, and roll fibers.

Tie down butts and
divide fibers.

X-wind between and
in front of the halves.

UPRIGHT ROLLED FIBER WING

Remove the down from
paired hackle tips and
stubble the barbules
along the butts.

Tie down the butts in
vertical plane.

X-wind between and
in front of the hackle
tips.

UPRIGHT HACKLE TIP WING.

Set paired sections back-
to-back, the curvature
upward.

Tie down butts.

Wind in front of sections.

UPRIGHT QUILL FIBER WING

FIG. 20. TYING UPRIGHT WINGS

JEL

Bivisible

The bivisible is as optical as its name suggests, being visible to both the fisher and the fish when light conditions are poor. It is simply a fully hackled fly, tied palmer fashion, with a few turns of white hackle at the eye of the hook. Some patterns are finished with light ginger, light dun, and light gray instead of white. At the very edge of darkness, following the course of the truly imitative dry fly, often dark brown or dark gray, is difficult. The two or three turns of white or very light hackle at the front of the bivisible can be seen under all but the worst conditions.

The original bivisible, as developed by E. R. Hewitt, was springy and light on its toes, quite unlike some of the creations one sees today; and it was always faced with white hackle. Hewitt also developed the Neversink Skater, described later.

Tying Two and sometimes three body hackles and one white or pale face hackle are sufficient. Whether to wind on a body is a personal choice, for many good patterns have none, except for that amount of the hook shank that shows through the hackle fibers. Gold and peacock-herl bodies seem to enhance the bivisible, however, and there are combinations of colors that hackles alone cannot provide: badger hackle, yellow body; grizzly hackle, red body; ginger hackle, green body are all good examples.

Start at the end of the shank, and tie in about eight glossy hackle fibers or the equivalent of squirrel, badger, groundhog or similar hair. Select two hackles, one with fibers slightly longer than the other. The smaller will be wound first, the larger last. Snip the fibers from the tip of the smaller hackle, and fasten the tip over the tail windings, the dull side to the left. Taper and tie on the tinsel, if called for, and fasten and wind the body. Rib the body with the tinsel, then counterwind the smaller hackle toward the eye of the hook. Tying the body hackle tip first is the benchmark of the well-made bivisible, because the fibers are shortest near the tip and increase in length toward the butt, giving the body gradual taper for proper poise on the surface.

Tie the tip of the body material over the tail windings, and wind the body no more than two thirds up the shank. Secure it with a half hitch; then wind the tinsel ribbing, and counterwind the hackle, securing it also with a half hitch. Trim the butt, and tie in the second hackle butt first. Wind this hackle three turns through the last of the body-hackle windings, picking free with the dubbing needle any body-hackle fibers that may have been

Hackle clipped flat at the
bottom lowers the profile.

Hackle wound then pulled
upward and divided into
wings.

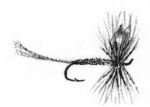

Baigent's style variant.

Reverse style preferred
by the author.

Hackle trimmed top and
bottom for spent wing
spread.

X-wound, 2-color hackle.

Notched hackle reveals
details of entire body.

JEL

FIG. 21. VARIATIONS IN HACKLE TREATMENT

wound under. Wind the remainder of the head hackle to the right, and tie it off with a half hitch.

Because there is usually little space left between the head winding and the eye of the hook, it is advisable to tie in the white face hackle by the tip. Little space is needed, two or, at the most three turns being enough to flag the wherabouts of the fly to the fisher, which is what the bivisible is all about. Trying to wind a whole white hackle at the head of the fly will destroy it.

A hackle trimmed to a stubble the size of the flues on peacock and ostrich herl is excellent for bivisible bodies. The stubble supports the body hackle wound through it and lends body color like no other material. Brown hackle wound through black stubble, or grizzly through orange, are examples. Furnace and badger hackles are simulated in this way. The mentioned brown-through-black looks as much like furnace as the original hackle; badger, of course, suggests a cream hackle through black stubble.

Some tiers counterwind the body hackle with gold wire, instead of winding a body. Counterwinding does hold the hackle in place but no more so than fine monofilament.

Fore and Aft

Hackle at both ends of the body is the earmark of this high floater, renowned for salmon in past years. It may resemble a joined male and female mayfly by a long stretch of the imagination.

Tying The order of tying is obvious. Fasten the tails, tie on and wind the aft hackle, tie on and wind the body, and finish with the head hackle and the head knot.

Skater

The skater was developed by E. R. Hewitt for the Neversink. By definition, the skater is a spider, in the fly fisher's vernacular, but it certainly is no representation of the real arachnid. Hewitt reputedly designed the skater to be twitched and skated across the surface, a tactic not espoused in those days, the downstream drift being preferred. The dry fly, was traditionally intended to float as willed by the currents, and every last effort was made to avoid "drag," that nemesis among the pocket currents that can snatch an otherwise perfectly drifted fly from the very mouth of the trout. There must have been occasions when a fly, pulled off course to skate across the surface—if it had not been dragged under—was taken in wild pursuit by a trout coming out of nowhere. It has happened so many times to me—the trout missing as often as being hooked—and I doubt that any flyrodder who knows a Blue Dun from an oyster cracker has not had the same experience. Yet, trouters did not stray from the dictum of the natural float, at least as far as I can determine, until the development of the skater, which soon set more than a few rods twitching.

History tells us that Hewitt's skaters were not varnished or cemented—the winding thread, that is—the idea being that the hackles could be spread out the length of the hook shank or compressed, accordionlike, to the fisher's fancy. Whip knots would survive the pushing and pulling, but I doubt that others would.

Tying The skater is tailless and consists of a short-shank hook and two oversized hackles. Color is optional, but the original was of one color: black, ginger or blue dun are traditional standards. Again, the strict adherence to tradition is curious. Hackles of *mixed* colors and markings are a benefit, because natural insects seldom, if ever, have legs without some markings, especially on the femur.

Spider

The spider, like the skater, is simply hackle tied on a short-shank hook. The tailed version rests on the water in the upright, conventional manner, the tailless in the hook-down, horizontal position. Sparseness is the rule. A size 18- or 20-spider coupled to a 6X or 7X leader point requires little to keep it afloat, and overhackling it defeats its purpose: to look like its archetype, a natural spider.

Badger and furnace hackles are sound favorites, for the small black or brown centers that develop around the hook when the hackles are wound. In the sparsely tied horizontal spider, the dull side of the hackle is down, and the dark center stands out. Getting the fly to light so that the hackles are spread out on the surface and the hook is down is not easy; it is likely the reason for the horizontal spider's unpopularity. Tying the horizontal spider on a regular-length hook with the two or three turns of hackle close to the hook eye will tip the fly over, leaving the hook vertical under the surface, as it should be.

Tying The difference between the tailed and tailless spiders is obvious. For either one, good, springy hackle is necessary.

Variants

The term "variant" often is applied to a dry fly tied with any of the variant hackles. It is a misnomer. The true variant is a dry fly tied

Tie both hackles,
dull sides to left.

Wind first hackle
and tie down.

Wind second hackle
through first, tie down.

VERTICAL HACKLE (MIXED)

Fasten hackle dull
side down.

Wind firmly around
projection on hook.

Extend tip over hook
eye and tie down.

HORIZONTAL HACKLE

JEL

FIG. 22. WINDING VERTICAL AND HORIZONTAL HACKLE

with short wings and long hackles, the wings upright, slightly divided, and the hackles a little shorter than those of the spider. According to some records, the variant was developed by England's Dr. Baigent, who named his version the "refracta." It featured double-hackle spreads: a short one having markings like the legs of a natural insect and a long, neutral-colored one for floating the fly high on the water. Of course, in those days, the fine-wire hook was still in the future, and a fly floated only if it was thickly hackled and somewhat waterproofed with mucilin. The wing length was the same for most fly styles, and any pattern could be made a variant simply by hackling it oversized. Adaptations changed the scheme of things, and some years later the variant appeared with short wings, as we know it today, and multicolored hackle—reportedly the product of one Albert Barrett of Pittsfield, Massachusetts. In that period, circa 1930, the variant was tied with the brown-grizzly hackle, sometimes called "cree," or it wasn't a variant. Today the variant is more a style than a color. The wings remain short, and the spider-length hackle appears in many variations: mixed solid colors like dun and brown, brown and black, ginger and dun; in grizzly, furnace, badger, ginger and dun variants, and in dyed solid colors and grizzly mixes.

Tying The variant differs from the standard dry fly only in the length of the wing and the hackle. The wings are short hackle tips or quill fibers tied upright or sometimes spent. Gold bodies are popular, as are up-eye gold hooks.

Baigent's technique of using long, pale, nearly colorless hackle to float the fly and sparse, short hackle to represent the color and markings of the natural's six legs has merit. I like the combination reversed: pale hackle at least one size smaller than the regular fly size and wound over a longer part of the body than usual, the "legs" of mallard, teal, mandarin, or short pheasant body plumage wound *one* turn behind the wings. The object here is to lower the position of the floating fly—hence the slightly smaller hackle—to cause the few fibers of the "leg" hackle to spread naturally on the surface, after the posture of the natural mayfly. Well tied on a 2X-long, light-weight size-12 hook, this attempt to imitate the mayfly is second to only one: the parachute.

Parachute

The resurgence in popularity of the parachute-hackled fly is interesting, for it seems to reappear in 15-year cycles, according to my findings. And each time it is reinvented, rediscovered, or renamed at least, the old "flat hackle" takes its place again as one of the best dry-fly types ever contrived. I have seen an orange-bodied, mallard-winged, furnace-hackled parachute convert June-shy brown trout into walloping monsters. More than a few times I was on the other end of the line. I have yet to see a dry fly of any other kind that will agitate a torpid trout as will the parachute. It is claimed by some to represent the cranefly, and well it does, but it doesn't stop there! If you are ever astream when the big Green Drake, *Ephemera guttulata,* is popping out of its nymphal bindings and happen to have a few parachutes in size 8 with pale lemon-grizzly hackle and straw-colored body, you had best beef up your leader tippets—and your leader, for that matter—if you plan to hold the trout that can all but rip the rod from your hand.

I first learned of the parachute in the 1930s, shortly after its first popularity. Doubtless through the evolution of the dry fly, the horizontal hackle—the key feature of the parachute—was contrived by some enterprising fly fancier before William Brush, the automobile great, popularized it to the extent of applying for and, in 1934, being granted, a patent on the hook, not on the fly dressing as such; but to the trade the parachute itself was considered patented.

There was a certain mystery about winding the hackle horizontally, and several methods emerged, each being claimed as the proper one. The Brush patent was for the hook, which had a short vertical projection about one fourth the shank length from the eye, the whole affair looking like a loop-eye salmon hook with the tip of the wire bent up, perpendicular to the shank. The "peg," which was integral to the hook, worked well because it was rigid, a decided advantage over some of the makeshifts that appeared later. Herter's of Waseca, Minnesota, markets a similar, if not the very same, hook as their Perfect Model 432. I concocted a few methods too, but none was equal to the real thing. Of course, all hook makers do not manufacture the parachute hook, perhaps owing to the patent conditions, which may account for the home-made doodads and gadgets that surface from the tier's bench from time to time: bent wires hot-soldered to the shank of a hook or simply tied to it with fine wire and solder-cemented. Hot soldering naturally burns off the bronze plating, and solder cement is messy and a far cry from good for the purpose. Using the base of the wings for an anchor is about the best substitute.

Tying Starting at the left, fasten on the tails, then the body, and half-hitch the winding thread about one third the shank length from the hook eye. Hackle tips for wings are the easiest to handle, and they occupy little space around the "peg." For the parachute the stems may be stiffer than for hackling conventional flies. Cut the fibers on the base of the quills to a short stubble, to help the wound hackle stay in place; then tie the wings in place immediately around the "peg." X-winds are no advantage. The point is not to thicken the "peg" with unneeded bulk. After the wings are in place, cement them well until their base is firm. Fasten the butt of the hackle close to the front of the wings, and wind it horizontally around the wing butts. Parachute hackle has a wider spread than that of vertically hackled flies, spanning from well behind the end of the body to beyond the hook eye. A good rule of thumb is that the hackle spread should be about three sizes larger than the spread of the conventional hackle. Large-sized hackle has a slight concavity on the dull, or inner, side; tying the hackle with its dull side down places the tips of the fibers on the water surface. Conversely, tying the glossy side down causes the tips to rise, and the load of the fly is supported by the curved inner portions. I prefer the former arrangement.

Wind the hackle carefully, starting the first turn about $1/16$ inch up the wing butts, and wind three turns toward the shank. Let the weight of the hackle pliers hold the wound hackle taut, and pull the forward hackle fibers up slightly, making room to tie the tip of the hackle to the shank. Finish with the head knot and a drop of cement.

Another method, in which the butts of the wing quills are pulled between the wings after the fly is tied, is useful if no parachute hooks are available. After tightening the hackle-tip wings in place, let the butts project vertically below the hook shank. Cement the windings well, and let the cement harden. Wind the horizontal hackle, and tie it down behind the eye. Grasp the two wing butts projecting below the hook, and bring them forward between the wings. This is a little tricky at first, because the butts tend to spread the wings too far apart. When pulling the butts up behind the wings, cross them twice, at the same time stroking out with the dubbing needle any wound-under hackle. Fasten the wing butts behind the hook eye, and cement the head knot.

Detached-Body Mayfly

The development of the detached-body mayfly over many years has been interesting. At one time the big No. 8 fly with translucent veined wings and the detached stick-to-itself-only latex body was heralded as the ultimate imitation of the huge Green Drake that everybody was bending feathers to imitate. To the human eye it seemed as natural as could be; yet for some inexplicable reason, despite its lifelike appearance, it never lived up to expectations. Various tubing, tapered cork, bucktail tied cone shape and cemented into a stiff, unlifelike body, and other materials were no better. Either the trout did not respond well to them, or the fishers simply did not like them. I had only spotty results with any of them. Like most tiers, I continued experimenting but eventually abandoned the whole effort, concluding that the detached body was too stiff and pulpy.

Ten or twelve years ago I was tying nymphs, pulling back the fibers on a ring-necked pheasant body feather for antennae, when the body and tails of a detached-body mayfly virtually popped out of the feather! There it was—a weightless, light-porous, mottled body having a fine, cream-colored center quill with the tails attached. I immediately quit tying nymphs and turned to tying what is probably the easiest-to-make mayfly I know about. Its advantages are so many that other efforts to devise a lifelike detached body seem a waste of time. The standard relation of fly size to hook does not apply. The body and tails are so light that hooks several sizes smaller than usual are preferred, as are hackle-tip wings and sparse hackle.

Tying From a ring-necked pheasant, mallard, teal, widgeon, or other duck, pluck several body feathers having the desired barring or mottling for the tail fibers. Strip the down from the base of the quill, and bend the remaining fibers toward the butt. Find fibers of the right length for the tail, and snip out the wedge-shaped tip of the feather continuing beyond them. The feather now should terminate in a V, with two or three tail fibers branching from each side. Pull the fibers below the tail fibers toward the butt of the feather. You now have the total body and tails of the mayfly. Hold it up to the light, and notice the porosity between the quill and the fibers.

Moisten the fibers bent back along the quill, which will become the body, and place the feather on the hook. Tie the feather with three or four turns of thread at about mid-shank of a size-14 hook. Then tie in the hackle-tip wings and the hackle. This type of fly needs no more than two or three turns of hackle.

I claim no authorship of this detached body, because certainly there have been others who have at least tried out the idea. One just discovers such things accidentally, as I did here. The tie may look a little fragile compared with solidly wound bodies tied on long-shanked hooks, but it is not as fragile as it may appear.

After all, what is the loss of a fly that brings up a brown trout that you weigh instead of measure?

The fibers can be stripped from the quill, leaving a white-to-gray or buff body, depending upon the individual feather. Stripping the fibers slims the body and, to some extent, may weaken it; fibers bent back along the body and tied down are naturally reinforcing. Short, stubby body feathers have stouter quills for the purpose, although the markings on the tail fibers may be absent. You will have to hunt for the feathers that tie best.

Midge Flies

The midge, a miniature version of the dry fly, was patterned originally after the blackfly, gnat, and mosquito—true two-winged flies—in sizes 16 and 18. Today the term "midge" includes any terrestrial or aquatic insect in sizes 18 through 28, although in some circles authorities on minutiae contend that a fly is not a midge if it is larger than size 20.

There are few real differences between midges and regular-sized flies. Except for the size and the care in tying it, the midge is simply a miniature. Pattern is another matter, for the tiny terrestrials and Caenis flies, archetypes for the midges, have distinctly different colorations; that is if the fisher is a stickler for imitation.

Use the finest tying thread you can handle well. The hooks are flea size and it takes time and patience to become proficient at tying materials on them. A magnifying glass clamped to the tying vise is a help. Perhaps the best way to develop skill in tying the midge is to lay out a series of hooks, beginning with size 12 through 24, and then tie the same pattern in declining sizes. Upright hackle-tip wings are ideal for midges because they lack bulky fibers. Hackle for legs need be a mere suggestion; in flies so small the relation of hook weight to body density is of no importance. A good fly dressing will keep the midge either on top or in the surface film, at least, which brings up the point that any distinction between a wet and a dry midge is more theoretical than real, provided, of course, that the fly has not been wire-weighted to sink.

Midge fishing has become a highly specialized art for which little splinter rods, shell-like reels, 4-weight lines and the finest of fractional-pound test leaders have been expressly developed. It has its place. For those with the light touch it can be phenomenally productive when ants, tiny caddis pupae, mini-mayflies, dull sowbugs, and the like, are the trout's forage of the moment.

Tail fibers too soft or
elevated too far.

Hackle too long and
slanted toward tail.

Fur body no-hackle
fly (emerged dun)
rests in/on surface
film.

Conventional, close-
packed hackle.

Sparse palmer hackle
aligns fly horizontally
and supports body off
surface.

Horizontal hackle spread
gives fly low profile.

Hackle clipped at bottom
lets fly rest on surface
film.

JEL

FIG. 23. HOW HACKLE AFFECTS THE ATTITUDE OF A DRY FLY

The Nymph, Larva, Pupa, and Crustacean

The largest part of the trout's menu consists of the myriad aquatic insects and crustaceans populating the pools, shallows, and runs of the trout stream; for in those three environments the nymphs, larvae, and pupae, the scuds, sowbugs, and shrimp, thrive in both separate and mixed societies, as best befit their kind. Some mayfly nymphs, for example, are equipped to burrow under the silt, others to flit comfortably amid the strong currents, still others to cling hidden within the creases of the rocks. Pupae of the caddisfly and cranefly may or may not inhabit the same waters; stonefly nymphs prefer fast water; the larvae and pupae of the midges, for the most part, reside in pools. Add the aquatic forms of the alderfly, fishfly, hellgrammite, dragonfly, the many beetles, the sowbug, scud, and shrimp, and the variety swells into a universe of fauna.

In earlier times the old wet fly served as a nymph or larva, and it brought many trout to the landing net. It still does and probably always will, but the advent of the nymph, as we now identify the type, is quite recent in the history of fly fishing. Now viewed by so many as the "fourth dimension" of fly fishing, fishing the nymph has become more scientific with the passing of each season, and well it should: It poses the greatest challenge to the serious tier-angler, who fortunately in recent years has had a world of good books on aquatic biology to support his own field work. Those who study their entomologies usually can identify a nymph, a larva, a pupa or a scud and take pleasure in recognizing it by its scientific name; and they think in terms of periodicity, refraction, density, translucency, prismatic effect, and the like. So it follows that tying simulators of such underwater creatures can be pretty exacting, requiring the knowledge of just about every skill that is part of the fly-making art. Subsurface fauna are subject to close scrutiny by the trout, and every effort spent in tying an imitation as lifelike as possible will be rewarded. The size; the shape of the body (whether it is round or flat); the translucency; the texture; the mobility of the legs, tails and antennae, and the sink rate—each of these can spell the difference between an effective lure and "just another bug" to clutter the fly box.

The size of the natural determines the shank length, but the substitution of a 2X-, 3X-, or 4X-long shank reduces the hook profile, a definite advantage most of the time. A No. 10 standard, for example, and a No. 12 2X-long, by Redditch standards, have the same length: $9/16$ inch. The gape of the No. 12 is shallower, and the wire gauge is finer. Therein lies one of the keys to good nymph design: selecting the hook with the least profile to match the size of the natural. But there is a practical limit: It is seldom necessary to exceed the length of the 4X-long shank.

Some nymphs are fished deep, others at mid-depth, still others—like the emerger—in the surface film. Regardless, it is better, I have found, to use a fine-wire hook and to weight it with lead or copper wire for faster sink rates than to revert to a heavy-gauge hook, although years ago I would have argued this point. By "heavy-gauge" I mean hooks of wire gauge larger than 2X-stout. Nymphing requires the fine leader, a soft rod and a gentle touch, and the finer-gauge hook sets with much less effort than does the heavy weight.

A rather recently developed hook is the English bait hook. It is deeply arched, almost sickle shaped, and is excellent for tying curled larvae. The eye is ringed. Some fly fanciers rebel at the thought of tying a nymph or larva on any but a down- or up-eye hook, but I do not. I like the shape regardless of its ring eye for several of the aquatics that I am never without when wading a trout stream.

Bending the hook shank to suit one's own notions has become popular of late. Some of the finest imitations are made that way. A long-shank hook bent to have a high arch as a base for the thorax of the burrowing mayfly is an example. But it is doubtful that small hooks, like sizes 16 and 18, bent in this way offer advantages over the unbent hook.

In addition to weighting the hook with lead or copper wire wound around the shank before the body material is wound, the sink rate of a nymph can be increased by tying small brads or brass pins on each side of the shank. Called "outriggers" by some, these small brads and pins serve the purpose of making a flat base for the wide, compressed-body nymph. A small split-shot sinker closed immediately behind the hook eye is good for giving the nymph a "heads down" attitude, and it is easily flattened to represent the shapes of the heads of so many nymphs.

Enameling the hook shank white helps to effect translucency. Rayon floss wound over the white enamel, then coated with clear acetone, produces most lifelike bodies. Monofilament in one of its many hues—pink, blue, green or amber—is ideal for its natural translucency. Wound over a shank enameled white or buff, it fairly rivals the body of the natural; and it is tough, beside being available in every useful size. Fur dubbed on the tying thread is somewhat translucent because the tiny air pockets in the fibers create underwater prismatic effects on the exterior of the body.

The majority of the materials in the tier's stock is useful, in one way or another, for artificial nymphs, larvae, and pupae. Hackle, for example, is most versatile. It can be trimmed close to the quill for narrow, fringed legs and is better than peacock herl for the purpose, or it can be left full to simulate hair-like gills. Or it can be stripped of all but the very few barbules at the tip, to form claws. Bucktail and other coarse hair can be tied and knotted to form joints; sections of wing fibers can be tied in at the tips and folded forward to represent wing pads and thorax. Possible methods and materials are almost limitless. The studious and enterprising tier can unleash his imagination without restraint when it comes to tying nymphs and the like. With today's man-made materials to supplement the proven standards, one may fashion a nymph so realistic that it might swim off, if clipped from the leader and given the opportunity.

An insect is comprised of three parts: the head, the thorax, and the abdomen. The head includes the antennae, the mouth, the compound eyes on the sides of the head, and a simple eye (the ocellus) in the center.

The thorax is the section between the head and the abdomen; it consists of three segments, each of which bears a pair of legs: the prothorax, nearest the head; the mesothorax, the middle segment; the metathorax, the third, next to the abdomen. The upper side, or back, of the thorax is the notum, and the underside, or belly, is the sternum. Both the notum and the sternum are subdivided into the pronotum, prosternum, mesonotum, mesosternum and so on.

Wings (wing pads in nymphs) have their origins in the second and third thoracic segments, the mesothorax and metathorax.

All insects have six legs (spiders have eight and are arachnids). The large joint nearest the thorax is the femur, the second the tibia, and the third the tarsus, which ends in the claw.

The abdomen is the part on which fly tiers spend the most effort to simulate the natural, doubtless because the segments, usually eleven in number, are so clearly marked and visible,

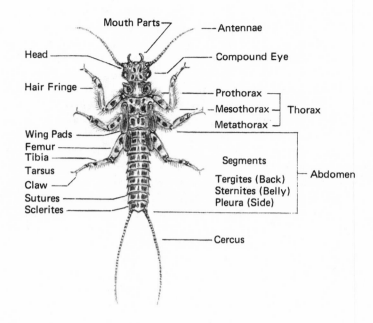

Mouth Parts

Antennae

Head

Compound Eye

Hair Fringe

Prothorax
Mesothorax   Thorax
Metathorax

Wing Pads
Femur
Tibia
Tarsus
Claw
Sutures
Sclerites

Segments

Tergites (Back)
Sternites (Belly)
Pleura (Side)

Abdomen

Cercus

JEL

FIG. 24. NOMENCLATURE OF THE NYMPH

although the first segment is obscured in some genera. The back (upper side) of the abdominal segment is the tergite, the belly (lower side) the sternite, usually paler in hue.

Two or three tails, cerci, tip the abdomen in lengths peculiar to the order and family of insects.

The nymph, pupa, larva, and crustacean are tied like the typical wet fly, from left to right, beginning with the tails.

Tails: Some nymphs have widely fringed tails for locomotion, others bristly or smooth tails. Smaller hackle feathers with flexible quills represent the fringed tails well, and if too wide they can be trimmed to size. Select hackle of dry-fly grade. Saddle-hackle tips may be too fragile for this purpose; much depends on the individual feather. Marabou is excellent, but again the strength of the quill must be considered. Bristly tails are simulated by trimming the hackle barbules close to the quill from the tip toward the butt. Smooth tails are various: moose mane, fine-stemmed hackle stripped of the barbules, caribou hair, horsehair, flank-feather fibers, and coarse hackle fibers. Naturally, not every one has the ideal markings and hue; so it becomes a matter of experimenting to find the right hair or fiber to do the job.

Abdomen: As already mentioned, the tergites are usually darker than the sternites. There are several techniques for simulating them. The following two are rather easy and satisfy all the requirements for dark-back, light-belly nymphs that I have encountered.

The first consists of winding the shank with material the color of the sternites, then folding over them, from tail to thorax, material that is the color of the tergites. A spiral winding of monofilament spaced increasingly farther apart toward the thorax (about ten spirals) represents the segments.

The second method is, perhaps, easier: The abdomen is wound the color of the sternites, and the tergites then are "painted" on by stroking the dubbing needle, tipped in enamel, across the back. Monofilament may be used in the same manner, for producing the effect of segments. The center quills of larger body feathers make lifelike sternites. Goose body-feather quills have both light and dark sides. If soaked well in water, they will flatten when drawn between the thumbnail and forefinger, so that the light and dark sides become parallel, contrasting bands.

Round Bodies: Round bodies are typical of many of the nymphs and larvae of static waters. Padding the hook shank is sometimes necessary for larger bodies. If the nymph is to be fished deep, the addition of a lead or copper underbody doubles as both weight and padding. Floss or yarn is the choice for padding the nymph body to be fished mid depth.

Flat Bodies: Nymphs frequenting lotic water have flat bodies for quick maneuvering. Their imitations are important to the serious fisher. There are several ways to tie them, none difficult. A few years ago the procedure was to tie the body "round" and to saturate it with clear acetate enamel, then, before the enamel had hardened, to press the body flat with smooth-jawed pliers. A second method, which is neater and more controllable, consists of winding a small brad or pin to each side of the hook shank and thoroughly soaking the winding thread with clear enamel or cement. Substituting monofilament for the metal pins reduces the sink rate. Polyurethane strips, used in the textile industry, are superb for flat bodies. They wind faultlessly with sufficient elasticity to form tight, well-shaped bodies. Coating the underbody with white enamel adds translucency to the finished body that is hard to duplicate with other materials.

Gills: Gills appear under the thorax and along the sides of the abdomen in a variety of forms, depending on the insect, which may account for the enduring effectiveness of the palmer-hackled body, standard for many of the older patterns of wet flies: Queen of the Waters, Wickham's Fancy, Male Beaverkill, Brown Sedge, and others. The tier's ingenuity can work wonders here. Some nymphs have gills like hairy tufts, others appendages resembling atrophied legs. Both are well simulated by small, mobile hackle tips tied laterally at the juncture of each body segment. Peacock herl is similar but is limited to metallic-green and bronze colors. Marabou, the immature, downy feathers of the turkey, is excellent and is usually tied along the median line.

Thorax: The length of the thorax varies among the orders of insects. The thorax is bulkier than the abdomen and significantly affects the profile. It is reasonably well represented by tying the tips of body feathers, deer hair, a tuft of hackle fibers, or the like, at the front end of the body and bending them forward over the hook eye behind which they will be tied down; the windings become the heads in many styles. Winding hackle around the forward part of the body before folding the tip of the thorax is common practice. The barbules, bent outward and downward by the folded thorax, assume the appearance of gills and legs. Hackle tips—short, stubby body feathers trimmed to shape if necessary—and folded sections of hair make good wing cases. Some effective patterns have painted wing cases as well; the stonefly, whose ornamental markings are a marvel of geometric design, is a fine example.

Shell Back: Crustaceans like the sowbug, *asellus,* and the scud, *gammarus,* have a continuous shell back or, more accurately, an articulated shell. Imitation is not difficult. A favorite method is to tie a slightly palmer-hackled body to simulate the legs and body, then to fold the back over the entire body, securing it behind the eye of the hook. The segments are easily formed by winding fine monofilament at the proper intervals—ten being about right.

Legs: Hackle of the right fiber and spread represents the legs of the nymph, larva, pupa, and crustacean about as well as any material, but it should be coarse and resilient. Yet, at best, hackle only suggests the shape of an insect's legs. Much effort has been spent on contriving better, and one often wonders about the need for it. Mobility, especially during a slow retrieve, is an asset to any underwater lure. Hackle has that quality like few other feathers or hair. If I were forced to choose between hackle and the most lifelike but inflexible imitation of a leg, I would choose hackle. It can be trimmed to shape, adding size where needed, as in the femur, or reducing it, as in the area of the tibia, by trimming the barbules proportionately. It can be bent at right angles in the shape of a nymph's leg and set in that attitude with a touch of cement applied to the joint. This is best done after the legs have been tied in place because it gives the tier a little more latitude in shaping the legs to suit the size of the nymph.

Antennae: Antennae add realism and mobility to the nymph and larva. Two thick hackle fibers are fine for the purpose, as are two flank-feather fibers. Moose mane, fibers from the pheasant tail, guard hairs from the groundhog and badger, and fibers from the body feathers of pheasants have their place. Medium-to-fine hackles trimmed close to the quill make good imitations of the antennae on some pupae. Ostrich and peacock herl is of ideal texture, but the tips that are the best size are usually too flimsy.

The following descriptions of the underwater phases of insects are general only, treating the *types* of nymphs and pupae.

The Mayfly Nymph

The large *Ephemera* and the still larger *Hexagenia* nymphs have many like qualities from the tier's point of view. What a pity more was not known about these great insects when I was a young fellow forty years ago. What a sight it was to witness those magnificent

Green Drakes jerk to the surface in numbers to the 10th power, the great brown trout of Penn's Creek flashing in pursuit—but always, always just a little too far down to take the big grizzly-yellow hackle dry flies we mistakingly drifted over them. The trout were simply taking the nymphs just before they had emerged, and we misread the slashes at the surface as meaning they were gorging on the popping dun. Sometimes a huge yellow-bodied Light Cahill wet fly cast far upstream and twitched furiously would tease a brown into thumping it; but, as a rule, the dusk-to-dark flights of the Green Drake were a sight to behold only and were seldom the hoped-for experience of swishing lines and throbbing rods that would have resulted had we been wise enough to fish a facsimile of the nymph. The wonderful Green Drake is as enigmatic now as it was then, even in its evidently declining population, which, regrettably, so like that of the trout, is the product of our time. It still appears sporadically in some of its well-known habitats, but seldom does the fisher see it emerge like a snow flurry in June, when the fingers of dusk reach across the pools to mark the moment of the fly man's hour.

If only then I had known the secret of the Green Drake! But that was long ago, and we learn only by doing—doing the wrong thing, eventually to grasp years later what was wrong about it. Like drifting a dry fly big as a Ping-Pong ball over trout feeding on Green-Drake nymphs a foot and a half below the surface.

Proportions: A tier may spend great efforts in gathering together materials with the right markings and hues to make a nymph, but the one characteristic he may disregard, for all his painstaking, is the relation of one part of the nymph to another. The proportions are just as important as the hues and the markings. A stonefly and a mayfly of equal overall lengths differ significantly in the lengths of comparable parts. Even genera within the same order vary. Just as the Green Drake has one set of proportions, so the other mayfly genera have theirs, as do the stoneflies and caddisflies.

A good mathematical system for establishing the proportions of the nymph is illustrated in Figure 25. It is based simply on the body length of the nymph as having the value of one and each of the body parts, the antennae, legs, and tails, as being a proportional part. If you have doubts about the values of these proportions, tie a Green Drake to those shown, and compare it with one tied with the lengths of the thorax and the abdomen reversed.

Tying A No. 8 4X-long hook is about right for this big

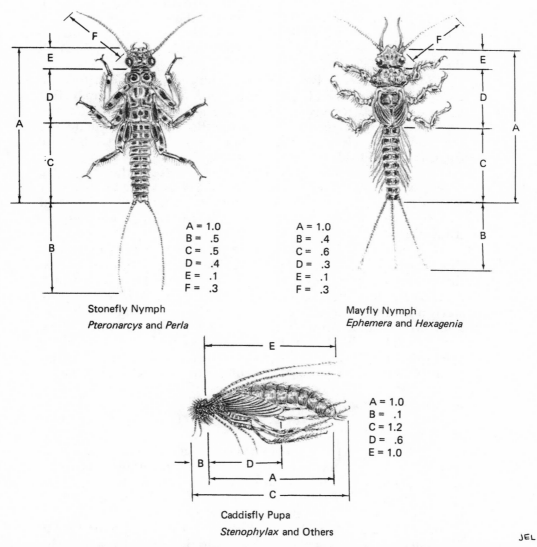

A = 1.0
B = .5
C = .5
D = .4
E = .1
F = .3

Stonefly Nymph
Pteronarcys and *Perla*

A = 1.0
B = .4
C = .6
D = .3
E = .1
F = .3

Mayfly Nymph
Ephemera and *Hexagenia*

A = 1.0
B = .1
C = 1.2
D = .6
E = 1.0

Caddisfly Pupa
Stenophylax and Others

JEL

FIG. 25. PROPORTIONS: STONEFLY, MAYFLY AND CADDISFLY

nymph. Enameled white it makes the body somewhat translucent, a desirable quality in the simulation of this particular insect. Start at the left, winding on for the tails three fine hackle feathers, the barbules of which have been trimmed to the size of peacock herl. Spread the outer two slightly, and secure them with X-winds so that they will close and open when the nymph is twitched through the water.

The sternites are lighter than the tergites, and the difference is obvious in the Green Drake. One good way to achieve this effect is to tie the body with two sections of bucktail, the darker on top, and wind monofilament spirally up the body to simulate the segments. Fibers from coarse feathers are a satisfactory substitute for the bucktail. Monofilament of 10-pound test is about right. Another method is to wind quill stripped from the stem of a pale-gray goose feather or the stalk of a peacock-eye feather over an underbody of pale-yellow rayon thread that has been soaked with clear lacquer or acetate enamel. The final appearance is quite translucent.

The abdomen is about 60 percent of the nymph's length. The thorax occupies the next 30 percent. The underside of the thorax, the sternum, sometimes is dubbed with fur, the texture of which entraps air, lending the aspect of movement. Before tying the sternum, fasten the tip of a section of wing or tail feather of appropriate color immediately in front of the abdomen. This section will be folded over the thorax, to be tied next, toward the eye of the hook, to form the notum, the *top* of the thorax. A few turns of hen hackle, duck breast, or partridge hackle around the thorax, before the notum is formed, will represent gills well—despite their being in the wrong place, if you are a stickler for exact detail. Those few turns add, however, the movement that any good nymph should have.

Chestnut partridge hackle, ring-necked pheasant body feathers, teal and mallard breast feathers, and hen hackle have good markings and texture for legs. They tie well and are the correct length. Three turns around the thorax (before the notum is bent forward and tied down) are sufficient. Secure behind the hook eye with a pair of half hitches. Two or three of the hackle fibers may be bent over the hook eye and tied there for antennae. A scant amount of cement or lacquer applied to the lower third of the fibers ensures their forward attitude yet leaves the upper two thirds free to vibrate.

Weight hook with
fine lead wire.

Start winding thread
behind wire and tie
down end of dubbed
thread.

Wind a small fur knob
and fasten flank
fiber on each side.

Tie down fur dubbing;
fasten 12-lb. mono-
filament ribbing, wind
dubbing and tie wing
section.

Wind dubbing toward
eye, spiral monofila-
ment, tie tip of hackle,
and trim tip.

Wind hackle 3 turns and
tie down butt.

Hold hackle fibers down
and bend wing section
forward.

Tie down wing section
behind eye; trim surplus,
tie on antennae and
finish with head knot.

JEL

FIG. 26. ONE METHOD FOR TYING THE STONEFLY NYMPH

The Stonefly Nymph

The large, ornamentally marked stonefly nymphs, *Perla* and *Pteronarcys,* are well known to the flyrodder. Some *Pteronarcys* nymphs have bodies close to two inches long, and the larger *Perla* have bodies as long as those of the largest mayflies, *Ephemera* and *Hexagenia.* So a No. 8 4X-long hook is the correct size.

Tying Figure 26 illustrates one good method for tying the stonefly nymph. Another way to weight the body is to tie a brad on each side of the shank, which broadens the abdomen and thorax (as shown in Figure 27). Fastening the flank fibers on the sides keeps them spread out. Brown mallard is a first choice. As mentioned, the proportions of the stonefly differ from those of the mayfly. The thorax is shorter, as are the tails and the abdomen. The antennae are slightly longer and more widely spread. Stripped quill from the stem of a wing feather also makes a good abdomen and thorax. Form the underbody with rayon thread, and soak it with cement or lacquer. Monofilament carefully wound between the quill windings represents the segments of the natural insect.

Dark, mottled turkey feathers are good simulators of the wing cases and the notum. They can be tied tip first at mid-body, one slightly overlapping the other, and folded forward to represent the notum, or V-notched and tied in place.

The legs of the stonefly are quite ornamentally marked, both the femur and the tibia being darkly blotched. Certain of the brown-black mottled body feathers on a ring-necked pheasant have similar markings. Wind three turns around the front of the thorax before folding the wing cases forward.

The antennae are widely forked. Two fibers from a ring-necked pheasant body feather or two from a brown mallard flank feather are equally good. The lower third of the fibers should be cemented or lacquered for holding their forward position.

Caddis Pupae

Caddis pupae are easily recognized by their banana-shaped bodies; long, gangly legs and antennae, oar-like wings projecting downward, and hunchbacked profile. Compared with the mayfly and stonefly nymphs, the caddis pupa is, indeed, a forlorn-looking critter. Yet, from the trout's point of view, the caddis—in any stage of its interesting morphology—is both succulent and abundant and able to survive a higher degree of pollution than can the mayfly.

Tying If your aim is simulation in every respect, the shank of the hook must be bent into the shape of a shallow arc, the body curvature typifying most caddis pupae. The large *Stenophylax* (see Figure 25) is a good genus to copy. A size 8 3X-long hook is about right. Bend the shank into a gradual arc until the hook is banana-shaped. There are no tails. Begin the abdomen slightly beyond the end of the shank, to emphasize the curvature. The abdomen is thickly haired, and brick-colored fur dubbed over brown wool is a good representation of the hard-to-describe hue sometimes called "rust" or "burnt orange," among others. Gold ribbing adds brightness resembling the flash of tiny air bubbles caught in the hairy, irregular body surface of the natural.

Use gray duck wing fibers for the wings, which are tied to slant slightly downward from the median line. The hackle, brown mallard breast or brown pheasant body plumage, is tied sparse and long, extending well beyond the tip of the abdomen. Wind two turns immediately in front of the abdomen, and pluck the upper fibers, leaving only those below the wing cases. The antennae are two large woodduck fibers tied in at the top. Brown hackle trimmed to peacock-herl size and wound behind the hook eye simulates the fuzzy head of the pupa.

Caddis Larvae

Decades ago anglers believed that the stick-and-leaf fragments found in the stomachs of trout lent credence to the contention that trout, like humans, needed some roughage in their systems, that the pebbles and sand proved the trout also needed ballast to withstand the surge of spring-swollen creeks. That was before the mysteries of the caddis were well understood; the unique caddis larvae are among the most skillful of nature's architects, building with remarkable accuracy their portable shelters of tiny timbers, thatched leaves, or cemented sand and pebbles—all meticulously contrived to precise structural plan—which they occupy and drag about until the time of pupation, when the worm "closes the lid" by sealing the entrance of the case with bodily secretions.

The larvae are of many sizes, from the tiny size 22 to the ample 3X-long size 8. The cased and uncased versions naturally differ, the former consisting of the case and the projecting head and legs of the larva, the latter of the larva alone.

Tying Constructing the larval case is a test in artistry. Many attempts have been made to imitate it, the earlier Strawman, a good example. Tied with clipped deer hair and trimmed to shape,

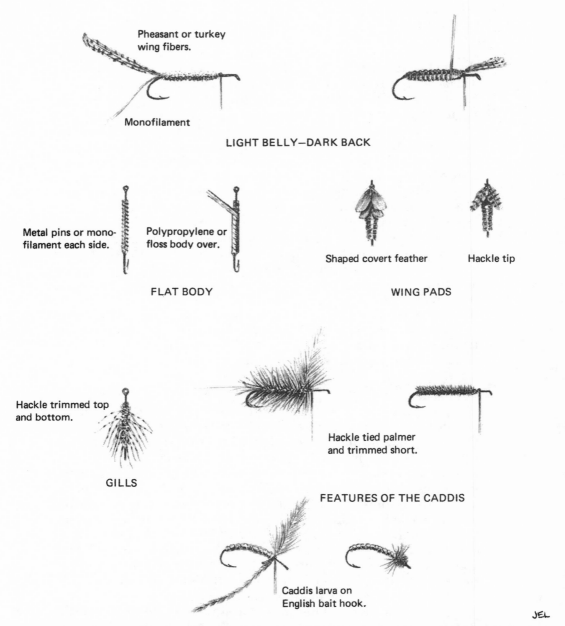

Pheasant or turkey wing fibers.

Monofilament

LIGHT BELLY—DARK BACK

Metal pins or mono-filament each side.

Polypropylene or floss body over.

FLAT BODY

Shaped covert feather

Hackle tip

WING PADS

Hackle trimmed top and bottom.

GILLS

Hackle tied palmer and trimmed short.

FEATURES OF THE CADDIS

Caddis larva on English bait hook.

JEL

FIG. 27. USEFUL TECHNIQUES FOR TYING THE NYMPH AND LARVA

it has fooled trout for close to half a century. More exact copies have been built of wool yarn saturated with cement and left to dry, after which they are recemented and adorned with bits and pieces of sand, sticks, toothpicks and the like while the cement is tacky. Coarse feather-fiber trimmings are good for the purpose; they adhere well to the cement. It is best to capture specimens for copying from the streams you fish because, as stated, the numerous genera of the caddis communities unwaveringly follow the case-building practices of their kind.

Weight the hook shank with wire. Form the head by winding two or three turns of fine chenille behind the eye of the hook and the legs by winding one turn of mottled pheasant body feather or partridge hackle immediately behind the chenille head. Trim out with tweezers all but the hackle fibers that project laterally.

One fast way to make the case is to wrap the shank with wool yarn, soaking it with cement, and forcing several coarse fibers into the yarn before the cement has hardened.

The larva, itself, is quite grub-like. A dubbed fur body ribbed with oval or wire gold tinsel of appropriate size, with partridge- or pheasant-body fibers for legs, and a tightly-wound chenille head make a good representation of the natural.

Crustaceans

The sowbug, *Asellus,* scud, *Gammarus,* and shrimp, *Palaemonetes,* are of genuine interest to the flyrodder. There are times when these small crustaceans are taken with rare selectivity by the trout, and the chap who does not have a few artificials that reasonably represent them in at least shape and size may find himself up a creek he never intended to fish!

The large thumb-size crayfish, *Cambarus,* is too bulky to be copied well at the fly vise—although big trout are partial to it, particularly after it has just shed, pink and vulnerable as a newborn field mouse.

The scud, sowbug, and shrimp, like other crustaceans, swim backward, a feature the tier should keep in mind.

The Scud: Scuds are amphipods, inhabiting cold, slow-moving streams. They are partial to hard water. Compared to the sowbug, they are colorful and agile, darting among the watercress and weeds. The body is arched and narrow, and the legs, capable of propelling these little crustaceans at surprising speeds, are draped below the body. The largest, *Gammarus,* measuring one inch in length, is gray throughout. Others of about the same size are olive or dull yellow. Hooks size 14 through 10 2X-long are appropriate.

Tying The artificial has to be a pretty good facsimile to be effective because scuds live in dense communities, and one that does not closely resemble the natural scud is apt to be ignored by the trout which are especially fond of scuds. The body is arched, clearly articulate and flea-like, the antennae curving inward and the two short tails bending outward. Start the work beyond the shank—about one third down the curvature of the hook—by tying two mottled pheasant wing fibers so that they project downward. Strip the quill from the stem of a white wing feather dyed yellow, and tie the finer end, dull side up, over the windings that secure the two pheasant wing fibers. Next fasten the tip of a gray partridge body hackle at the point where the shank begins, the quill end toward the eye of the hook. Tie on a 6-inch length of 10-pound monofilament, to be wound later to form the back segments. Dub the shank length with yellow fur, and pick it out with the dubbing needle. Wind the partridge hackle around the body palmer style, and secure it with a pair of half hitches just short of the hook eye. The lay of the barbules should be toward the hook eye. Fold the stripped quill over the body and hackle, tying it in place with two half hitches. Wind the monofilament up the body spirally and finish with a whip knot at the eye of the hook. A stroke of clear enamel or lacquer will add desirable luster to the quill back.

Scuds vary in color according to their environment and the alkalinity of the water. Generally they are yellowish, olive, or tan. Combinations of partridge, grizzly and brown hackle and fur dubbing of the right hues will be most useful.

The Sowbug: Sowbugs are small, gray isopods that are common to most waters. Seldom exceeding one inch in length and averaging only half that, the flat, wide sowbug is a staple part of trout diet. Hooks size 12 and 14 are ideal for the sowbug.

Tying First broaden the base by fastening two metal pins to the sides of the shank. The sowbug subsists on decaying vegetation on the stream bottom, where the artificial is best fished, and the additional weight of those two small pins is just enough to get it there. Except for the wider body, the sowbug is tied the same as the scud. Use muskrat fur for the body and grizzly hackle for the 14 legs which project laterally. The sowbug is a dull-colored creature, and the imitation should be dressed accordingly.

The Shrimp: The shrimp is a branchiopod and somewhat

resembles the scud but is longer and slimmer, most being brassy olive. Like the scud, the shrimp has its legs under the abdomen, and the overall profile is slightly S-shape. A No. 8 2X-long hook is the right size. Like other crustaceans, which seem more interested in where they have been than in where they are going, the shrimp swims backward; moreover, it swims upside down. The offset Keel hook, with its lowered center of gravity, is a good shrimp hook. The shrimp can be tied in the conventional manner—not upside down, as with the regular hook—because the lowered center of gravity of the Keel hook will flip it over in the water.

Tying Follow the plan for tying the scud. The body is greenish-gray fur dubbing; the legs partridge hackle dyed light green, tied palmer and trimmed blunt; the back stripped light-gray quill, segmented with 10-pound nylon monofilament (a lighter weight is optional); the thorax greenish-gray fur dubbing, and the antennae partridge hackle dyed light green.

Midges

Because they are minute, compared to the mayfly, stonefly, caddisfly, and crustacean, which receive so much emphasis as the bases for the creations in the angler's fly book, the larval and pupal stages of the midge fly all too often are overlooked—but not by the trout. There are times when trout seem to ferret them out, ignoring larger insects that, by human definition, should be preferable.

True to their name, midges are tiny, and just about the smallest stream-inhabiting creatures the tier-angler need be concerned about imitating. They are easy to tie but difficult to fish; yet, cast upstream on the finest leaders and allowed to glide motionless in the surface film, they often reverse the course of otherwise fishless days.

The black fly, *Simulium,* is a diabolical sneak, half corkscrew and half vampire; it headquarters in Maine, and is taken avidly at times by the trout. Its vertically ascending pupal stage is well worth learning to copy. The pupae rise to the surface with the help of a gaseous shroud generated as they ascend. Those that attain the surface soon emerge to begin their torment of mankind. Those that do not end in the gullets of rolling trout. The "smut" rise of the trout for the midge is maddening at times, unless it is recognized for exactly what it is. Until anglers learned to tie the tiny mushroom-shaped pupae, they were tormented, cast after cast, hour after hour, by these hardly perceptible rises.

The Midge, *Chironomus,* is more widely distributed and ranges in color from white through black. The pupae are important to the flyrodder because the trout are selective about them at times. Black, deep red, herl bronze and yellow are effective colors for imitation.

Tying Pupae are easy to tie. Sizes-18 and -20 2X-fine hooks are right for most conditions. Midge pupae drift vertically in the surface film, their gills uppermost; it is this position that the artificial will take ideally. The gills are represented by peacock herl or hackle clipped to the same size as the herl. The body is simply tapered from the tip, becoming larger at the gills. Tie the body of floss slightly conical and rib it with fine gold wire. Lacquer the body, and allow it to dry before tying the gills. The lacquer and gold wire simulate the tiny gas bubbles generated by the natural during its rise to the surface. Tie the herl immediately behind the eye of the hook, and finish the pupa with a head knot. If you use hackle for the gills, trim the barbules before winding it in place.

Leader tippets no coarser than 6X are necessary to fish the midge properly. Lightly dressed hackle flies without tails often will work well during the smut rise. I have seen a Royal Coachman, size 20, stripped of its wings and golden-pheasant tippet tails, take trout like no other fly in the book.

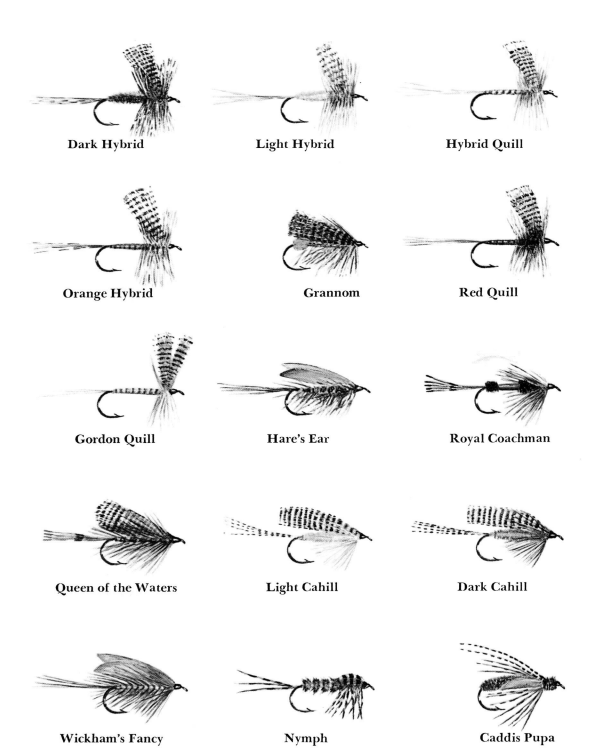

Dark Hybrid

Light Hybrid

Hybrid Quill

Orange Hybrid

Grannom

Red Quill

Gordon Quill

Hare's Ear

Royal Coachman

Queen of the Waters

Light Cahill

Dark Cahill

Wickham's Fancy

Nymph

Caddis Pupa

Woodduck and Gold

Black Ghost

Carson

Mickey Finn

Golden Demon

Jane Craig

Black Demon

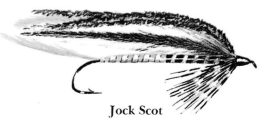

Jock Scot

Red Owl-Eye Optic

Edson Tiger (light)

Rat-Face MacDougall

Lady Caroline

Blue Charm

Pink Lady

Enfield Shad Fly

Typical Shad Fly

Silver Grey

Logie

Butterfly

Yellow Palmer

Leonard's Galli-Nipper

Gibbs' Striper

Brooks' Platinum Blonde

Kreh's Cockroach

Big Boy

Bonbright

Rhodes' Tarpon Fly

Loving's Striper Fly

Lyman's Terror

Leonard

STREAMERS

If it weren't for the streamer, hosts of flyrodders would know more fishless days. No other fly-rod lure is so versatile and productive, for the veteran or newcomer. From the tiny 3X-long 16 to the cigar-long 6X-3/0, the streamer represents dozens of life forms such as nymph, minnow, saltwater shrimp, squid, and baitfish. It also represents some types fished on top, like the grasshopper and cricket. Many anglers use the streamer exclusively, flailing away all through trout season until they put away the rod and turn to the shotgun in the autumn.

When the minutes without a strike have lengthened into hours, and casting the wet fly, dry fly, or nymph has become simply an exercise, the change to a streamer very likely will ferret out a good fish from waters seemingly barren of anything with scales. Doubtless, that is the reason why all but the most devout dry-fly purists have at least one or two tucked away in the folds of their fly books—and I sometimes wonder about the purists!

Time was when the "bucktail" and the "streamer" were considered separate forms, but when hair from animals other than deer became popular for its barring, texture, and other properties, and hair and hackle feathers were mixed to represent the markings and shapes of the dace, sucker, sculpin, and fingerling, the distinction between the two types all but disappeared.

Streamers customarily are tied on long-shank hooks, 4X- and 6X-long being the most popular, although there is no hard-and-fast rule governing the choice. The long shank is necessary if the body is to be long and detailed, and the pattern calls for full-length silver or gold tinsel. Shorter hooks, on the other hand, are effective for short strikers, notably the smallmouth bass and the striped bass, both of which strike at the heads of their prey a large part of the time.

The length of the hook has a lot to do with the "fishability" of the streamer. The relation of hook length to streamer length is critical for more than mere appearance's sake. The abominable combination of a hook that is too short and a streamer that is too long causes the streamer to corkscrew between the shank and the return bend of the hook. No amount of catering to the back cast helps either. The best remedy is to tie the streamer on a hook almost as long as the streamer itself or on a hook short enough to keep the streamer from becoming fouled on it.

The effectiveness of any streamer rests in its profile, markings, and mobility, not necessarily in that order. Originally designed 75 years ago to simulate the bait fish that landlocked salmon and "squaretail" trout feed on, the streamer has come a long way since the day when Herb Welch of Mooselookmeguntic, Maine, turned out the first one. Apparently, hackle feathers seemed the likeliest candidate to impart the wriggle of a fleeing minnow, for they have been used ever since. But I have always reserved the opinion that, despite the records, some of those old, long-winged wet flies of nearly 200 years ago were streamers in effect, if not in name.

There is little that is formal or traditional about the streamer. Imagination and the abilities to select the most suitable materials, and to tie well, are the only qualifications needed to turn out anything from the drabbest to the most bizarre. As to which is more useful—the drab or the bizarre—there are those who claim that fish accept a streamer only for its size and action, that the colors, how they are blended, and the other intended lifelike values satisfy the angler more than the fish. I have mixed reactions to that claim. A whole book could be written on color alone, for there is so much that can be said about it. Some anglers stress color over all other ingredients; and there are sticklers for the *exact* hues, who fret that the yellow, for example, is too dark, or that the blue should be more greenish. There probably is no right or wrong to their contentions, which obviously are a matter of preference. I, for one, know that the fisherman who has confidence in his tie—whether it is of stork dyed indigo or giraffe whiskers dyed azure—will fish it more deliberately and expectantly and will catch fish with it.

Streamers patterned after the life forms existing in any given water are usually successful—if properly fished—although some patterns resemble nothing that ever was hatched or that ever lived, and they sometimes, inexplicably, lure fish. I refer especially to the black-and-orange combination for largemouth bass, the black-and-red for rainbow trout, the yellow-and-red for pickerel and others that, for one reason or another, have become reliable on any stretch of water.

Overall length may have as much to do with the success of a streamer as any one of its qualities. This is borne out when schools of fish are feeding on pods of baitfish. There have been times when striped bass persistently refused a well-placed streamer 3 inches long but took another in the same pattern a half-inch shorter as if they would never have a chance at another. Interestingly enough, the lengths of the minnows in the pods were just about 2½ inches! Had the patterns been different, these comments would not be worth writing.

Fishing depth is governed largely by the weight of the hook or, more exactly, by the weight *added* to the hook—wire, lead shot, or metal pins fastened to the shank of the hook, to increase the sink rate. In open water especially, it is futile to cast a streamer that fishes too near the surface when the fish are feeding deep; and it is just as futile to work a deep-swimming streamer when the fish are herding baitfish to the surface. In current and tidal waters, upstream casts will allow for deeper sinking without any extra weight built into the streamer; still it is better to have both kinds: those that fish deep and those that fish from mid to shallow depth.

Streamer patterns are legion, many being fine examples of the fly maker's art. Some are highly specialized, embodying the same meticulous material arrangement that is prerequisite for the well-made salmon fly. Each year the array becomes more complex. One new to the game might conclude that he would need at least two or three dozen patterns just to get started. That is far from the truth! The logical approach is to pattern your streamers after the fauna in the waters you fish. "Pattern" does not mean "imitate." If the shiners in your favorite pond are of the typical gold-and-white and silver-and-blue hues, excellent simulations can be achieved with hair and tinsel. The addition of a few fibers of mallard to lend the appearance of scales is a plus, as is a little artistry in spotting a small eye on each side of the head windings. Study the fauna where you fish, that is, the fauna you know your quarry prefers. Catch a few and measure them; examine their color markings and their scale patterns. Then make a sketch of the principal features, and record their colors.

I must admit to being a staunch believer in the streamer. It has served me well in both familiar and strange waters, freshwater and salt. In one form or another, it has brought to the net or gaff my most prized fish, from 3-pound Maine brook trout to a 28-pound white sea bass off the coast of Baja California. And I am quick to add a 14-pound musky—not big as muskies go but still a lot of fish on a fly rod—a striped bass of the same weight (I once struggled for over an hour with one that may have tripled that weight), bluefish up to 11 pounds, dozens of pickerel over 24 inches, scads of smallmouth black bass up to 4 pounds, large-mouth bass to 8 pounds, landlocked salmon, barracuda, bonita, yellowtail, lake trout, fresh and saltwater panfish of every kind, walleyes and even channel catfish and one snapping turtle.

This list is not meant to parade my personal accomplishments in fishing the streamer; rather it is meant to illustrate that the streamer is, perhaps, the most useful fly-rod lure ever contrived. In passing, it is particularly fond of the trouts and they of it. Try it at night on the edges of the dark pools where the big brown trout hold. Perhaps the following pages will give you some ideas.

Tying the Streamer

In the beginning, start with relatively simple types—the bucktail or hackle feather—with tinsel or Mylar bodies. Tie several as nearly alike as you can, to get the "feel" for handling the longer hair and feathers and proportioning the streamer to the hook. As mentioned, the size and length of the hook must be right for the streamer, 4X- and 6X-long being preferred for most conditions. Regardless, choose the hook to match the streamer, not the converse unless the fish to be caught dictates otherwise.

Hackle-Feather Streamer

The "wing" of the hackle-feather streamer is tied in the vertical plane, to flutter and to let the barbules open and close, or in the horizontal plane, like the wings of the stonefly, to create striped effects, such as lateral lines. The former is the original, the latter an innovation of about 30 years ago. Hackle is an almost endless source of materials for the streamer. It comes plain, mottled or barred; takes dye well, and is available in about every size and quality. The neck hackles have stronger center quills than saddle hackles have and are better tapered after the shape of minnows. Saddle hackles, however, are more flexible, owing to their fine quills, and are more finely barred, especially those from mature grizzly cock birds.

Hackle Feather

Injured Minnow

Flat Wing

Tandem

Hair

Feather-Hair

FIG. 28. SOME STREAMER TYPES

JEL

Tying The streamer is tied like the hackle-wing wet fly. Tying begins at the left, as usual. A No. 8 4X-, 5X-, or 6X-long hook is a good size. Tie on the tail, in this instance just a stub of red feather, wool, or hair. Form a base for the tinsel body by adding a small amount of dubbing fur to the tying thread, or winding a little wool on the shank. Either will serve as a cushion over which the tinsel can be more smoothly wound than if it were wound directly on the hook. Fasten the tinsel behind the eye of the hook, and proceed to the left to where the body should end; then wind back toward the eye. The double layering will give the body a superior smoothness, especially if the tinsel is of narrow width. Sometimes it is advisable to wind four layers, if the smoothest possible taper is the objective. Wider tinsel is fine for *ribbing* flies, but the narrower is better for making a smooth, continuous body. Counterwinding with gold wire reinforces the tinsel and adds to the appearance of the finished product.

Floss, herl, chenille, and fur (or wool) bodies are tied in the same manner as wet-fly bodies. The only difference is the length. The distance between ribs is much discussed; if there is a preference, it is strictly a personal one. Some patterns call for hardly any spacing between the ribs; instead of the body being black with a silver rib, for example, it really is a silver body with a narrow black rib!

A little hackle wound on before the streamers are tied adds much to the mobility of the streamer. Here is the place where the mallard and teal breast feathers, the hen grizzly, the pheasant rump feathers, and the short guinea plumage are superb for streamlining the profile of the fly and adding just enough motion in the area of the gills to make it all the more credible to a well-educated trout, salmon or bass. Just two or three turns are necessary, but what a difference those turns make!

Tying the hackle by the tips slants the fibers rearward, the longer covering the shorter. After winding the hackle, binding the quill, and clipping the butt, wind two turns of thread through the fibers to separate them; then push the fibers down between the left thumb and forefinger, securing them with two more turns of thread. Apply a drop of cement to the windings.

Select hackle feathers having little, if any, curvature for the streamers. The straighter they are, the better. Neck hackles have stronger quills and fibers than do saddle hackles. Midget streamers are dressed with only two streamers each; those ranging in size from 10 to 6 have four each, and those larger than six 6 have four or sometimes six each. With scissors trim the down from the base of each streamer, but leave enough stubble to be caught by the working thread. Stripping against the lay of the feather leaves the quill smooth with a tendency to roll out of position when tied. Hold one feather over the hook and approximate its tied-down position. If it is too long, trim it to the right length. Place the inner (dull) sides of the two feathers together, and trim the second feather to the same length as the first.

Locate the feathers with the first of the fibers immediately behind the last windings holding the hackle. Holding them firmly, bind the butts in place, checking after two or three turns of the winding thread that the feathers have not slipped. If they have, unwind until they are free (or loose), and cant them slightly in the direction opposite to the one in which they slant. Wind and taper the head, and finish with the whip-finish and a drop of cement. Later coat the head a second time.

Injured Minnow

The hackle-feather streamer can also be tied as an injured minnow. When twitched slowly, this variation swims in short arcs, simulating a crippled minnow. This fetching action results from tying the streamers on one side only.

Tying Tie two streamers of the same length and resiliency, one on top of the other, with their dull sides facing the hook. When they are in place, touch the first of the barbules behind the windings with cement to stiffen the streamers. Whether the streamers are tied on the near side or the far side is a matter of ease in handling.

Flat-Wing Streamer

The flat-wing streamer features horizontally tied hackle feathers that, if arranged carefully, effect the narrow striping of some minnows and fingerlings. Glossy dry-fly hackles of the same size give the best results.

Tying Select good-grade cock hackles having stiff fibers of medium to short length. Apply two each, one on top of the other, of each color desired. The curvature of the feathers should be down.

Tandem Streamer

The tandem streamer is an old style, reputedly originated about 75 years ago for trolling for salmon in Maine. Similar streamers appeared in Europe about the same time, but they had three, rather than two, hooks, the center one tied point up. They were known as "Demons" and "Terrors."

The tandem is effective for hooking short-striking fish. The second hook adds extra flash and movement. The extent of the body dressing varies. Some prefer an undressed hook; others like the second hook full size and well dressed, particularly for big, brackish-water largemouth black bass.

Tying The so-called "standard tandem" was tied with two hooks, the trailer smaller than the front one, the two connected by a suitable length of silkworm gut, which was later replaced by fine, dull wire and eventually by monofilament.

There are two methods for tying the tandem. They differ only in the fastening of the hooks. In the first, monofilament of 15- or 20-pound test, depending on the hook size, connects the two hooks. Tie a 10-inch length of monofilament to the second hook, as if tying a snelled hook with a whip knot. Pass the forward end through the eye of the first hook from the top, and bend it back along the bottom side of the shank. Space the hooks the desired distance for the proper length of the streamer, which will be the length of a smelt, herring, or whatever is being copied. Tying the trailer hook first is the only sure means of controlling the space between the hooks and the overall length of the finished streamer. Hold the free end of the monofilament tight against the hook shank, and bind it tight with tying thread. Use cement liberally, and wind the thread evenly, as when winding a rod guide. Trim the tip of the monofilament after whip-finishing the head knot. It is best to prepare the hooks for the streamers you intend to tie all at one time; otherwise, no two will be the same.

Tie the body of the trailing hook, and add the tail and wing sections—generally a few fibers of hair. This will seem awkward with the connecting monofilament and front hook in the way, but with patience you can do it. Locate the front hook in the vise, and tie the body and hackle. Use one of the selected hackles for measuring the correct distance the streamers should extend beyond the end of the trailing hook: about a half-inch for most patterns. If too long, the streamers may corkscrew around the hook. Trim the barbules from the butt of the hackle feather accordingly, and make the remaining ones the same length. Four or six feathers are usually called for, two or three on each side. Place them with their dull sides facing the hook shank. If tying six at one time is difficult, try tying them in pairs, one pair on top of the others. Finish with the whip knot, and cement or lacquer the head twice.

In the second method, the trailing hook, which is long-shanked and ring-eyed, is fastened to a monofilament loop bound to the front hook, the loop extending about the length of three hook eyes. The trailing hook is generally finished as a complete fly, headed and lacquered. The front hook is prepared by tightly binding the monofilament loop to the shank. Cement the windings thoroughly; then prepare the front hook as already described.

Tying The tandem is tied with a fine wire connector in a similar way. Fasten the trailing hook by passing the wire from the front through the hook eye, over the shank, back through the eye, then back over the top of the shank. Cement and bind the wire tight. Fasten the wire to the front hook by passing the wire from the rear through the hook eye, over the top of the shank, back through the eye, then along the shank. Secure it with well-cemented windings. Avoiding the use of solder is better for the bronze plating on the hook.

Hair Streamer

Hair streamers, whether of bucktail, squirrel tail, calf tail, or whatever, have in common an opening-and-closing action that is most effective, particularly when twitched during a slow retrieve. Hair ties well and is durable—some kinds more than others. Very dense hair is difficult to handle sometimes when tapering the head. The solution is to taper the butts with scissors, wait for the first coat of cement to become tacky, then carefully wind the head. The tier's own technique for selecting and tying hair will evolve through trial and error; I know no written description that is a good substitute for experience.

A tuft cut from a bucktail, for example, consists of individual hairs of many lengths. Some tiers like their bucktail "wings" to contain hairs all the same length and make efforts to rearrange them that way. Instead of cutting the tuft and binding it to the hook by the butts, as most do, they first make the hairs the same length. A simple way is to cut the tuft close to the skin, then grasping the tips between the left thumb and forefinger and, with the right hand, pulling the shorter lengths out by the butts, adding the tips to the longer ones already held. Repeat the process until the "wing" is of the desired thickness. I prefer a mixture of short and long hairs for the resulting overall shaggy appear-

ance, which seems to me essential to bringing out the best be-
havior of the hair streamer.

Tying Except for the wings, the feather and the hair streamers are tied the same way. Cement the butts of the hair
thoroughly. A little cement stroked a short distance behind the
windings will do no harm. After the butts are firmly set, trim the
surplus so that it tapers toward the hook eye. Do not trim the tips;
much of the weaving and working action of the hair will be lost.
Tying contrasting bands of color, one on top of the other—as in
the Mickey Finn—is effective: yellow over red over yellow, black
over yellow over white, white over red over white and so on.

Feather-Hair Streamer

Of all the long-winged streamers, the mixed feather-hair type
offers the tier the most opportunity to indulge his creativity. It
may not be a distinct type by strict definition, but I consider it
such, for it embodies all that is good in both the hair streamer and
the feather streamer—and adds values of its own to the finished
product. There are few if any standard patterns. Let the tier
contrive his own to represent the shiners, daces, smelt, and other
baitfish abounding in his own waters. The following suggestions
are merely guidelines, outlining a few techniques for blending
hair and feathers in minnow-like lures, many of which are as
killing as any lure yet devised. Tying takes a little longer because
there are more parts to prepare, proportion, and blend.

If possible, have a shiner, dace, or whatever, to copy—or a
good illustration of one. Studying the colors of the scale arrangement, the translucency of the abdomen, the lateral line, the markings on the fins and head, and the shape and gills will reveal some
surprising qualities that you may have missed before. Several of
the daces and shiners, for example, have strongly marked stripes
from gill cover to dorsal; chubs and minnows have pink- to rose-
colored fins; sculpins have brown-mottled, fan-like gills. They can
all be imitated with feathers, hair, tinsel and the other materials
on the tier's work table.

Tying The tendency is to crowd too much material into this
streamer or into any streamer, for that matter. Tie a little on the
sparse side; otherwise, by the time all the materials are in place, no
space will remain for shaping and finishing the head.

Fasten on the tail fibers—hair, hackle, or two flexible hackle
tips—and wind the body to the point where the first of the hair
sections will be tied, roughly three fourths up the shank. Tie on

the first layer of hair—perhaps clear nylon—over the cemented turns of thread binding the body. Nylon sometimes may curve slightly from handling and storage. If so, in the piece you are using, turn the curve inward so that the ends turn away from the shank of the hook. This will simulate the lower curve of the long oval shape of the minnow. Translucent nylon hair complements the glint of tinsel or Mylar. Ideally, the second layer will be of animal hair: white goat, polar bear, or high-quality deer tail, serving more as a filler than as a visible part, since it will be covered by side feathers. Tie this layer slightly forward of the nylon-hair bindings, and use cement or lacquer liberally on the butts and windings.

At this point, Mylar strips can be tied in among the second layer of hair. The $1/32$-inch width is ideal for flexibility. Three or four strips the length of the hair and tied on each side add unparalleled glint to the finished product.

The top layer is usually darker, and several long teal or mallard fibers are excellent, as is peacock herl or the guard hairs from the foxtail, badger and so on.

Simulating the markings along the side of the minnow has challenged streamer tiers for years, and the best approach has been to use grizzly hackle feathers, natural or dyed, one on each side. In many instances they obscure the banding of the hair layers and detract from the intended overall effect. I have found that a good way to solve this is to trim the grizzly hackle with scissors along the quill to the needed width. Placing the hackle carefully along the middle layer gives a most realistic minnow-like appearance. The barring is more distinct and blends well with the other materials without changing their values.

Use two strong-quilled peacock-herl strands for the lateral line, one on each side. They should edge the top side of the trimmed grizzly feathers. Gill covers are represented well by duck breast feathers—finely marked mallard or teal—or white, dyed pale yellow or olive, to match the gill covers of the natural minnow. Open gills can be simulated by placing a white breast feather dyed red under the gill cover. Only the outer edge of the red under feather need show.

Heads and eyes can be simple or elaborate, or they can be deleted. Painting eyes directly on the gill covers (cheek feathers) is easy. Use no more than two dots of lacquer for each eye: a large one for the iris and a smaller one for the pupil. For the sake of appearance, locate the pupil in the center. Many tiers prefer to

Muddler

Mallard Minnow

Palmer

Marabou

Optic

FIG. 29. OTHER STREAMER TYPES

JEL

paint the eyes on the head windings, which, of course, must be smoothly finished if the results are to be worthwhile. Then there are those who will shoulder a streamer with nothing less than jungle-cock feathers, for so many years a standing tradition.

Use cement liberally, even when preparing the shank for the body material. A streamer is exposed to rough fishing and bigger fish, both of which make short shrift of a poorly tied one.

Muddler Minnow

The Muddler received its name in a curious way. By dictionary definition, the word "muddler" can mean a stirring stick, a person who muddles through his day or a miller's thumb—any of several, small freshwater sculpins of the genus *Cottus,* whose heads are thumb-like. Don Gapen, the reputed creator of the Muddler as a superfly for brook trout, patterned it after the sculpin. But, depending upon its size and the way it is fished, the Muddler can be much more than a "sculpin"; it can be a grasshopper, a stone-fly, a caddisfly, any minnow, or just about anything short of a mayfly spinner or a midge, at the election of the user.

Patterns are far from standard. Basically, the Muddler is a feather-hair streamer with a clipped deer-hair head. The body often is tinsel. The tail is speckled turkey and the wings are mixtures of hair (calf tail or squirrel) and speckled turkey. The clipped-hair head finishes the fly. Years ago, before the Muddler was so named, it was called "ball head." There was a slight difference: The "ball head" had hackle streamers instead of turkey-quill fibers.

Tying Fasten the winding thread, and wind from right to left. Fasten the fibers from a brown-speckled turkey wing quill at the tip of the shank. Wind back to the right, and tie in the tip of the tinsel. Wind firmly back to the tail; then return to the point where the tinsel is tied in. Secure the work so far with a pair of half hitches. Clip the thread, and remove the work. Coat the body with cement or lacquer, and set the point of the hook in cork while the cement dries. Start the second body.

After the cement is bone dry, replace the hook in the vise, and resume. Retie the thread, and wind three or four turns over the front tinsel windings.

The wing arrangement varies among tiers. I doubt that there is a right or wrong way to tie it, but some prefer the turkey-wing fibers on each side of the hair and others prefer them on top.

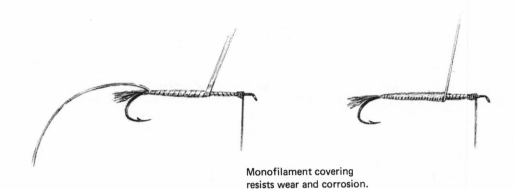

Monofilament covering
resists wear and corrosion.

Slip de-cored Mylar over hook,
tie down ends and whip finish.

A single strand of peacock
herl becomes a lateral line.

Light feather tip over dark
gives gill effect.

A half hackle trimmed to
length simulates dorsal fin.

JEL

FIG. 30. A FEW TECHNIQUES THAT MAKE STREAMERS EFFECTIVE

Take your choice. Either way, the tips of the turkey fibers should point down.

The deer-hair head is tied like the body of a bass surface bug. Clip a tuft of hair close to the skin about the diameter of a pencil. Try to arrange the hair with the tips together so that they will be the same length when fastened in place. One way to do this is to grasp the tips between the thumb and forefinger of the left hand and, with the right hand, pull out the shorter lengths by the butts, and align the tips with those held between the left thumb and forefinger.

Place the hair on top of the hook and in front of the wings, the tips of the hair extending close to the hook point. Hold the hair firmly between the thumb and forefinger, and wind two turns. Still holding the hair, snug the thread with gradual force; it should fan around the wing and become hackle-like. Check that the fanning out is uniform; then secure the hair with two more turns over the previous turns. Keep them close. Now wind the thread through the butts and toward the hook eye.

Pack the butts against the front of the wing with pressure from the thumb and forefinger, to clear space for the second tuft of hair. Locate this tuft against the butts of the first, and wind it in place, three turns being about right. Hold the hair butts back, and tie two half hitches behind the hook eye. Then whip-finish, and cut the winding thread.

With scissors shape the head until it is uniform. Leave the longer fibers of the first tuft untrimmed. The Muddler is considered correct if the head is trimmed blunt at the front. Why, I do not know. I trim the heads of the Muddlers that I tie in rather roundish form.

Mallard Minnow

The mallard minnow is an easy fly to tie. For all its simplicity, it is one of the most productive fly-rod lures I have ever used. The word "mallard" is misleading, however, because the finest mallard minnows are made of teal feathers.

From right to left, tie on the tail fibers—red wool or deer tail are always good—and build up a tinsel body. Select two or three flank feathers, well-marked mallard or teal, having long, even fibers.

Cement the windings at the front of the body thoroughly. Tie two sections—one on top of the other—horizontally over the hook, then two sections vertically (as in a down-wing wet fly) over the horizontal sections. Tie two wider sections, one on each side, with the lowest fibers in the same plane as the body. Wind the head, whip-finish and lacquer or cement the head windings.

The mallard (or teal) minnow will tempt about everything that can be taken with the fly rod. It is a *darting* type of lure, the type that represents minnows as few others do.

Palmer-Hackle Streamer

Palmer-hackled streamers simulate shrimp and are easy to tie. The tails are hackle streamers, and the body hackles, tied palmer, are wound over gold- or silver-tinsel bodies. Counterwinding the tinsel through the hackle is a technique espoused by many tiers, to reinforce the hackle.

Marabou Streamer

Marabou "breathes" like no other material. Dry, it looks like nothing that a fish would flick a fin at; wet, it flows back in a quivering, weaving mass that often is irresistible to game fish. It is excellent for making the slinky, hard-to-simulate sand eel.

Tying Clip several flues from the stem of the marabou feather, and tie them in place like hackle streamers or bucktail. A few strands of peacock herl mixed in with the marabou flues, or placed over the top of them, are effective. One strand tied at each side becomes a lifelike lateral line when the lure is wet. A few mallard or teal fibers lend the appearance of scales.

Optic Streamer

"Optic" pertains to the large head and eye on this type of streamer. There are no hackles and tail, at least if the lure is to be tied after the style of its originator, C. Jim Pray of Eureka, California. The hair wing is rather sparse, even in the larger sizes. First a steelhead wet fly, the Optic became a streamer as soon as the success of its big head and eye was publicized. Consequently, it was adapted to simulate saltwater jigs having dime-sized heads and eyes as big as peas. Hooks 3X-long are necessary to compensate for the space occupied by the large head.

Tying Wind the tinsel body from right to left and back. Tie in the hair wing about one third the shank length from the eye. Cement it thoroughly, and allow it to dry. If the hook is size 6 or smaller, build up the head with the winding thread, cementing the turns frequently until the right size is attained. If the hook is larger than size 6, form the head with hollow brass beads especially designed for the purpose or split-shot sinkers for deep swimmers. Plastic solder, available in tubes, is good for the purpose but a little troublesome to handle. Fine-diameter chenille builds the head quickly and easily and tapers well. Cement or lacquer the windings frequently; then coat the head in the desired color. After the head is dry, spot the iris on each side, and spot a small drop of contrasting color for the pupil.

Another method for building the large-eye Optic is to tie wire-stemmed glass eyes to the shank before tying the remainder of the fly. Herter's sells such glass eyes, and they are excellent. The most practical sizes are 4 or 6 millimeters. Bend the wire at right angles close to the glass eye; tie it to the shank, and clip off the surplus. Build up the tinsel body, and fasten the hair wings; then tightly wind fine chenille to form the head, X-winding between the eyes. Whip-finish the head, and cement or lacquer the knot.

PANFISH FLIES

Some flyrodders look on panfish as substitutes for the real thing—the trout, salmon, and bass that men spend fortunes to pursue and write about. To me panfish occupy a very special place in the order of things, for they are a fisherman's delight and no more a substitute for trout, salmon, or bass than woodcock is a substitute for grouse. They simply are different.

Panfish are colorful little clowns, inhabiting waters nearly everywhere. They take the fly gratifyingly well and are not easily depleted from fishing pressure. Perhaps their most laudable virtue is that they offer rewarding fly fishing to the many thousands who are not able to travel to trout streams or are just satisfied to fish for their local bluegills, perch, crappies, and rock bass.

Not at all fussy about the patterns of flies they strike, panfish do prefer the smaller ones—sizes 12, 10 and 8, with a sprinkling of 6s and 4s. Rubber-legged types have become popular of late, but I always have questioned which really preferred them: the fisher or the fish.

When bluegills and sunfish are on the spawning beds in the spring, they are as aggressive as game fish many times their size. Any bluegill guarding a nest will take a twitched fly in sheer fury! Small bluegills will strike the fly almost as soon as it touches the water. But the larger ones, broad as a cigar box, will stalk it, waiting and peering for the first movement. When it comes, they will bang the fly with a "spat" that will raise the hackles on your neck.

No, by no means are they a mere substitute for the "real thing." They have their own place in the scheme of things. The same can be said of the yellow and white perches, the rock bass, the white and black crappies, the white and yellow basses. Even

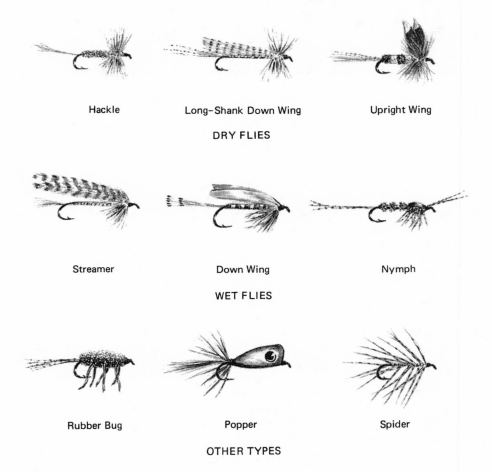

Hackle   Long-Shank Down Wing   Upright Wing

DRY FLIES

Streamer   Down Wing   Nymph

WET FLIES

Rubber Bug   Popper   Spider

OTHER TYPES

FIG. 31. PANFISH FLIES

JEL

the occasional catfish that will take a surface fly can have surprising strength.

Most dry flies and wet flies will take bluegills. Trout flies of all kinds are good, especially the hackle types. I doubt that pattern alone is a determinant. Some fishers claim so, but the record book is rather open on that score. Its tallies about like this:

DRY FLIES: (1) *Black hackle,* peacock body, size 12; (2) *Gray hackles*—red body and yellow body, size 12; (3) *McGinty,* size 10; (4) A light colored *spent-wing,* size 12.

WET FLIES: (1) *Royal Coachman,* size 10; (2) *McGinty,* size 8; (3) *Brown hackle,* peacock body, size 10; (4) *White Miller,* size 4; (5) *Yellow May,* sizes 10 and 4.

NYMPHS: A matter of choice, but one dark and one light in size 10 are effective.

STREAMERS: Any trout streamer size 10 will do.

If panfish are taking the fly—and seldom do they refuse—one or more of the listed patterns will interest them. Bluegills are the most consistently responsive, rock bass the most gluttonous, crappies the cagiest, yellow and white perch the most unpredictable. As a rule, the bluegill and crappie take surface flies more readily than the other panfish. Seldom will a perch take a floater. Southern sunfish generally concentrate on underwater life forms.

Many tiers of trout flies began their benchwork turning out panfish flies. The procedures are the same, as are the materials, and it is but a short step from the bluegill "hackle fly" to the Hendrickson, Cahill, or Gordon Quill of troutdom. Comfortingly, any trout fly that has gone awry in the vise is entirely satisfactory for panfish. As mentioned, they are not fussy and will gnaw the hackles off a lopsided fly as quickly as those of the perfect dry fly.

There are "freak" times when the little clowns *will* refuse the best-placed fly. Arming the barb with a smidgen of garden worm will turn the situation around: an old wrinkle that I learned while fishing for perch, both yellow and white. It works wonders with all panfish.

Tying There is no reason to consider special techniques for tying panfish flies, unless you want to explore the rubber-bodied, rubber-legged bug. The body can be sponge rubber or any of the durable expanded synthetics. Many tiers simply run the hook through the body material, trim it to shape with sharp scissors, and position the rubber-band legs by threading them through the body with a needle. Your imagination will guide you here. As I see it, there is little if anything that a rubber-legged bug will do that a hackled fly cannot do. But that is my bias. Make your own choice. The chances are that you will catch panfish regardless; that is, if you can cast where you are looking.

Dry Flies

If you can tie a trout dry fly, you can tie a bass dry fly. The difference is size. Spent wings are always good (they represent dragonflies and damselflies), and the palmer-hackle flies are hard to beat at any time.

Tying The double spent wing is ideal for smallmouth. Tie it on a 3X-long hook in size 10 or 8, and wind the hackle at least one third the length of the body. Patterns are legion and largely a matter of personal choice, for bass are not nearly so discriminating about the pattern of a dry fly as they are reputed to be. A scientific list of sure-fire patterns would seem appropriate here, but I do not give one: It would be more fanciful than real. Experience shows that one dark and one light pattern are needed. For the dark, a spent-wing Royal Coachman has served well. For the light, any one of several patterns is as good as another: the Light Cahill, Grizzly and yellow, or an all-white fly. If you see a smallmouth rising to surface flies and it will not take one of those patterns, the chances are slim that it will take any surface fly, and you had best switch to something representing an emerging nymph of good size or to a streamer, maybe even a wet fly.

Wet Flies

In wet flies again the size determines the makeup of the fly. From sizes 8 through 2, the tie can be similar in all respects to the trout wet fly. If the fly is larger than size 2, the wing treatment will be different, for the fibers of some wing quills are too short for the length of the fly. The solution is to select full hackle tips or the longest breast and side plumage with center quills for the wings. Hair wings are always good. In fact, the hair wing is dependable at any time.

For many years I have had the opportunity to pursue the smallmouth in creeks and rivers, ponds and lakes throughout the Northeast. I have always felt adequately equipped if there were McGintys and Jock Scots, in sizes 6 and 2, in my fly boxes, when the bronzeback were so disposed to take wet flies. If challenged about which of those two patterns is better, I would hesitate to say.

Tying The techniques for tying the bass wet fly follow the general lines for tying the trout fly. Do not be concerned about thickening the hackle only because you are tying a bass fly. If you are using wing feathers with center quills and the wings stick up too high, strip the fibers from the lower parts of the feathers.

Some tiers of bass flies like to wind the hackle in front of the wings; others wind it before fastening on the wings. Flies for connecting to spinners should be tied on ring-eyed hooks. Up or down eyes cock out of line. While on the subject, the fly-spinner combination is one of the deadliest fly-rod lures known for bass.

Streamers

Bass streamers are structurally the same as trout streamers. The hackle may be a little fuller, but the dressing is proportionally the same. Decades ago it seemed that the object was to crowd as much material on the hook as possible. Today's bass streamer is slim and active when retrieved, as it should be.

The streamer is a principal fly-rod lure for the largemouth bass. It is even better trailing a double spinner in size 1. This rig is a hunter of bass and will turn many an otherwise poor day into a good one. Although the plastic worm has become a standard in recent years, the streamer-double spinner combination, in the hands of a knowledgeable flyrodder, will hold its own when fished side by side with the "worm."

In the longer streamers, color combinations seem to be important. Largemouth are more responsive to some color mixes than they are to others—yellow-black, red-gray, and red-white the ones most cited. I certainly do not disagree. On the other hand, I have yet to see a feeding smallmouth or largemouth that would hesitate to make a pass at any wriggling, pulsing streamer placed to the fish's advantage. An angler may be gliding along quietly with the aid of a competent oarsman and casting his favored streamer among the stumps or lily pads. Suddenly he sees and hears the "swoosh" of a feeding largemouth and quickly drops his streamer into the center of the rings bulging from the rise. The bass takes with a jolt, and the angler smiles, laying all the credit to the pattern and, strangely, not to his own ability to put the streamer where it ought to be. I often wonder what the angler might think, had he tied on another pattern and still hooked the bass. I know some who would consider such an incident a fluke, because the bass had taken the wrong fly!

This book is on flies, not tactics, although I find it difficult to think in terms of one and not both. Probably the key reason why patterns seem so important to the angler is their eye appeal. Some feathers and hair, dyed or undyed, seem to tie and mix better than do others. When the fly or streamer is finished, it has singular appeal; the shape is right, the colors blend well, and the tie has a really "fishy" appearance. The tier thinks, "That has to catch a bass!" The chances are that he is right. Thereafter, if he is a systematic fellow, he will continue tying that pattern, putting emphasis on exact duplication each time he ties a few. But why not? He has caught bass with it. What might have happened, had he made the streamers of badger instead of grizzly? Or had wound on a brown instead of a yellow hackle? Would his creation have been any less effective? I doubt it.

Tying Tying the bass streamer follows the same procedure as for tying the trout streamer, previously described, although one type deserves special mention: the fly tied on the Keel hook. This hook rides point up instead of down because the shank has been offset, lowering the center of gravity. Any bass fly fished under the surface, if cast to the right spot, is apt to become snagged in the lily pads, or stumps and vines making up the bass's hideout. In reversing the position of the hook point so that it rides up, the Keel shape deflects the point much as the housing around the lower unit of an outboard motor protects the propeller. It is a great hook for a lure fished on the popular sinking line.

Tying the streamer on a Keel hook is different from standard procedures in one respect: The hook is mounted in the vise in the conventional manner while the tail, body, and hackle are being tied in place, then reversed when the wing material is fastened on.

As already pointed out, bass *flies* (not surface bugs, which will be treated in a following section) are really larger editions of trout flies. Except for local variations and colors, they are much the same everywhere.

SALMON FLIES

Fly tying as an art form is best illustrated in the elegance of the classic salmon fly, which is slow to tie but beautiful to behold, if tied well. Steeped in tradition, the classic melded imported feathers with expensive furs, tinsels, and the like, all fashioned to a precise prescription that once made mastery of the art a long process completed only through strictly monitored apprenticeship. For its exactness and complexity, the classic stood forth among all others. It is not surprising that the sport of fly casting for salmon became rather exclusive.

At first glance, one might ask, "Why all the color combinations and just a fiber or two of this and a few of that?" The answer depends upon the emphasis the owner chooses to place on such values. If he holds that the particular fly under discussion, say a Jock Scot, must be dressed exactly in agreement with the technique of T. E. Pryce-Tannant, then those values are important.

There is much to be said for both for holding to and for departing from the Victorian classic. If the colors alone seem to have a special mystique, that might be reason for holding to it. If the difficulty in tying one with the specified materials resulted in effects not attainable with more common materials, that might be another reason. But there has been a shift in thinking in recent years, and with it came substitutions, skimping and even omissions and simplifications of style that violate the character of the classic in many minds. Today the classic still is available; it has endured for more than a century. So has the "short cut" version. Both will bring salmon to the hook. That being the case, it is apparent that those who will have no less than the classic are a breed apart and will continue to use it, whatever their reasons or lack of them.

The correct styling and proportioning of the classic are essential if the fly is to have eye and, hopefully, fish appeal. Length, profile, hackle arrangement, the curve of the tail fibers (or lack of it), and the body taper must be in accord with each other and with the hook itself.

The classic is actually not a single type, despite its name. For example, the wing arrangement may be one of at least six forms. Somewhere in the process of making salmon flies progressively difficult to tie, it seems that difficulty itself and the really unnecessary expense of materials became the governing criteria for too many years; but this occurred during the Victorian period, when owning exclusive trappings and enjoying the pursuits of the privileged were hallmarks of success. Perfectionism flourished then, and well-tweeded flyrodders vied to have the most impressively stuffed fly cases. Even today there are those of the salmon-fishing clan who shudder at the thought of bending on a pattern whose lineage is too proletarian for the heralded salmon.

Patterns like the Durham Ranger, the Silver Doctor, the Dusty Miller, the Thunder and Lightning, and the Beauly Snow Fly are generally considered classics when dressed with the original ingredients. As expected, the steps in tying them are many. Styling is rigidly held. The locations of the tip and tag with respect to the barb and point, for example, are as precisely set as a draftsman could draw them. The tag (almost always tinsel) starts directly in line with the barb of the hook, and the tip (usually floss) ends immediately in line with the point.

Sparse dressing is a mark of the classic. The wing is placed low and close to the hook, over which it never should extend according to formula. Curvature in the wing is another. The top, or "roof," and the bottom, or "foundation," must curve gracefully rearward, to streamline the finished wing into a smooth oval. However, wings from pheasant tippets are blunt and do not contribute to that oval shape; the wings are accepted without the ideal profile, although no moment is made of it. Marrying dissimilar fiber sections from wing quills is favored for many patterns, like the Silver Doctor.

The lay and the length of the hackle fibers, the exactness of the hue (not only of the hackle, but of every part), the character of the ribbing, the location of the center joint, the curvature of the crests topping the wing, the blending of the shoulder feathers, the veiling of the inner wings—each of these and many more not mentioned here are the elements that gives the classic its elegance and symmetry.

Feather Wing

Hair Wing

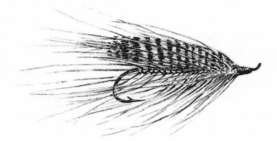

Spey

Dee

Low-water

FIG. 33. SALMON-FLY STYLES

JEL

American, Canadian and some Scottish and Irish fly dressers modified the classic, to the dismay of many who still hold to the guild-like traditions set by the early fly dressers. Whole series of patterns evolved based on simplicity and better available materials, challenging the historically ornate designs. Nearly 40 years ago, when I was writing the manuscript on *Flies,* I corresponded with two expert salmon-fly tiers, Joe Aucoin and Peter Cartile, both of Nova Scotia. Each related that for years the hairwing had been popular there and that it was far and away more productive than the classic. It was simply more mobile, and faster and easier to tie than the stiffer-winged classic.

Today the larger percentage of salmon flies has hair wings or wings fashioned from the flank feathers of the mallard or teal. For practical reasons, such styles will be considered here. Add the hard fact that more than a few of the materials called for on the classic wing come from endangered birds, now fortunately protected by strong laws, and the reasons become doubly practical.

In addition to the classic, salmon flies of the wet class divide roughly into five other types: the Spey, the Dee, the low-water fly, the hair-wing, and the streamer.

Spey

Originally the Spey was dressed on the earlier long-shank, fine-wire Dee hook, which was about 3X-long. The Spey probably was the progenitor of the low-water fly. Although it has distinct characteristics that set it apart, *in some patterns* the Spey dressing is considered a classic in some quarters.

Characteristics:

Tail. None.

Body. Tag or butt, none. Slim, with closely spaced flat tinsel of medium width; counterwound with oval tinsel spiraled around the body and hackle after the hackle has been wound. Because the two tinsels, fur or wool for the body, and the butt of the large hackle are apt to form a knob when tied close together at the end of so slim a fly, they are best tied sequentially, the oval tinsel to be counterwound last.

Hackle. Spey hackle comes from either the head and shoulders of the heron or from the section behind the saddles of a gamecock. Because the fibers are to be long and flowing, the hackle is tied on butt first. There is disagreement about the hackle treatment, however. Some contend that it must be folded as it is wound; others believe that it should be stripped on one side. The difference is obvious: Folded hackle doubles the number of fibers; stripping one side halves them. If sparseness is the objective, and stripping one side achieves it, I fail to see any flaw in stripping. A stickler for formality may. I am not one, and I seriously doubt that the salmon has a check list for evaluating hackle windings. Furthermore, stripping one side of the hackle makes the winding of two or more hackles together possible, or at least simpler, when several colors are called for. Unstripped hackles add too much bulk, preventing the glint and the colors of the body materials from showing to best advantage.

Some patterns have throat hackles of teal and mallard, even of gold-pheasant tippets. Several fibers tied beard fashion in front of the body hackle are all that is required.

Wings. The wings are of gray and brown mallard, sometimes teal, flank fibers, dyed or undyed. They are tied slightly divided in the vertical plane.

Tying Use the finest tying thread you can handle comfortably, to avoid the formation of lumps when fastening the body materials to the hook. Start at the right, and wind to the left. Tie in the tip of a strand of wool or dubbed fur, according to the pattern. Taper the tip of the flat gold tinsel with scissors, to reduce the tendency to bulk and to prevent cutting the fine thread at the edge of the tinsel. Tie the tapered tip immediately in front of the wool or fur.

Strip the down from the butt of a spey hackle, and fasten the butt immediately in front of where the tinsel was tied. Taper the tip of the tinsel to be counterwound after the hackle has been wound in place, and tie it in front of the hackle butt. Each of the materials now should be to the left so that the building of the fly can begin.

Wind the body material, ending well behind the hook eye. Next, spiral the flat tinsel around the length of the body winding, and secure it with a half hitch.

Spey hackle folds best if it is wet while being wound. Wet the fibers in short sections by moistening the left thumb and forefinger in water and stroking the fibers rearward as you spiral the feather along the edges of the tinsel ribbing, folding and bending the fibers as the spiraling progresses (see Figure 34). Secure the hackle with a half hitch, and trim the tip.

Counterwinding the oval tinsel through the hackle may seem awkward at this point, but it can be done easily with the aid of the

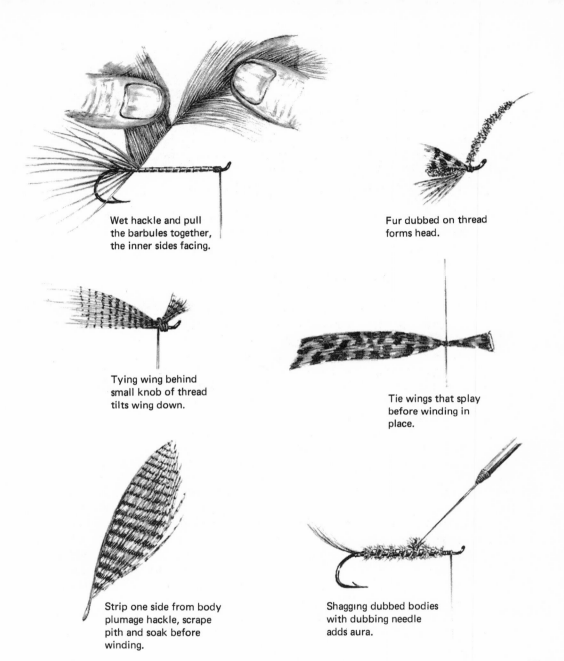

Wet hackle and pull the barbules together, the inner sides facing.

Fur dubbed on thread forms head.

Tying wing behind small knob of thread tilts wing down.

Tie wings that splay before winding in place.

Strip one side from body plumage hackle, scrape pith and soak before winding.

Shagging dubbed bodies with dubbing needle adds aura.

JEL

FIG. 34. BASICS FOR TYING THE SALMON FLY

dubbing needle to hold the fibers clear with each turn. The final effect is like cross hatching, the oval tinsel crossing the flat tinsel. Secure the tinsel with two or three half hitches and a touch of cement.

Winging the Spey correctly requires care. The wing strips are not placed on top of the body but slightly on the sides. According to formula, they must not obscure the body.

Dee

The Dee is a long fly having horizontal (flat) wings tied on a 4X- or 5X-long hook. The wings are horizontal and rest close to the body quite like those of the stonefly.

Characteristics:

Tag. As a rule, oval tinsel.

Tail. Generally one golden-pheasant crest topped by about 7 tippet fibers half the length of the crest feather.

Body. Always slim but often two colors, the aft body tinsel-ribbed only and the forebody palmer-hackled with heron or spey hackle and tinsel-ribbed, the hackle flowing back to the tip of the wing and even beyond the hook.

Hackle. Folded or stripped, long-fibered and palmered as required by the pattern.

Throat hackle tied beard fashion is often called for, folded teal, mallard, and pintail being preferred. It is always tied in front of the body hackle.

Wing. Paired, narrow strips tied horizontally, are standard and are clipped from matched wing quills—all white, gray, or brown from turkey, peacock, and pheasant or the quills from any large, suitable bird.

Tying The major differences between the Spey and the Dee are the wing treatment and the inclusion of tail fibers on the Dee. Some authorities claim that the hackle on the Dee must be shorter. Others say, the longer, the better. It's a toss up. For all intents and purposes, one might conclude that, so long as the fly has a pair of long, slim, *horizontal* wings, it is a Dee, and if it has a pair of long, low, *vertical* wings, it is a Spey.

Low Water

The low-water fly is small for the hook on which it is tied, the body only about one half to five eights the length of the conventional fly; the wings, tails, and hackle are proportioned accordingly.

This leaves a lot of hook uncovered, which is the objective: a small fly with no sacrifice of hook power. The low-water hook is longer than standard, as illustrated in Figure 6 in the hook section. Even so, the exact relation between fly size and hook size is not easily fixed because the shorter, regular salmon hook, scaled to Redditch standard length, also is used for the low-water fly.

There has been a trend toward a style that falls between the low-water and the fly of standard size. Although slightly shorter, it still retains regular proportions. One might say that it is scaled just about one size smaller than the hook size: a size-6 fly on a size-4 hook. Dressed on the light-wire, low-water hook, this style may be a full-fledged classic or a modified version of any style to suit the intent of the tier. Regardless, it is good-looking and deserving of its laurels.

Characteristics:
The low-water fly is a fully proportioned fly approximately one size smaller than the hook size. It is the ideal type for illustrating the techniques of tying and proportioning.

Tying Wind the tying thread down the shank, and fasten the tapered tip of the tinsel for the tag on a perpendicular line just edging the hook point. Wind the tinsel back to a point midway between the hook point and the barb. Counterwind back to the starting place. Trim off the remaining tinsel, half-hitch, and apply a drop of cement.

Fasten the tip of a section of floss to form the tip. Wind the floss smoothly until its length is about two thirds that of the tag. Secure the floss with a pair of half hitches, and apply a drop of cement. Select a golden-pheasant crest with slight curvature extending to a perpendicular line midway between the outer edge of the hook and the barb. Wind in place, half-hitch, and secure with a drop of cement.

Next tie in the tapered end of the tinsel for ribbing the body. Let it hang free to the left. Wind the tying thread forward to the point where the body floss will be tied in. Take pains to ensure that the floss is wound smoothly from right to left and back again. Tie off the floss, half-hitch, and apply cement. Now wind the tinsel ribbing, slightly increasing the space between each succeeding spiral. Five, or sometimes six, ribs are customary. The key to good appearance here is to match the width of the tinsel to the size of the fly. Tie off the tinsel, clip the remainder, and apply cement.

Hackle can be tied in a bunch, or it can be folded, the ideal

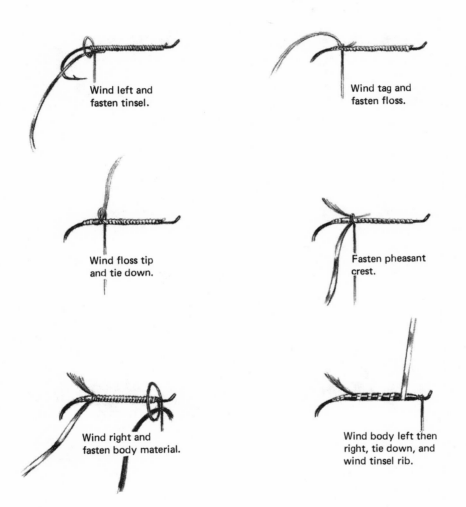

Wind left and
fasten tinsel.

Wind tag and
fasten floss.

Wind floss tip
and tie down.

Fasten pheasant
crest.

Wind right and
fasten body material.

Wind body left then
right, tie down, and
wind tinsel rib.

JEL

FIG. 35. TYING THE SALMON FLY

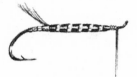

Leave space behind
eye for hackle and
wings.

Turn hackle in horizontal
plane before tying down.

Tie down hackle and
trim quill and butts.

Place wings with natural
curvature upward. Trim
butts.

Tie crest over wings
or one at each side.

Whip finish and
cement head.

JEL

FIG. 36. TYING THE SALMON FLY

"beard" resulting. Another way is to snip out the tip of a soft hackle or body feather and to tie the remaining part of the feather—now in the shape of a V—to the throat of the fly. Wind two loose turns around the feather and pull it slowly into position, making sure that the fibers are approximately horizontal. Tighten the winding thread, and fan the fibers into position with the left thumb and forefinger. Wind two more turns, half-hitch and apply a drop of cement. Mixed hackles are fastened the same way, one layer of color overlapping the other.

The wings have been simplified in so many patterns that it seems pointless to treat the very involved ones here. In some of the traditional types the first fibers to be tied in are from a golden-pheasant tippet. They form the foundation on which the other wing parts are built. For practical purposes the following description includes only the wing proper and the golden-pheasant crest topping.

Select matching sections from a pair of brown or gray mallard or teal flank feathers. Carefully match them with their concave surfaces together, the slight longitudinal curvature of the fibers inclining upward, the tips extending to a perpendicular line falling on the barb. Cement the area where the wings will be tied.

Wind two loose turns around the butts, and hold the wing fibers firmly between the left thumb and forefinger. Snug the wings into position, and check that they are aligned with the body and that the fibers curve upward. Secure the butts with several more turns of thread and a half hitch. Select one golden-pheasant crest (two, if the topping is to rest on each side of the wing), and place it over the top edge of the wing. The tips should reach to the end of the wing. The fibers of the crest will naturally incline a little down the sides of the wing. Trim the butt, taper the head neatly, and apply several coats of cement or lacquer. Black and red are the preferred colors, some fishers holding to the idea that red will enhance any salmon-fly pattern.

Because the jungle cock is protected, fewer patterns will be adorned with the beautiful, wax-like black and tan-spotted shoulder feathers that have been the hallmark of the classic and other salmon-fly types for so many years. Many tiers have turned to the black-and-white tipped feathers of the mandarin, and the effects are excellent. However, the need for shoulders seems to diminish each season. It seems the salmon rise to the shoulderless dressings just as well, and they act none the wiser.

Those who insist that shoulders are absolutely necessary can find all kinds of suitable substitutes for jungle cock among the materials that the average serious tier stocks. A touch of colored lacquer or enamel will add the "eyes" that many feathers do not have.

If you are fortunate enough to have some jungle cock from previous years, use it wisely. If some of the feathers are split, touch the inner surfaces with cement, and stroke the split closed. Other feathers can be treated similarly. In fact, some of the body feathers from a ring-necked pheasant are ideal for the purpose of shouldering. They just don't have the eye.

Here are some other wrinkles that may help you tie a tapered, well-proportioned salmon fly:

1. After building the body and winding the hackle with fine thread, switch to stronger thread for fastening on the wings, which require firmer pressure than fine thread will stand without breaking.

2. Remove the tinsel from the tip of the thread-core types before fastening to the hook, tying in the tip of core only, to minimize bulking.

3. Tie the tips of the hackle after winding *under* the body, to avoid objectionable bulk where the wings will be tied.

4. Long, webby saddle hackle is excellent for palmer-hackling salmon flies; it is fine-stemmed and occupies little space, although it should be counterwound with fine monofilament for reinforcement unless the pattern calls for tinsel counterwinding.

5. Body feathers from the partridge, guinea, golden and Amherst pheasants, the breast and flank feathers of the many ducks, some covert feathers, and the like, are the secret to hackling many patterns, but they must be stripped on one side and the pith removed with a razor blade.

6. Flank feathers from the mallard or teal have a tendency to split. Try tying inner wing sections from gray turkey feathers, the fibers of which remain intact; then tie the mallard or teal flank sections against them.

7. Two hackles of different colors and wound palmer style are best wound together, but, if the fibers from

one side of each of the hackles are stripped, the result will be superior—especially if the body dressing is complex and is to show through the hackle fibers clearly.

Hair Wing

As already mentioned, the use of hair and the mixtures of hair for the wing is actually many years old. The hair wing was first developed in the 1930s, and perhaps earlier, among fishers of the Miramichi. Black or brown bodies with tinsel ribs were first choices. Jungle-cock shoulders were all but disregarded. One innovation was the almost constant use of butts on all patterns. The butts later were tied with fluorescent materials—chenille, yarn, and floss. This practice was so common that patterns dressed in this way came to be known as "butt flies." Another innovation was tying the hackle dry-fly fashion in front of the wing, then sloping it slightly rearward to blend with the wing and body to provide a pulsing motion when the fly was retrieved.

Hair wings simplify the building of a salmon fly and add lifelike properties far and away superior to the relatively stiff wings of the classic, regardless of its elegance. Mixtures of bear, squirrel, goat, calf, groundhog, skunk, and badger, natural and dyed, with topping of peacock herl or sword, and outer wings of mallard, teal, mandarin and the like will build excellent, mobile wings, not only rivaling the classic in appearance but surpassing it in results.

Tying Because the hair wing is American in concept, it is almost casual in its makeup, compared with the classic. There is hardly a set of rules to follow, except that some patterns have an individual twist or two; you will have to compare the pattern lists for specifics. Some require sparse, long-hair hackle extending to the hook point. Others have bushy hackle resembling that on a dry fly. As for technique, tying the hair wing is easy.

Streamer

The "Long Tom" of flies, the streamer, is strictly an American invention. Records show that it was originated as a tandem or two-hook affair for fishing landlocked salmon in Maine, to compensate for their notoriously short strikes. Whether the streamer was adapted for the black salmon at that time or appeared simultaneously is arguable, to say the least. But we do know that Herbert L. Welch of Mooselookmeguntic, Maine, was tying

Feather Wing

Hair Wing

Feather Wing
(Cain River)

Sparse Low-Water

JEL

FIG. 37. SALMON STREAMERS

streamers for landlocks shortly after the turn of the century and that Fred Peet of Chicago was using salmon streamers in the Cain River, New Brunswick, in the early 1920s. The style was out of the Middle West: double pairs of contrasting streamers, collar hackle of banded colors, tinsel body, and barred feather tails. It became known as the "Cain River Streamer" and was the basis for several series of patterns.

The long-shanked variety, including the hair wing and feather streamer, is hardly different from the trout streamer except, perhaps, for the patterns. In Maine the everyday trout wet fly and the classic Salmon fly preceded the streamer—and with the good results one might expect in those days. But after the long fly, imitating the bait fish of that region, came into being, the wet flies and classics received only casual attention. Fishing for the landlocked salmon had taken on new values, and the authorities of that day expounded on the distinction between the "ouananiche" and the so-called "landlocked," using as their basis the reaction of the fish to the choice of remaining landlocked—if it had such a choice—or returning to the sea.

Many great patterns, still as effective as when first contrived, grew out of that period: the Edson Tigers, light and dark; the Supervisor; Warden's Worry; Nine-three; Moose River; Gray Ghost; Black Ghost; Welsh Rarebit, and hosts of others. As was to be expected, human nature and fly tiers being what they are, each pattern became subject to improvement and modification: the addition of a black butt, a gold- instead of a silver-tinsel rib, a touch of this, and a touch of that, as anglers and fly tiers tried to make a good thing better. Interestingly, the flies survived, doubtless because they were devised to satisfy genuine needs. Their enduring success is good evidence.

Streamers are not general-purpose flies but seem most fetching when the waters are discolored following a quick rise. In this respect the salmon respond no differently than the trout. Streamers also are ideal for deep waters.

Dry Fly

Colonel Ambrose Monell is credited with being the originator of salmon dry-fly fishing on the Miramichi some time after 1910. Dry flies were large then, about the size of bass surface bugs —thickly hackled and palmered for many patterns—but they were used by few. Today trout patterns as small as size 12 are not unusual. The majority falls between sizes 8 and 4.

Large Trout Fly

Down Wing (hair)

Deer-hair Body

Horizontal Hackle
(parachute or glider)

Palmer and Bivisible

No body Hackle fly

FIG. 38. SALMON DRY FLIES

JEL

In a general sense salmon dry flies divide into five classes: the typical trout dry fly in many of its forms; the hair-winged fly with upright or down wing; the clipped deer-hair body; the hair-tailed, and the palmer-hackled. These classes are not entirely specific because their features often are combined to form other types, but they do at least suggest the characteristics one might expect to see in each of the five.

The typical trout fly, for example, includes the full spectrum of both winged and wingless styles, especially the horizontally hackled "parachute" which, as a salmon fly, was renamed "glider"—at least in the state of Maine. Whatever the name, the horizontal hackle belies the long-held assumption that a salmon dry fly *must* rest high on the water to tease a strike. Standard patterns—the Gordon Quill, Cahill and Hendrickson, drab as they are, and the Royal Coachman, have been popular for many years in sizes as small as 12.

Hair-winged flies, like the Lee Wulff upright patterns, are based on the principle of "riding high," the very principle that made the Wulff trout versions so productive. Built for long floats, these thick-bodied flies deserve their reputation as first choices for coaxing strikes when the trout are sulking. Lee tied his creations without the aid of a vise, a practice few tiers follow successfully.

The Cosseboom is an example of a successful wet fly that has been converted to a floater. Dating back to the early 1920s, when it was first tied as a wet fly for the Margaree River, the original Cosseboom soon existed in no less than eight distinct dressings. It is a squirrel-tail down wing. The originator, John C. Cosseboom, contributed much to making the hair wing an important class of salmon fly, despite his seeming adherence to the complicated principles of the classic: His original pattern was a hair-wing streamer containing no less than eight layers of peacock herl and squirrel-tail. The pattern later to be known as the Cosseboom was an entirely different fly, indeed. The whole color scheme had changed, and the new version was olive-bodied, winged with sparse gray squirrel, and hackled with a collar of yellow saddles tied to slant slightly rearward. Making it into a dry fly was a rather simple operation: adding more hackle to the collar and tying it dry-fly style.

Clipped deer-hair flies are represented by the Rat-faced MacDougall, the Bomber, and the Irresistible. The wings are upright and divided, usually of bucktail, calf tail, or squirrel tail.

Bodies are clipped cigar shape, and the hackles are three to six neck or saddle feathers. The tails are hair, sometimes hackle fibers, if the pattern specifies them.

Another class is the fly sometimes tied without a body. It consists of a bunch of hair fastened at mid-shank to project well beyond the end of the hook and a burr of hackle filling the space between the eye of the hook and the windings securing the hair.

Palmer-hackled flies have been favored by salmon dry-fly fishers for decades, some preferring them to the hair-bodied styles. Old patterns like the Pink Lady, Colonel Monell, and the Soldier Palmer head the typical list. Some patterns are "faced off" with hackle of contrasting color and resemble bivisibles. The Pink Lady's ginger hackles, for example, are faced with a turn or two of yellow.

Tying The salmon dry fly is simply an overgrown trout dry fly, regardless of its particular style or class. Tying procedures are the same, but the patterns differ greatly—not only in color but also in shape and fullness. This difference sets salmon dry flies apart. Not patterned after natural insects as are trout flies, they are largely the fancies of their originators.

Sizes range from 12 to 2, the majority spanning 8, 6 and 4, although local conditions and preferences may dictate otherwise. Black, light-weight salmon dry-fly hooks are first choice, but there is a place for the 2X- and 3X-long trout dry-fly hook. In recent years it really has come into its own.

A good example of a high floater is the Rat-faced Mac-Dougall. With clipped deer-hair body and abundant saddle hackles fortifying its ability to float, the Rat glides along like a Ping-Pong ball. It is tied like many hair-bodied bass lures.

Wax and fasten the winding thread to the tip of the shank. Tie about seven white bucktail hairs at that point, and cement the windings. The building of the body requires strong thread, so increase the size after securing the tail fibers. Tie in a length about 12 inches, and wax it thoroughly, if it is not prewaxed.

Cut a tuft of deer-body hair about as thick as a pencil, and hold it firmly between the left thumb and forefinger. Place the tuft lengthwise on top of the hook, with the center above the windings that secure the tail fibers. Wind two loose turns around the shank and the hair. "Snug" the turns by drawing up on the thread until it is tight. Remove the thumb and forefinger, but keep the thread tight. The tuft of hair now should have fanned out. Still holding the thread tight, adjust the position of the hair by stroking the tips with the dubbing needle.

Wind two or three more turns in front of the hair, and tie a pair of half hitches. With the thumbnail of the right hand, push this first section of hair toward the tail windings to make it compact. Apply a drop of cement to the half hitch. Clip another tuft of hair, and place it in front of the first tufts, repeating the same procedure until the body is full and firm but extends no more than two thirds the length of the shank. Secure the winds with two final half hitches, cement them thoroughly, and clip the thread.

Remove the work from the vise, and trim the body to shape by clipping the bottom flat and blending the sides into an oval crown at the top. The profile should resemble a tear drop. Place the work in the vise for winging and hackling.

Retie the winding thread to the shank immediately in front of the hair body. Place a drop of cement on the windings. Clip a tuft of bucktail thick enough to form a divided wing—the amount depending upon the size of the fly and your ability to "set" the hair in the space between the body and the hook eye. Hold the tuft firmly by the butts, the tips extending flat over the hook eye. Wind the butts tightly in place, and half-hitch the thread forward of the wings.

Clip the surplus from the butts, shaping the hair to match the body contour. Grasp the tips of the hair between the left thumb and forefinger, and pull them into a vertical position; then divide and set them with X-windings. Fasten two or three saddle hackles by the butts between the wings, and wind them separately behind, between, and in front of, the wings. Secure with two or three half hitches, and cement the head.

STEELHEAD FLIES

Opinions about hooks for steelhead have changed. In the 1950s the swing was to the short-shank, wide-gape hook for leverage, strength, and fast sinking; but the sinking line changed the steelhead fly as it changed the shad fly. As dressed by some tiers, steelhead flies look so much like salmon flies tied Spey fashion that one is hard pressed to tell the difference between them.

The trend to hair wings has been widespread except for some fishers who favor the veiled wing copied from the classic salmon fly. C. Jim Pray was tying hair wing, hair-hackle steelhead flies at least 40 years ago, and it was he who introduced me to the short-shank, gold-plated hook favored then. His methods for building the Carson, Thor, McGinty, Golden Demon, Black Demon, and Railbird were new at the time, and I doubt that they have ever been surpassed. At one time, any angler whose fly book contained those patterns and Enos Bradner's Brad's Brat and Preston Jennings' Lord Iris was considered well equipped for steelhead.

No longer. Now the number of patterns and styles of flies for steelhead fairly rivals those for trout and salmon. Still, one man fishing a Thor, and another working the bottom with a brand-new tie, can stand within rod's length of each other and catch steelhead in equal amounts and sizes.

If man's assumptions are right, that the steelhead, like the salmon, is incapable of digesting what it ingests after leaving the sea, then the old question arises: Why does a steelhead (or a salmon) take the fly? Biologists say that neither fish *can* eat after ripening into sexual maturity. The answer would be nice to know, but I doubt that it would shed much light on fly patterns because they vary so much regionally—red, yellow, white, orange, black, and some brown predominating. Sparse dressings have replaced bushy ones.

Conventional size 6
fly on size 6 hook.

Size 6 fly on size
1/0 hook lowers center
of gravity for keel effect.

Spey-type salmon fly

FIG. 39. STEELHEAD FLIES

JEL

Bright, colorful patterns are "attractors" and meant to be representative of fry. As with the trends in salmon flies, the hair wing, for its toughness and mobility, is becoming almost standard; still, streamers and typical wet flies remain effective. Again, locality and time influence the selection. There are those who dress steelhead flies without hackle—on the order of shad flies. And they work, which lends more credence to the idea that holding to the old conventions is not above question.

Tying There is little, if any, real difference between the steelhead and regular trout wet fly, except for the patterns. The drab Eastern patterns representing insects are ineffective. In steelhead patterns, copper- and brass-wire bodies are old-time favorites. The wire is wrapped on the shank first (if the body is to be slim), and the tail fibers—a generous number of hackle barbules—are wound on next. If the body is to be thicker, tie the tail fibers on first in the usual manner, letting the butt ends extend up the shank. Then build up the diameter with tying thread or any hard filler like floss to form a neat, tapered base for the wire body.

Saddle hackles are liked by many for their luster and lack of bulk, but it is well to counterwind with fine monofilament, to reinforce the center stem of the hackle. Because they are fine-stemmed, saddle hackles occupy little space, and two or three bands of color can be wound in the space normally taken up by a single, thicker-stemmed cock hackle.

Recently the salmon fly has been adopted for steelheading; the Spey type with its long-barbuled saddle, heron, and rooster (spey) hackles is the most popular, especially for patterns tied after the prawn. How opinions change! Not so many years ago the salmon fly was denounced by steelheaders because it was not tough enough to withstand the power of the steelhead.

Pray was at least among the first, if not the very first, to develop the steelhead fly as an individual style. Because conventional wet flies rolled in fast steelhead water, Pray built his patterns on short-shanked hooks several sizes larger. The size of the *fly* remained the same, but the deeper bend in the hook added the keel effect he wanted. The majority of his ties were developed as size 6 on 1/0 short-shank hooks, which generally were gold-plated. Pray was largely responsible for introducing tough hair hackle for steelhead flies. His Thor a good example.

Steelhead dry flies are styled after the salmon dry fly. The hackles are bushy, often hair-winged and hair-tailed, to float high and dry. But the wet fly is really the big gun for steelhead.

SHAD FLIES

The sinking line has given fly fishing for shad a new perspective. Before the sinking line was developed, the shad fly was weighted with an underbody of lead strip or copper wire, or with beads —glass, lead, or brass.

The bead-head flies were attached to a leader (snell fashion) on which the beads—usually three—were strung. Some tiers preferred to wrap a few turns of winding thread in front of the third bead, to keep the three in place. The hook was tinned and became quite brilliant for a while after exposure to the salt water. One successful pattern was devoid of adornment by today's standards, having no more than a pair of yellow-quill down wings.

Forty years ago the shad fly was hardly known as a type. In fact, size-4, -6 and -8 trout wet flies were considered ideal for shad, so long as they were white-winged, the Royal Coachman, Parmacheene Belle, and White Miller being first choices. After the advent of fluorescent materials, red, orange, yellow, and light greens became prominent colors, some fishers claiming that flies tied with them were all the more effective for their new flash.

Tubular Mylar, which replaced the tarnishable metallic tinsels, appeared in the majority of patterns. Its many facets, whether it is slipped on over the hook or decored and wound, add brilliance that is hard to equal with other materials; that brilliance is essential to the shad fly.

Tying Start with either a tinned hook or a stainless-steel hook, size 6. Tying is fast and elementary, because there is relatively little sizing and trimming to do.

Artificial polar-bear hair is always good for the tail; it is metallic, bright and tough, and forms a good base for building up the Mylar body. Fasten a length of it, that extends beyond the hook one third the shank length from the hook eye. Cut the

203

Palmer Hackle

Trout Wet Fly

Snelled Bead Fly

Optic

Lead Head Jig

FIG. 40. SHAD FLIES

JEL

surplus ahead of the winding. Holding the rear portion between the left thumb and forefinger, continue winding left to the end of the shank, and the clip the extending hair the length of the tail—normally a bushy stub.

The Mylar body can be slipped on over the hook eye after its wick-like core has been pulled out, or it can be decored first, tied in at the tip and wound up the shank to that point where the work began. In the former method, tie the tip end, and spiral wind the thread up the body. In the latter, wind the thread to the starting point before winding the body. Cement the windings thoroughly at that point.

Calf-tail (straight-haired, by all means) has become the popular wing material for shad flies, replacing wing fibers and bucktail. It is ideal because it is tough and of the right texture for tying flies of this size.

Clip a tuft long enough to extend a little beyond the tip of the tail, and fasten it where the front of the body was tied down. Be sure that the cement is still tacky—even add a little while building the neat taper toward the hook eye with the winding thread. The old theory that the beads add something is still valid! The long, tapered head virtually duplicates them. Finish the head with several coats of cement or lacquer.

Shad flies, incidentally, are effective crappie, perch and bluegill flies. Smallmouth bass, walleyes and even pickerel respond well to them—often when typical lures, including streamers, fail to produce so much as a nudge. Fished deep and slow, they have a way with the fish.

PIKE FLIES

Northern pike and pickerel offer the flyrodder an interesting change of pace. And while I am well aware that pickerel are not pike, I include them here only because their habits are similar. They react to the same colors and types of flies as do their cousins, the pike, and sometimes the biggest pickerel in the pond will do everything that a pike will. The pickerel is a redoubtable fish without question.

Pike and pickerel leave no doubt that they are tough, analytical breeds capable of exercising the fisher and his rod. These long-billed uglies will take *big* streamers skirting the snags and lily pads in shallow bays. Here "shallow" means water about 10-feet deep. The streamer performs best within that limit.

Pike flies are large—even larger than many saltwater flies. Five and 6-inches long (some span 8), they are, in the strict sense of the word, more lure than they are fly. It takes a good rod to push the 10-weight, forward-tapered line needed to switch such big flies to the target.

Hooks for these fellows range in size from 1/0 to 3/0. Larger sizes are not needed. I like the 1/0. Hooks larger than that are too gross, as I see it. A slight offset is an advantage; the pike's jaws are long and bony, and the offset will steer the hook home, regardless of its position at the time of the strike. As mentioned in the section on hooks, my personal preference for hooks without offset has only two exceptions—those for striped bass and those for the pike and pickerel.

Long shanks are best for long, tinsel- or Mylar-bodied streamers. The tandem or trailer-hook streamer has two regular-length hooks, size 2, 1 or 1/0, connected by nylon or wire. Adding Mylar strips to the hair or feather wing increases the flash that both pike and pickerel like. While on the subject of nylon or

Hackle Streamer   Hackle-hair Streamer

(Double) Hair Streamer

FIG. 41. PIKE FLIES

JEL

wire, I would like to mention that there *is* a place for wire at the terminal end of the leader. Soon as wire is mentioned, many "experts" sneer, insisting that the teeth of the pike and pickerel will not cut through monofilament of 20-, 30-, or 40-pound test. Of course they won't; and I doubt that any flyrodder who has tangled with more than a few will contend that they will. But fine, dull wire, practically invisible in clear water, is a positive asset at times. It does not streak like heavy nylon, which sometimes will flag the pike or big pickerel about to strike that there is a man on the other end of the whole affair. Wire has one failing: in small diameter, it may wind knot and become worthless. Therefore, the shortest reasonable length is recommended at all times. Two feet is about right.

Few colors are necessary. Red, yellow, and white head the list. It is doubtful that you will need others. Dual colors *seem* to attract the pike and pickerel better than single colors. Yellow with a red center stripe, and white with a yellow center stripe will fetch pike out of their dens if any color combination will—so far as streamers go. Mixed hair and feathers are effective. The hackle gives the streamer a few more undulations and an extra kick or two that pike and pickerel look for.

As mentioned, pickerel flies follow the scheme for pike flies, except that the pickerel fly is scaled down a little—unless the angler is concentrating on the pike-size hermits that few anglers ever see or know about. Then he will bend on the same slinky, 6- or 8-inch long Tom that he would use for pike. Big pickerel stay close to their dens in wait for frogs, fish smaller than they are, and other passersby that they can cram into their gullets. But they are not easily fooled. Often they will swim parallel to the lure for many feet, then seize it quickly or sink into the shadows, as if having determined that the lure is a fraud.

Tying Building length into the long pike streamer is the first consideration. It can be a problem. Instead of trying to get the length in the wing only, tie half of it into the tail. If the streamer is to be 6-inches overall, tie 3-inch tails and 3- or 4-inch wings. You will be able to use more of the regular stock on hand (mainly bucktail) because most bucktail is not 6 inches long. The same applies to hackle feathers.

At first glance, the finished streamer may look too sectional, but when well soaked and in action, everything will blend together into the long, slinky fish-getter that you want it to be.

Pike and pickerel mangle streamers quickly, the bodies especially. Although Mylar has the advantage of not tarnishing, it does tear, unless reinforced or well lacquered. Ribbing the Mylar with 15-pound test nylon also prevents tearing, and I prefer it to coating the body with lacquer. Fact is, a few frayed bits of Mylar protruding from between the nylon ribbing adds flash to the fly. And for pickerel and pike, that is what streamer fishing is all about. Without silver or gold bodies and wings and tails laced with bright Mylar, the streamer for pike and pickerel lacks a principal property.

In passing, I add that muskies sometimes take the streamer. It is rather rare, and fly fishing for this member of *Esox* is even rarer. To be truthful, I cannot even guess about the type or color that might be considered a "muskie" streamer. The only muskie I ever caught with the fly rod was a fourteen-pounder—a little fellow by any standard—that took a huge hackle streamer wobbling behind the rumpus kicked up by a willow-leaf spinner. It may have been one of those "things" that people talk about. I include the instance here for what it may be worth.

SALTWATER
FLIES

The subject of saltwater flies is deserving of a whole separate volume. There is so much to be said—and left unsaid. In recent years, there has been an overwhelming flood of "new" patterns, "new" techniques, "new" ways for doing this and doing that. Some chap who never caught anything larger than a 2-pound small-mouth bass will, after taking his first striper or two, a weakfish, or a bluefish, dash off to his typewriter and compose a most scholarly account on why a particular fly, tied a certain way, is the best lure for the kind of fish he caught—because he happened to be using that fly when the stripers, weakfish, or bluefish were taking. It is regrettably misleading but mighty good business for those who stand to profit by it.

Far too much nonsense about flies has been written, even about the flies that will and will not take saltwater fish. This is largely a holdover among the clans who departed from the pro-gressive shrinkage of freshwater fishing to tackle the briny kinds. They stuff their Wheatleys and leather books with hundreds of creations they have read about but never used, positive that one or another of them (it's usually another) will always have the magic touch.

If it were only that simple! I have been fishing in salt water for most of a lifetime, and with the fly rod. I know of no sure-fire patterns, although there were years when I believed that I did. If asked today what I would choose from among the countless patterns of striper flies tied by both Eastern and Western tiers, I would say, "A streamer fly." In the final analysis, it boils down to what pattern a fisher *likes* to fish with.

On the other side of the coin is the practicality of choosing one streamer over another. Given enough publicity, any fly or lure will appear almost overnight coast to coast. But then consider

211

the fellows who do not belong to the clubs, who do not read the magazines and books. Quietly, without the huzzahs and the horn blowing, they continue to tie the streamers and lures that work. As a rule, the typewriter fishermen seek them out to filch their knowledge and write with authority.

I have written often of Harold Gibbs, perhaps the best-informed flyrodder for striped bass who ever lived. He was a private person, given to truth. He possessed the finest flyrodding equipment made, knew his way with the fish, and was quick to ferret out the real from the imagined. If he had written a book, it would have been a best-seller for decades. But Hal was not so disposed. Hal Gibbs taught me more about flyrodding for stripers than I could have learned from every book written about the subject.

We discussed flies hour after hour—the pros, the cons, size, colors, shape, sink rate, in fact every aspect of the subject that could be recalled. Out of our long association surfaced one of those comments that Hal will always be remembered for: "It's not so much the pattern—it's you and the fish." There is the crux of it all. And I am sure it applies to every fish, every fisher.

The Gibbs' Striper caught stripers everywhere, when they were responding to streamers. I still have a Striper that Hal gave me in 1949. It is a handsome tie, having a bright-blue feather strip along the side of the white bucktail wing, a gill-like barred cheek, a silver-tinsel body, and a sparse red throat. It needs no extolment from me, for it has long since earned its own. The point is, Hal confided in me that he liked to see some "forethought" in the makeup of a streamer; the Striper embodies forethought beyond question. More important, Hal said that, despite the success of the Striper, a plain white bucktail would have done as well—if the stripers were working in the shallows. He grinned when he said he had proved it to himself countless times. And there was a man who doubtless had caught more stripers on the fly rod than anyone else has!

Then there was the chap who used nothing but long, furnace-hackled streamers. When we met for the first time on the Palmer River, he had a great string of stripers wallowing from a heavy line tied to his waist. I had a few, too, which had taken the first of the pattern I had been developing to represent the spearing. There was absolutely no similarity between his dark-brown streamer and the lightly barred, silverish streamer I was using. We agreed that the bass were feeding on pods of spearing and that my streamer was closer in appearance to the spearing than was his furnace-hackled fly. Apparently the stripers could not have cared less; perhaps they accepted the brown streamer for another kind of critter that was not as visible as the pods of spearing.

Color may be overemphasized for the reason that *anglers* react to it so strongly. *Size* in streamers, however, really seems to make the difference. There is always the chance that some lunker will rise from the depths to gulp down a lure the size of a Polish sausage, but, by and large, the lure that is the same *size* as the fauna the fish seem to be taking at the moment will consistently take fish, if anything will.

Most saltwater flies represent bait fish, eels, shrimp, squid and, in fewer instances, small crabs. Tying techniques are the same as for tying equivalent flies for other fish. Shrimp, for example, are tied like several of the shell-back nymphs for trout. Many streamers have both hackle feathers and hair, and materials like peacock herl for topping and striping.

Streamers that include bucktail are far and away the principal type of fly on which the saltwater flyrodders rely. There are many variations, from the simplest "no-body" fly to ornate examples that rival the salmon fly. Some are carryovers from more than 50 years ago, when flyrodding in the salt had become a way of life for a very few who had discovered the art was without equal.

Tying Regardless of what saltwater fly you tie, use materials that will survive long, hard casts; corrosion from salt water and the powerful jaws and teeth of saltwater fish. The following descriptions take those points into account.

For flashy bodies avoid metallic tinsels; use Mylar tubing. Mylar is practically impervious to salt water, and stands up well after hard fishing. Reinforce the body with spiraled monofilament of 12- or 15-pound test. Bucktail and calf tail are good wing materials but lack the flash of nylon hair, about the toughest (if the least flexible) of available wing materials. If not brittle, goat hair makes a splendid wing, superior to any other hair I have found, natural or synthetic.

Saddle hackles are more mobile than neck hackles and have naturally weaker stems. Wound as hackle at the head of the streamer, they are fine, if reinforced by counterwinding with light-weight monofilament. As long, trailing streamers they are easily severed or torn loose. Some excellent saltwater flyrodders specify them, however.

Shoulders and eyes appear more and more, but their worth is hard to evaluate. If you like them, by all means include them in the patterns you tie. Two of my top producers have both shoulders and eyes, and I would consider both of them unfinished without the added features.

Shredded wool or nylon hair (artificial polar bear) makes good throat and tail fibers, blending into a blob of color, red being the first choice for many patterns, for its resemblance to blood.

Peacock herl, weak as it is, makes excellent topping over a streamer. The bronze-to-deep-green color scintillates, and the fibers cling together in an overall back stripe that enhances many minnow-like lures. A single strand placed on each side gives any streamer a lifelike lateral line (see Figure 30).

Try trimming the barbules from a pair of grizzly hackles to within ⅛ inch of the center quill. Tied along the sides of a bucktail or other hair wing, these trimmed feathers add barring hard to equal; and they are stronger stemmed than saddle hackles.

Tying the Streamer

The Galli-Nipper is a good example of a bucktail with overwings of hackle. I claim only part authorship for this creation because its principles are almost as old as the wet fly itself.

The hook is size 1/0, 3X-stout, ring-eyed, stainless steel. The tail is a short bunch of imitation polar-bear hair dyed bright red. Fasten a length of 10- or 12-pound test monofilament at the tip of the shank, immediately after securing the tail fibers, for counterwinding the body. Clip and decore a length of Mylar tubing a little shorter than the shank length, and slip it over the hook eye. Now tightly counterwind the Mylar with the monofilament at ⅛-inch intervals; secure it with winding thread one fourth the shank length from the hook eye. Lacquer or cement the winding thread.

Tie at the throat a short section of the same red imitation polar-bear hair used for the tail. It need not be thick—just enough to suggest the opened gills of a baitfish. Lacquer the windings again in preparation for tying in the bucktail.

Select matched grizzly hackles with strong but not stiff quills, and trim the barbules from the butts so that the finished hackles are three fourths the length of the bucktail. They can be tied in place individually, or paired, to suit the tier. I tie first one and then the other. The hackles should adhere to the bucktail, and tying them separately is the best way to get that result. One tight

Streamer
(Galli-Nipper)

Shrimp

Sand Eel

Rock Crab

Squid

FIG. 42. SALTWATER FLIES

JEL

winding *behind* the windings holding the bucktail will draw the hackles tight against the bucktail.

After securing the hackles, lacquer the windings thoroughly; while they are wet, fasten the thread tip of a length of gold Mylar chenille, and build the head with two or three turns, leaving sufficient space behind the hook eye for whip finishing. Lacquer the Mylar chenille thoroughly. The chenille will fill and become a gold bead.

Another treatment of this same pattern reduces the width of the hackle feathers, sometimes an advantage, when the water is clear and the fish have become selective. Trim the barbules until the overall width of the feather is about ¼ inch. When wet, the narrowed feather represents the subtle barrings of the silver-sides baitfish.

Tying the Sand Eel

The sand eel is a principal part of the diets of many saltwater fish. The striped bass, for one, always seems to have an eye cocked for sight of it.

Streamers representing the sand eel are slim and tied on tandem hooks joined by nylon monofilament. The body is decored tubular Mylar, and the streamers are paired hackle feathers either tied by their tips to the shank of the trailer hook or left trailing. Badger, grizzly, and light-furnace hackles are popular. I have had success with light grizzly dyed pale blue.

Tie a 10-inch length of monofilament to the second hook, as if tying a snelled hook. Use limp 30-pound test. Measure the desired distance between the end of the shank of the forward hook and the tip of the trailer hook. Cut a length of Mylar tubing that length. Decore the Mylar. Place the hook in the vise, and slide the Mylar tube down the monofilament to the end of the shank. Fasten the tip of the body at the end of the shank with winding thread, and lacquer the windings.

Position the forward hook by inserting the monofilament through the hook eye from the rear. Tie a simple half hitch in the monofilament behind the hook eye, and securely wind the part extending behind the knot to the shank, at the same time closing the forward part of the Mylar tubing. Cut off the surplus, and cement the windings thoroughly.

Decore a length of Mylar, and fasten the tip end over the windings at the end of the shank. Wind the tubing up the shank, but leave sufficient space for tying the streamers, throat and head. Half-hitch the winding thread, and cement the knot.

Fasten the butts of a pair of hackle feathers over the windings. Their tips should extend slightly beyond the end of the shank. Tie them neatly with several turns of thread, and cement the windings. This point is a good place for the whip knot.

Soft hackle or peacock sword enhances the appearance of the sand eel. If hackle, three turns of long hen feather will do well. Tie them to lie back. If peacock sword, a bunch of six fibers is enough.

Build the head with winding thread, and cement it. After it is dry, spot the eyes with lacquer.

Tying the Shrimp

The shrimp swims backward, and some descriptions for tying it are written that way; the tail of the shrimp extends over the eye of the hook, and the antennae trail beyond the end of the shank.

Striped bass and weakfish (sea trout) feed heavily on grass shrimp. Weakfish in particular ascend the bays and rivers inhabited by the grass shrimp. The little creature is a good indicator of the level of pollution filtering into the water. It is no coincidence that, when certain insecticides are curtailed, the grass shrimp reappear, to be followed by the weakfish.

Hook sizes 1/0 through 4 approximate the size of the grass shrimp. I prefer black salmon or regular bronzed hooks, despite their lack of resistance to saltwater corrosion, for weakfish are wary at times of a bright, stainless-steel hook, especially when they are feeding in shallow flats. Size 4 is better for depths of a foot or so, the larger sizes for deeper water, although this should not be considered a rule by any means.

The antennae are tied where the curvature of the hook begins, to add the effect of the slight S-shape peculiar to the shrimp. Several hairs from a bucktail or mixed light and dark moose mane are good. The hairs should measure about the same length as the body.

The back (carapace) is well represented by bucktail. Tie a bunch at least three inches long and wide enough to cover the body directly over the antenna windings. Remember, the shrimp swims backward, and the thicker part of the body is to the rear of the hook. So let the butts of the bucktail extend halfway up the hook. Saturate the windings with cement.

Tie a hackle feather by the butt at midbody, then a length of wool yarn behind the eye of the hook. Wind the yarn back over the butts of the bucktail, and hold the hackle feather clear so that it is not wound under by the yarn. Wind the yarn back to the hook eye. The body now should be slightly conical, the thickest part over the hook point.

Palmer-wind the hackle toward the hook eye, leaving sufficient space for the body to show through. Cut the surplus hackle, and half-hitch the winding thread behind the hook eye. Now bend the bucktail back over the body, and tie it behind the hook eye. Lift the tips of the bucktail, and tie several half hitches; whip finishing is difficult here.

Next trim the tips to a stubble, so they protrude about ¼ inch. Lacquer or cement the windings thoroughly. Do not build up a head; the head is at the other end over the barb. The eyes are located above the hook point. Spot them with a drop of black lacquer on the wool body, slightly below the center line. After they are dry, apply another drop to each to increase their protrusion.

Tying the Squid

The squid is to the saltwater fish what the garden worm is to the sunfish. When the stripers, blues, weaks, bonito, kelp bass, yellowtail, and albacore are slashing for the rubbery little squid, the flyrodder can do wonders with long-hackled imitations. One remembers his banner days, and I am no exception. The Pacific was as blue as its name suggests—glassy, warm, almost lazy. Schools of bonito began to close in on masses of small squid, which arched rhythmically free of the surface when the flashing "boneheads" drew near. The live-baiters on a nearby party boat were striking fish only occasionally. But a size 1, stub-tailed blue-and-white streamer kept my line whizzing until the bonito had surfeited or had simply moved on to explore new places. For at least an hour the bonito massacred those blue-and-white stub tails almost before they had settled in the water. Ever since, I have believed in the value of "squid flies."

Easy-to-tie, the squid consists of hackle feathers, a little bucktail, chenille, a few marabou fibers, and a pair of eyes. The squid, like the shrimp, swims backward; therefore, the eye of the hook is at the rear of the squid.

Overall, the squid is long for its mass, and the long-shanked hook is necessary. A size 1/0, 3X-long, is long enough.

Cluster 8 white hackles, and tie them where the curvature of the hook begins. Do not attempt to arrange them in an orderly manner. Two inches are right for the size 1/0 hook. Cement the windings. Select a pair of strong-stemmed saddle hackles about 3 inches long, and tie one on each side of the other hackles, to represent the tentacles.

Clip a few fibers from a marabou feather dyed deep pink, and space them around the white hackles. Add short white marabou in the same way. Next, fasten wire-stemmed, flat glass eyes about two thirds the distance from the hook eye to the shank, first bending the wire stems at right angles one eighth of an inch from the back of the eye. (Herter's of Waseca, Minnesota, stock these glass eyes in 4-mm, 6-mm, and 8-mm diameters.) Bent in this manner, the eyes will be the right distance from the shank for building up the chenille body around them. Clip the surplus wire from the eye stems.

Fasten the tip of an 8-inch length of thick chenille behind the eye of the hook, and wind it to the left and the edges of the marabou, X-winding between the glass eyes en route. Wind back to the right, again X-winding between the eyes. Secure the chenille behind the eye of the hook with a pair of half hitches, and clip the surplus chenille. Cement the windings, and cover the cement with white lacquer.

Tying the Crab

The crab is tied like the shrimp but it is bulkier.

Many types of flies are not described here, simply because they are variations of ones that are. The combinations of materials and shapes are without limit. The best approach to tying lifelike saltwater flies is to copy from the natural. It takes patience and time to do it well, but it is worth the trouble. The art of *fishing* the fly is another subject; for imitating the movement of the natural probably has as much to do with the success of the artificial as does color, shape, or any other feature.

Large bass, pike, and salmon streamers are as effective as any lure you can tie to the leader. Saltwater fly fishing began with the use of such flies. The major difference between freshwater flies and saltwater flies is the hook. Bronzed hooks simply will not stand up in salt water. Tinned or stainless-steel hooks will.

Grizzly and yellow, red and white, and yellow and white are

Gibbs' Striper

Bonbright's Tarpon Fly

Loving's Striped Bass Fly

Joe Brooks' Platinum Blonde

JEL

FIG. 43. FOUR SALTWATER CLASSICS

the predominant color mixtures. They have proved effective for over 50 years. The embellishments added in recent years, which are so attractive to the angler, may be equally attractive to the fish; my own experience more than suggests that they are of marginal value.

SURFACE BUGS

Fishing with surface bugs—those hair, cork, and balsa-wood creations that are as much fun to make as they are to use—has come a long way since they first appeared before the twentieth century. In those days the angler "jigged" his lure, which dangled on a short line fastened to the end of a long cane pole. The lure was a gob of chicken feathers wrapped on a huge hook; sometimes it was buoyed up by a wedge of cork. The angler simply pointed the long pole over the pothole between the lily pads or stumps and "jigged" the lure up and down, or round and round, until the inevitable happened! The water would erupt, and a bucket-faced bass would blast the lure; the angler would haul back, slide the pole over the gunwales of the boat, and horse another fish aboard for the stringer or fish bag.

Tactics today are more refined. The fly rod has replaced the cane pole, and the lures themselves possess a certain elegance. Yet there is no standard for surface bugs—hair bug or otherwise—for saltwater or freshwater fish. Much imagination enters into the design of every type; and there are many types. Moreover, the "popper" in all its many forms has become a favorite with saltwater flyrodders. Some versions of the small crab, for example, are designed after the clipped-hair bass bug and versions of the surface minnow after the crippled minnow, which is at least 50 years old.

All that you may have learned from tying trout, salmon, panfish, and other types of flies is useful for tying surface bugs. At least you will have gained the feel of materials and the sense of proportioning required of the well-made surface bug.

Surface bugs divide roughly into two classes: those made of deer hair and the like and those made of cork or balsa. Both classes have feathers in their makeup, as a rule.

Hair Popper

Hair Frog

Cork Popper

Swimmer

JEL

FIG. 44. TYPICAL SURFACE BUGS

The shape and angle of the head, the taper or fullness of the body, the appendages—wings, legs, arms and tails added to suit the tier's fancy—affect the motion and the sound of the surface bug during retrieve. If the shape of the head is blunt and the angle slants forward from the top, the bug will dive with a gurgle. If the angle is reversed, the bug will "push" water and "talk"—one of the most exciting adventures in flyrodding. If the shape is round, the bug probably will have a rolling or swimming action. Whether hair, cork, or balsa, makes no difference.

Hair-body lures are not difficult to tie. With a little practice the tier can turn out one in short order, including one with glass eyes and a pair of legs. Attempting to list all the known hair-body types would be foolish. I certainly do not know them. And any listing would be obsolete before it was finished. Examples of a few types and their features should be sufficient to rouse your interest and cause you to set up your tying vise.

Tying Hair-Body Bugs

There are three essentials in tying hair bugs: The hair for the body should be thick and coarse, it should be tied full and compact and the bottom of the body should be clipped flat and close to the hook.

Hair from the hide of deer and caribou is ideal for the body. Being coarser than bucktail, it flares and packs better. Some of the long, white belly hair, if it is of fine texture, is superior for tails and wings, however, and should be set aside for that purpose.

Start the work from the left. Tails are all-hackle, all-bucktail, or mixtures of the two. Cement or lacquer the shank before fastening on the tail. Building the body may appear difficult, but it is not. Clip a tuft of hair about as thick as a pencil, and bind it at the middle to the shank immediately in front of the tail windings. As you let go of the tuft when making the last turn with the tying thread, notice that the hair will flare out (hopefully) completely around the hook. If a bald spot remains, add another smaller tuft to fill it. Half-hitch the tying thread, and, with the nails of the right thumb and forefinger, jam the hair tightly to the left. Complete the body in the same manner, adding small tufts here and there to fill voids, if necessary; then tie off with a pair of half hitches about one quarter inch from the hook eye. Cement or lacquer the winding thread at that point.

Trimming the body is the next step. Remove the work from

Tie first tuft in front
of tail windings.

Draw thread snug and X-
wind through ruff. Pack
ruff tight towards tail.

Tie second tuft against
first and pack tight.

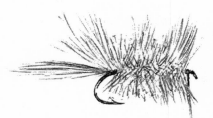

Continue building body
to hook eye. Tie head
knot and cement.

Remove from vise and trim
in successive cuts until
bottom is flat and sides and
back are to shape.

Spot eyes to suit.

JEL

FIG. 45. BUILDING THE DEER-HAIR BODY

the vise. With sharp scissors, trim the bottom flat, snipping off successive layers until a short, even stubble remains. Hold the tail sections between the left thumb and forefinger, and clip the sides toward the front, forming a straight or curved taper. Trim the back arch shape.

The chances are the first shaping will be rather rough. So trim where needed until the body is symmetrical and evenly formed.

The hair-body bug is winged in several ways, each one serving the purpose as well as another. Deer-body hair, with ends clipped, can be placed in the space between the front of the body and behind the hook eye and tied with X-windings. Or another tuft of hair can be held upright, tied in place and divided with the tying thread. Some tiers prefer two or three layers of hackle tips on each side; others wind three full collar hackles to add bulk and motion to the bug; still others trim the bottoms of the collar hackles flat and snip a V from the top. Wings are what the tier wants them to be.

Tying the hair-body frog centers on the appearance of the legs, which are tied on first. Clip a tuft of bucktail thick enough for the two legs when divided. Fasten the butts to the rear of the hook, letting the tips extend beyond the hook eye. Cement or lacquer the windings.

Separate the bucktail into two equal sections, and pull them rearward. Hold them in place with X-windings, half-hitch the thread and apply a touch of lacquer. Do not trim the butts yet. About two-thirds down each leg make the "knee" joint by inserting a short length of wire. Wind the tying thread around the bucktail and the wire, whip-finish the winding, and lacquer the joint thoroughly.

Build the body by winding on tufts of deer-body hair clear to the eye of the hook. Lacquer the head knot, and remove the work from the vise. With scissors taper the body to a flattish oval, the shape of a frog. Lacquer on a pair of eyes and a few spots on the back to suit. Taper the ends of the legs to represent feet.

The body of the frog can be made more realistic by tying on tufts of deer hair dyed green and light yellow, the green for the back, the yellow for the belly. The same applies to the legs. When tying the body, control the revolutions of the hair with the fingers of the left hand so that the green tufts remain on the top and the yellow tufts on the bottom.

If you prefer the lifelike appearance of flat glass eyes, fasten

Insert wire in leg at joint, wind tight and bend to shape. Cement.

Leave untrimmed hair for wings. Trim to shape.

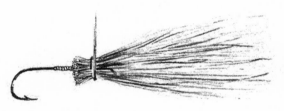

Fasten bucktail behind hook eye and X-wind in place.

Wind tight several turns toward hook eye and half hitch.

Pull back feathers and bucktail and wind collar of thread. Whip finish and cement.

FIG. 46. HAIR-BUG TECHNIQUES

JEL

them on before building the body. First bend the wire stems at right angles so that the eyes project only as far as the body hair when clipped.

Bands of alternate colors are interesting to tie and attractive to the fish. Three bands are popular: red-white-red, black-yellow-black and so on. A hair-body McGinty size 4 is a good summer bug for smallmouth bass, and an all-yellow bug with a red center band size 1/0 will coax largemouth into striking like few others. An all-black, wide-winged bug often is deadly at night.

Tying Cork- and Balsa-Body Bugs

Because they are easily shaped by filing and sanding, billets of cork and balsa offer the fly tier (bug maker, in this instance) unlimited opportunities to test his imagination. The effects produced by the shape of the head and the body are almost self-evident, as examination of several types will prove.

The direction and depth of the slope of the head, the contour of the body (slim, broad, round or flat), the pitch of the body with respect to the hook shank—each greatly alters the action and the sound of a bug.

The "pop" that is so desirable at times is the result of dishing out and slanting the groove in the head *rearward* from top to bottom. The short, diving action, with its equally desired "plunk," is produced by slanting the groove in the head *forward* from top to bottom. The "spout" that is so irresistable to a lethargic bass is caused by hollowing out the sides of the head. And the "sneaky-Pete" action of a slow-swimming bug, which a bass is prone to watch for long moments before walloping it into kingdom come, results from rounding and tapering the head. Even additions of bucktail and feathers alter the action and sound of a bug as a tail will change the flight of a kite. Trailing hair and feathers, if too long, will all but eliminate the provocative action a surface bug should have.

You will have to add new tools and materials to your regular list for tying flies. Cork- and balsa-bodied bugs are constructed more than they are tied and require entirely different treatments from those given to the trout, salmon and other types of flies. So include the following items: a fine, flat file; a small rat-tail file; a fine triangular file; medium and fine sandpaper; a pack of single-edge razor blades; small drills $1/16$-, $3/32$-, $1/8$- and $5/32$-inch diameter; a fine-gauge saw blade; artist's paint brushes; rubber

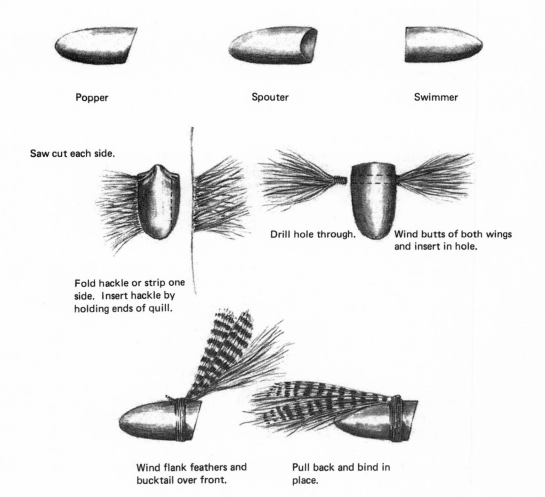

Popper

Spouter

Swimmer

Saw cut each side.

Drill hole through.

Wind butts of both wings and insert in hole.

Fold hackle or strip one side. Insert hackle by holding ends of quill.

Wind flank feathers and bucktail over front.

Pull back and bind in place.

JEL

FIG. 47. CORK-BUG TECHNIQUES

bands; spring-actuated clothespins; lacquer or enamel, and the correct thinner for either.

Here are a few basic guidelines that may save you time, disappointment and a little money.

(1) Try making a few "standards" before inventing others.

(2) Match the hook to the body. The hump-shank hook is essential to keep the body from twisting on the hook. 2X- and 3X-long hooks are usually better than regular lengths. The shape of the body determines the hook size, which the following list of hook-body relationships takes into account:

BODY DEPTH	HOOK SIZE
$5/16$–$7/16$ inch	2 3X-long
$1/2$–$9/16$ inch	1 2X-long
$5/8$–$11/16$ inch	1/0 2X-long

(3) X-wind the tying thread around the hook shank. Never expect a bare shank to "stay put"—the odds are against it.

(4) Use only quality cork. The ordinary stoppers found around the house are not suitable for good bug bodies. Already-shaped bodies or quality billets supplied by the tackle houses are superior in every respect, have little, if any porosity, and cut and sand better. Some firms list plastic bodies, which are said to be superb.

(5) Cut the angle(s) of the head, and taper the body like the original you are copying. The slightest variation will change the action or the sound of the finished product. If a lure produces well, copy it to the last detail. Change for the sake of change serves little purpose.

(6) Set the body at the correct angle on the hook shank. The pitch of the body has much to do with the sound effects during retrieve.

(7) Set the hook shank well below the center line of the body, to leave adequate space between the point of the hook and the body for hooking the fish.

(8) Save cork dust for mixing with cement to fill voids and porous spots.

Preparing the Hook

The bare shank—even with the hump—is too smooth for secure bonding to the body. Criss-cross windings of medium-size thread increase the bonding surface. Start immediately behind the eye of the hook, and wind back to the point where the body will end. Cement the windings, and set the hook aside.

Shaping the Body

Shaping the body with a single-edge razor blade is easy. A cutting board is an advantage. Place the billet upright, and with a razor blade slice it square to the approximate size of the finished body. Next slice off the corners of the square, leaving an octagonal shape. Taper the rear in like manner, and round the remaining eight edges with medium-coarse sandpaper or, if you prefer, a fine-cut machinists' file. Cork, too, has a grain, and the only way to find it is by stroking the body with the sandpaper or file, first one way and then another. If you can buy it, rub rottenstone on the surface with a dampened cloth.

The example of the round-faced "sneaky Pete" has been selected for its simplicity. Smooth the cork until it is symmetrical, and polish it to a fine surface suitable for lacquering.

Preparing the Body for the Hook

There are many methods for drilling and cutting the body to take the hook. The two easiest to control are, as one might expect, the least involved. The first is the simple operation of drilling a hole lengthwise through the body at the exact angle at which the hook will be placed, then slitting the body from the underside with a razor blade up to that hole. The second consists of slicing a wedge lengthwise from the bottom of the body and later setting the hook at the apex of the cut and cementing the wedge back in place. The former is more accurate for the reason that the drilled hole controls the placement of the hook better than does the latter. Drilling with a small power drill is more satisfactory than locking the drill in the fly vise and turning the body manually.

If you make the body of balsa, drilling a slightly oversize hole is all that is required. Wrapping the hook with chenille and cementing both the chenille and the interior of the hole will hold the hook in place for the life of the bug.

Bonding the Hook to the Body

Following the drill-and-slice method, thoroughly coat the drilled hole, the slice in the body, and the windings on the hook with plastic resin or an equivalent bonding cement. Slow drying is essential. Fast-drying glues glaze too quickly and lose their bonding properties. Insert the hook lengthwise into the slot until it is firmly set in the drilled hole. When the shank is so located, the thin slot will close, and little force will be needed to seal it. A few turns with a rubber band will do nicely.

At this point set the body aside to dry, and repeat the preparations for as many bodies as needed.

Preparing the Body for Lacquering

Remove the rubber band, and sand any surplus bond that has oozed from the slot. A file may be necessary if the bond has hardened beyond the ability of sandpaper to remove it. There may be a few holes or irregular surfaces remaining from shaping the body. Plastic wood, cork dust and cement, or even ordinary putty will seal them. Allow any of these fillers ample time to set before giving the body a final polishing with sandpaper.

Lacquering the Body

The natural color of cork is excellent for many purposes, and a coat or two of clear lacquer is all that is required to seal the body surface from water. Lacquers and enamels sold by the tackle houses are more reliable for making fishing lures than are the kinds you will find in the local hardware store. They are consistent, their colors are suited to tackle making, the flat-white undercoat is ideal, and they are bottled for the convenience of the bug maker. Furthermore, the companion thinner has the same base. Always have a sufficient quantity of it in stock; you will use a lot of it. It is the key to smoothly finished bodies.

Dipping the bug body in thinned flat-white lacquer or enamel starts the coloring process. Dipping is the cleanest method for producing a smooth finish. Thin the lacquer to an almost water-thin consistency. Dip the bug headfirst into it. After dipping, rotate the body so that the remaining drop (it's always there) flows away from the area of the hook eye. Tip a clean brush with thinner, and brush the hook eye. Then hang the body by the hook on a thread stretched conveniently across the work bench. Allow about 20 minutes for the undercoat to dry. Then repeat the process.

At this point the work can be set aside as "stock" and other bodies undercoated in the same manner and made ready for final coloring and feathering.

The final coloring of a bug usually consists of a one-color base, with spots or stripes added, and, of course, a pair of eyes, the character of which is determined by the bug maker, who can have a field day displaying his ingenuity.

Spotting the Body and the Eyes

Spotting is simple. Just avoid using too much lacquer or enamel. Two or three ordinary lead pencils and your dubbing needle will do the job. Wooden dowels are better than pencils. Shape the ends in a pencil sharpener, one to a point, the other to a tapered but blunt end, the diameter of the iris of the eye. The pointed end is for spotting the pupil. A good idea is to sharpen both ends of a dowel about 4 inches long to the desired amount—one for spotting the iris, the other for spotting the pupil.

Dip just the tip of the blunt end in lacquer the color of the iris, and touch it to the spot where you want the eye. Spot the other side, taking care that it is aligned properly. After letting the irises dry for about 15 minutes, dip the tip of the pointed end of the dowel in lacquer the color of the pupil, and carefully center it in the iris.

Feathering the Bug

Set the hook in the vise, and wind several turns of tying thread at the tip of the body. Select the hackle feathers, bucktail, or whatever fibers your pattern calls for: paired hackles with matched curvature are naturally better looking than those picked at random. Whether the bass will object to unmatched hackles is moot, but your fishing companion may, especially if he is a stickler for details.

Paired hackles in two layers trim a bug nicely. A common practice is to tie on a section of bucktail and the paired hackles on each side with their curvature outward.

A full hackle collar wound close to the tip of the body finishes the feathering. Two hackles are preferred for their fullness. Complete the tie with the whip knot, and cement it thoroughly. A coat of lacquer the same color as the body adds a professional touch.

Other Features

Naturally all billet-bodied bugs are not shaped and feathered or haired in the same manner as the one just described. The shape of the body, as previously mentioned, has much to do with the arrangement of hair, hackle, and plumage that follow.

Because they include *general* structural features, the following descriptions may be helpful as guidelines for the bug maker to follow when designing and building the particular surface lure he has in mind.

Continuous Side Legs

One of the deadliest of all surface bugs has hackle legs extending along the sides of the body, which is flat and only slightly tapered. This requires that the body be cut lengthwise on each side. Mark the cuts with a pencil. With a fine-gauge hacksaw blade or an artist's saw, cut slots in each side to the depth that will allow the insertion of the center quill and the barbules of a stout hackle feather.

Fill the slot with cement. Hold the hackle feather by the tip and the butt, and insert it from the side into the slot. Do the same to the other side. Let the cement harden, then clip the butt of the stem close to the head. The tip at the rear need not be cut. Seal the slots with cement applied by the dubbing needle.

Inserting Wings and Legs

Some styles of bugs require the insertion of wings and legs of bucktail or equivalent hair. With a pencil, mark the spots where the legs or wings are to be inserted. Carefully drill holes of a diameter large enough to take the tufts of hair, which must be wrapped with tying thread at the butts. With the dubbing needle coat the windings and the holes. Then insert the wound butts into the holes, and wipe off the displaced cement.

Tying Wings Over the Back

Other styles of bugs call for wings extending lengthwise over the back of the body. The combination of bucktail and flank feathers is good. Tying requires that thread be wound around the entire body, which points up the advantage of recessing the body circumferentially for the thread. With a pencil, mark the line for the cut, and follow it exactly with a fine triangular file. Make the cut deep enough for several complete turns of tying thread. File a notch at the top to receive the butts of the wings.

Tie a slip knot in the winding thread, and pass it over the head of the body. Secure it in the recess, and draw it snug. With the dubbing needle, cement the entire recess.

Next select a pair of flank or breast feathers (the size and fullness depend upon the size of the body and the hook) from a mallard, teal, pheasant, or whatever, and arrange them one over the other, in a slightly V-fashion. Place them upside down—that is, with the dull side up—so that they extend forward beyond the hook eye with the butts over the recess and the notch. Wind the thread over the butts and around the body, keeping tension on the thread by adding the weight of hackle pliers to the thread, if necessary.

Clip a tuft of bucktail or similar hair about the size of a soda straw, and place it on top of the feathers. Secure it in place with two or three turns of thread. Trim the surplus close to the windings, and coat the butts with cement.

Holding the tying thread firmly, bend the bucktail and feather wings back over the body. Bind them down with two or three turns of the winding thread—no more because the whip finish to follow will add at least four more turns, enough to secure the wings.

Thoroughly cement the windings after whip-finishing, and with an artist's brush apply two coats of body lacquer over the windings.

Eyes

The addition of eyes has much to be said for it. Any of the varieties of eyes—painted on or otherwise—adds appeal, particularly from the point of view of the bass or pike, which have strange senses of discrimination at times. Painted eyes are the easiest to add; they have already been described. Wire-stemmed glass eyes take more time to apply and finish, but they are worth it, for they are bulbous and more lifelike. Glass eyes do require that the body be prepared for them.

Mark the spots where they will be located with a pencil. Place a fine-cut countersink in your drill, and gently recess the spots to the diameter of the glass eyes. Next clip off the wire stems to the length needed to extend into the body, allowing, of course, for the depth of the countersinking.

With a fine file, taper the ends of the cut stems to a point. Then try the eyes for fit. Apply cement to the countersunk hole and to the backs of the eyes. Firmly press each eye in place. Let the cement harden before checking it for adhesion of the eyes to the body.

In some designs the butts of hair wings, for example, are ideal for blunting with scissors and coloring to represent eyes.

There are many possibilities for making a surface bug, and listing them would fill a book. The fundamentals set down here should be more than adequate to arouse your curiosity. After all, you are the one who will do the experimenting, the tying, the shaping and painting and—even more important—the fishing. After many years, if you still like this fascinating business of fooling fish with hair, feathers and cork, you will continue to experiment. It's an endless process, and only you can set your course.

EFFECTIVE
PATTERNS

If the effectiveness and the popularity of a fly were one and the same, compiling the names of effective patterns would become the simple task of checking lists. But effectiveness is not so easy to measure. More than a few of the most effective patterns ever developed never became popular simply because they had not been publicized. Some of the popular patterns became *accepted* as effective, only because they had been.

Is a pattern effective because it brought to strike three fish on a particular morning? Because it floats well or sinks fast? (Floating and sinking are properties of a type—not a pattern.) Because it looked like one of the duns popping to the surface that the trout were taking? Because it was light against a dark background, or the reverse? Because your fishing partner swears by it and has enviable results with it, while every time *you* use it, you swear *at* it? Or simply because it has a good all-round reputation? The answers are thought provoking.

A good many of the trout, salmon, and bass flies we use today were contrived decades, if not centuries ago; and it follows that by rote they were duplicated to the hair, the doing handed down as rock-ribbed tenets, holy as all get out, if the purity and fish-getting properties of a particular pattern were to be preserved. History tells us, however, that those patterns of old really were not the products of research; they were notions—mixtures of this and that, appealing to the originator at the time he sat down before his vise. I have often wondered what some of those patterns may have looked like, if the tier had not had on hand the exact materials that he used to tie them the first time. There were exceptions, of course, as many of the old partridge- and grouse-hackled patterns more than suggest, for they were surprisingly good representations of the emerging caddis pupae. Perhaps the credibility of holding to the original is worth at least a second thought, however. If the first Hendrickson had been tied with finely barred guinea fibers (you have to sort them out), would it have been any the less effective? I tie "Hendricksons" that way for the properties of the guinea fibers, although archives on the development of the Hendrickson show that golden-pheasant crest fibers tailed at least the first of that excellent dry fly. Along the way, the golden-pheasant crest fibers became blue-dun hackle fibers for the dun and woodduck fibers for the spinner; the hackle darkened from almost "water clear" to hues of brownish-gray dun, and the body fur became "urine-stained fox belly" instead of the simple fawn-colored fox fur. So my preference for guinea fibers may not seem like such a departure, after all. But I'm not tying *Hendricksons* if I tie them with guinea-fiber tails!

A pattern is not a *type* of fly. The Royal Coachman is a pattern; but it has been tied (and very successfully) as virtually every *type* of fly to fly from the tier's vise. So long as a fly has white wings, brown hackle, a peacock herl body with a red center section and gold pheasant tippet tails, it is a Royal Coachman, whether dry fly, wet fly, streamer or whatever. It has been both popular and attractive for many, many years. So has the Cahill, the well-spring for such a vast variety of representations of the myriad mayflies (and caddisflies, too) common to most rivers and streams.

Why the Royal Coachman, the Cahill, the Hendrickson, or any other pattern has met the test of time and become labeled "effective" is always debatable. Some contend that the white flag of the Royal's wing, seen so easily during the float or the drift, is the reason; that because the Cahill simply represents so many kinds of emerging duns and pupae, it is almost universal in its appeal, as an acceptable facsimile of the natural, to the trout and other "fly fish."

During my comeuppance years ago, I became obsessed with the idea of encapsulating all the rules about fly selection that my mentors recited so easily. One such rule that I tucked away —always to remember—was the then recently acquired one about fishing a light fly on a dark day and a dark fly on a light day. It never occurred to me that dark flies might hatch on dark days, the same as light flies might hatch on light days. I was too preocupied with the rule, itself.

One bleak morning on Penn's Greek I somehow mixed the

rule, for I bent on a pair of size-8 dark Slate-Wing Coachmen with which I had remarkable success. It was not until several hours later, when my companions and I had returned to camp, that I learned of my error. I had fished the formula completely backwards, and every one of the eight fat brown trout in my creel was an outlandish mistake; they simply should *not* have happened. "I don't believe it," one chum said. "You need a light ginger-colored fly on a dark day like this." He showed me the light honey-hued fly in his fly keeper. He had taken two trout with it.

When once abundant trout and salmon began to deplete, and the population of flyrodders began to peak (one was not necessarily a function of the other), the emphasis seemed to shift from fishing skills to concentration on the perfection of the fly, itself, becoming a sort of nostrum for all fly-fishing ills. Swarms of new patterns and types of flies, each labeled with a fetching name, appeared; and if you did not have a few of the best known of them, you were ill equipped.

The recent trends are toward precise imitation, as evidenced by the dry flies, wet flies and nymphs that have become the epitome of realism. Some imitations of the larger nymphs all but bite the hand that ties them! Many anglers believe such realism in fly design and dressing is essential, and they become almost tyrannical about it: the hue of a hackle, the translucency of the body, the curvature of the tails, the web-like properties of the wing. They are the true proponents of realism and their painstaking produces flies that, by human definition, leave nothing to be desired.

An example is the classic Gordon Quill, long since considered the imitation of *Epeorus pleuralis* that begins emerging early in spring. But *is* it an imitation of that important insect? The beautiful *Epeorus* has grayish-blue wings and gray-and-tan mottled legs and tails. Yet every good representation of a Gordon Quill has exactly the opposite: woodduck (mottled tannish-gray) wings and solid dun hackle and tails! As for the body, the body varies from bleached peacock-eye quill to bluish and olive quill, dyed of course.

The Light Cahill, *Stenonema canadense* and *Stenonema ithaca,* is another example of intended imitation, which it is not. The natural has buff legs with brownish markings on the femurs, and the wings are like a foggy window pane. But who would think of tying a Light Cahill with other than woodduck wings and the prescribed cream hackle without brown markings? Here again the colors and markings of the legs and wings are reversed. One theory contends that the barred woodduck fibers in the wing lend the appearance of motion.

It is strange indeed that the Gordon Quill and the Light Cahill, both so effective when their natural counterparts are hatching, do not imitate them. But they must *appear* real to the trout, even to the selective feeders.

It is worth repeating that the type and the pattern of a fly are not the same. Some mayfly patterns, for example, if tied down-wing style, become reasonable simulators of adult caddisflies, as attests the Light Cahill which serves admirably. Size plays a prominent role in this double duty, of course. The *Stenonema ithaca* or *S. canadense* represented by the Cahill is generally size 12. But the Cahill scaled down to size 20 doubles well for many other surface flies.

The legs and tails of natural insects are seldom monotone. Adding a few turns of grizzly hackle to flat-toned hackle lends a suggestion of the spots on the legs of natural flies. In the same way, substituting finely barred feathers of guinea, partridge, and woodduck, or combinations of brown and grizzly, dun and brown, grizzly and ginger fibers for the flat-toned hackle fibers adds realism.

As for the bodies, the tergites (the back segments of an insect's body) usually differ from those of the sternites (the belly segments), which are lighter. Yet the standard dressings for the best (?) imitations do not differentiate between the two, and it would be next to impossible to tie a fly in any of the small sizes having a body so clearly defined. Rather, the banding is continuous around the body. From the trout's view, this is unnatural; from the angler's view, looking down on the fly, it is a good imitation. The fur-bodied Grey Fox is a better representation of the *Stenonema fuscum* than is the Ginger Quill, for this very reason. However, the Ginger Quill was and still is effective, despite the fact that its quill body is the same—top and bottom. Again, "imitation" is relative.

It is logical to tie your flies with as much realism as needed —that is half the fun of it, although you may have to depart from duplicating the "classic" standards and create patterns of your own after the natural insect—that is the other half of the fun. If you do, the chances are that you will end up with fewer patterns tied in those sizes that you have learned are correct.

Four such dry-fly patterns, developing through the years, reflect this reasoning. They are hybrids, according to standard designs, but, in crossing the lines of species, family, and even the order of insects, those four patterns proved effective because they are so versatile. They are good "hunters" and they are productive even during periods of selective feeding; and in size 20 they will perform beautifully as midges. Here are the four:

1. Wings: barred teal flank, upright and slanted slightly to the rear. Hackle: grizzly and brown mixed, wound sparsely over the front half of the body. Body: muskrat fur dubbed sparsely on red tying thread. Tails: mixed grizzly and brown hackle fibers. Sizes: 8, 12, 16, 2X-long.

2. Wings: pale mallard flank, upright and slanted slightly to the rear. Hackle: pale grizzly (salt and pepper) and ginger mixed, wound sparsely over the front half of the body. Body: opossum or equivalent fur dubbed sparsely on yellow tying thread. Tails: mixed ginger and pale grizzly (salt and pepper) fibers. Sizes: 10, 14, 2X-long.

3. Wings: lemon woodduck or the barred tannish feathers from a mallard drake. Hackle: pale grizzly (salt and pepper) and ginger mixed, wound sparsely over the front half of the body. Body: a broad fiber from the short side of a goose or duck flight feather. Tails: mixed grizzly (salt and pepper) fibers. Sizes: 12, 16, 2X-long.

4. Wings: barred teal flank, upright and slanted slightly to the rear. Hackle: mixed brown and grizzly, wound sparsely over the front half of the body. Body: raffia dyed dull orange. Tails: mixed brown hackle and teal fibers. Sizes: 8, 12, 2X-long.

The "standards" are not to be deemphasized, and for that reason including them here is in order. Fish historically have accepted them and will continue to do so with measurable regularity. Whether similar patterns would be equally effective is always an interesting supposition. One's own research will determine that. Mine already has. I am far less demanding about exactness in a fly than I once was. So the following groups of flies may seem sparse to those fishermen who feel short-handed without a full spectrum of patterns from Abbey to Zulu. As for a comprehensive list, I do not think there is one.

Trout Dry Flies

ADAMS: Wings: grizzly hackle tips tied spent wing for mayflies and down wing for caddisflies. Hackle: mixed brown and grizzly. Body: muskrat fur dubbing. Tails: mixed brown and grizzly hackle fibers. The Adams and the Dark Cahill are similar but the addition of the grizzly makes the Adams more versatile. Sizes 10 through 20.

GRANNOM: Wings: brown mallard tied down wing. Hackle: slate gray tied palmer. Body: dark peacock quill with greenish-yellow fur egg sac. Sizes 12 and 14. An even better tie has partridge hackle trimmed flat across the bottom.

LIGHT CAHILL: Wings: woodduck. Hackle: cream ginger. Body: cream fox-belly fur. Tails: cream hackle fiber tips or light woodduck fibers. Sizes 12 through 20. In size 4X-long 10, the Light Cahill does well when the large drakes appear.

GINGER QUILL: Wings: light duck quill. Hackle: ginger. Body: light peacock eye quill. Tails: ginger hackle fibers. Woodduck wings and bleached quill body are better for the spinner phase. Sizes 10 through 16.

GORDON QUILL: Wings: woodduck. Hackle: blue dun. Body: peacock eye quill counterwound with fine gold wire. Tails: blue dun hackle fibers. Sizes 12 through 20.

HENDRICKSON: Wings: woodduck. Hackle: pale blue dun. Body: fawn fox belly fur. Tails: pale blue dun hackle fibers. This is close to the original Steelrod pattern. The hackle became changed to the indescribable hue, then ascribed to this pattern by others: brownish-dun and so on. For those who insist on the off-color, the mixture of brown and blue dun will do. Sizes: 10 through 14.

RED QUILL: Wings: woodduck. Hackle: slate gray. Body: brown hackle quill stripped. Tails: slate gray hackle fibers. Sizes 10 through 14. I like this pattern tied with peacock eye quill dyed red for the body and rusty dun hackles and tail fibers.

MARCH BROWN: Wings: darkest barred woodduck. Hackle: mixed brown and grizzly. Body: fox belly fur with ruddy-tan (or gold tinsel) rib. Tails: brown hackle fibers. I prefer partridge hackle fiber tails. Sizes: 8 through 12.

GRAY AND BROWN HACKLES: Tied with grizzly or brown hackle tied palmer over red, yellow, and orange fur bodies with gold ribs, these old standards still out-perform many winged patterns. Add peacock herl for the body to round out the assortment. Sizes: 12 through 20.

BIVISIBLES: The Royal Coachman adaptation is always good. Substitute two turns of white hackle in front of the brown for the white wings of the winged type. The peacock herl body with the red floss center joint, and the golden pheasant tippet tails lend visibility to both the fish and the fisherman. Sizes: 12 and 14.

Trout Wet Flies

HARE'S EAR: This angler's facsimile of the emerging Gordon Quill is most dependable. The original is tied with dubbed hare's fur—ideally from the mask—the projecting hairs left as hackle. The body is ribbed with gold tinsel. Wings: gray duck quill. Tails: brown hackle fibers. Sizes: 8 through 14.

ROYAL COACHMAN: A good "hunter" that has withstood the test of time. Wings: white duck quill. Hackle: brown. Peacock herl with red floss center joint. Tails: golden pheasant tippets. Sizes: 6 through 14.

QUEEN OF THE WATERS: A reliable simulator of the caddis pupa. Wings: gray mallard flank. Hackle: brown palmer. Body: orange fur or floss with gold tinsel rib. Tails: gold pheasant tippet. Sizes 6 through 14.

LIGHT CAHILL: The grubstake of any wet-fly fisherman. Wings: woodduck. Hackle: cream ginger (light partridge is better). Body: fox belly fur, gold tinsel tip. Tails: woodduck. Sizes: 6 through 14.

GRAY QUILL: Wings: light mallard (or pale gray duck quill). Hackle: badger. Body: peacock eye quill. Tails: badger hackle fibers. Sizes 10 and 12. This pattern simulates many of the grayish emergers.

WICKHAM'S FANCY: A reliable standard but seen less as

seasons pass. A great dusk pattern. Wings: gray duck quill. Hackle: brown palmer. Body: gold tinsel. Tails: brown hackle fibers. Sizes: 6 through 12.

CAHILL: Versatile, occupies a special spot in the wet fly fisher's box of tricks. A good nymph simulator. Wings: woodduck. Hackle: brown. Body: muskrat belly fur, gold tinsel tip. Tails: woodduck. Sizes: 4 through 20.

WOODDUCK AND GOLD: This lightly dressed wet fly is similar to a streamer and is most successful for northern brook trout and frequently landlocked salmon. It is a good "twitching" fly for probing strong waters along the edges of which the big squaretails hold. Wing: black-and-white barred woodduck dressed sparse with gold pheasant crest over. Hackles: short gold pheasant crest fibers splayed under the body. Body: gold tinsel. Tail: gold pheasant crest over short ragged-out red fur or wool. Sizes: 6X-long 10 and 8.

CADDIS PUPAE SIMULATORS: These are tied with grouse, partridge, and woodduck hackle over orange, brown, olive-green, and yellow fur bodies. The hackle must be *sparse*—two turns being sufficient. Tie it at the front and let the fibers extend naturally. There are no tails. Gold wire ribbing adds flash for deep, dark water.

Nymphs and Larvae

Nymph patterns differ in color according to the water: freestone or limestone. For this reason, the following list is quite brief; attempting to describe the nymphs and larvae populating each type of water would be a life-long task, one that would serve little real purpose, except from an encyclopedic viewpoint.

The actual difference between a nymph and a sparsely dressed wet fly is quite academic when it comes to catching a trout. Catching the eye of the fisher is something else. If a sparsely hackled wet fly of the right size and approximate color fails to interest trout feeding on nymphs, the chances are that an angler's facsimile of the nymph being taken will do no better.

If I were required to choose between color and size (including shape), I would choose the latter. The section on tying nymphs describes the differences between the mayfly, stonefly and caddisfly with emphasis on the typical proportions for each. Building your nymphs accordingly is, at least, a starting point.

The following patterns should serve most purposes, if tied in keeping with those proportions.

GENERAL NYMPH: Tails: pheasant or dark-barred wood-duck fibers. Abdomen: hare's ear or fox fur dubbed body ribbed with gold tinsel. Thorax: same as abdomen, pheasant or brown turkey feather fiber over for wing case. Legs: two turns of brown partridge, all fibers of which are displaced to the sizes and bottom when the wing case is folded over and tied down. Sizes: 8 through 12, 2X-long shank. This pattern, or rather this type, will serve for stonefly and mayfly nymphs. An alternate color, buff, for the body, is advisable.

CADDIS LARVA: Tails: dull fur dubbing, shagged out. Body: shagged-out fur dubbing wound loose, counter-wound with quill stripped from the stem of a duck or goose wing feather. In small sizes the short, broad fiber from a flight feather will do well. Legs: the predominately black fibers from a guinea feather tied short behind the hook eye. Sizes: 10 and 12, English-type bait hook. Yellow, green, and orange fur are good alternate colors for the body.

CADDIS PUPA: This abundant, interesting emerger calls for special attention from the angler. The pupal wings are close to the body, are shorter than the wings of other emergers the same size, and are sloped downward. The body is banana-shaped. The trick in tying the pupa is to let the hackle fibers extend long and gangly. Body: brick-colored fur dubbing wound over brown wool, counterwound with gold tinsel. Legs: two turns of woodduck, brown mallard, or brown-gray mottled pheasant body feather *untrimmed*. Antennae: two fibers of woodduck on top. Head: brown hackle trimmed to herl size behind the hook eye. Sizes: 8, 10, and 12 on English bait hook or 2X-long regular hook bent banana-shape.

OTHER: As already mentioned, patterns tied on small hooks, 16, 18, and 20 are effective. Simulating their size is far more important than faithfully trying to copy the entire natural. Even size-18 wingless wet flies are good pupae. Fish the proper depth by using sinking line or wire-weighted hook (or both, if necessary). But this is an angling technique, not the prescription for a pattern.

Streamers

Streamers are principally representative of minnows. They should have the overall appearance and flash of the natural minnow which has a dark back and a silver or gold belly with markings and streaks peculiar to each type. Head and gill markings, eyes, and the like, are quite individual and are natural targets for the fly tier.

Streamers are probably the most attractive of all the creations contrived for fly fishing. Patterns are deceptive, however; many are virtually the same, a touch of this, or a little of that, being the only ingredient that causes one pattern to differ from another. But that can be said of all flies! It is true that some color combinations represent no minnow that ever lived, and the reason for their effectiveness is largely a matter of opinion. Whatever it is, the fact remains that specific color combinations work, often superior to colors that have been researched in the efforts to simulate the minnows that inhabit a particular body of water.

Here are some that have earned the reputation of being reliable.

MICKEY FINN: Wing: yellow over red over yellow bucktail or other suitable hair. Body: silver tinsel with a silver twist rib, or Mylar counterwound with narrow flat silver tinsel.

EDSON TIGER (Light): Wing: yellow bucktail topped with short red section of duck quill fibers. Body: peacock herl counterwound with monofilament for strength, silver tinsel tip. Tail: woodduck or silver pheasant tippet fibers.

BLACK GHOST: Wing: four white saddle hackles. Hackle: yellow bucktail or equivalent at throat tied long. Body: black floss, silver tinsel rib. Tail: yellow bucktail or feather fibers.

GRAY GHOST: Wing: four blue dun neck hackles, silver pheasant body shoulder. Hackle: few strands of peacock herl, about 10 white bucktail fibers, and gold pheasant crest. Body: yellow (or orange) floss, silver tinsel rib.

JANE CRAIG: Wing: four white saddle hackles, peacock herl over. Hackle: white at throat. Body: silver tinsel, round silver rib.

JOCK SCOT: Wing: two yellow saddle hackles with two badger saddles outside, peacock sword topping. Hackle: guinea pulled down below throat. Body: black floss front half, yellow floss rear half, both silver tinsel ribbed. Tail: gold pheasant crest fibers.

Steelhead Flies

BLACK DEMON: Wing: black hair—dyed polar bear or bucktail. Hackle: black or badger. Body: oval silver tinsel. Tail: silver pheasant crest.

CARSON: Wing: white bucktail or polar bear hair over scarlet hair. Hackle: brown. Body: peacock herl with red floss center joint. Tail: bright red hackle or silver pheasant crest fibers.

GOLDEN DEMON: Wing: brown bucktail or bear hair. Hackle: orange. Body: oval gold tinsel. Tail: golden pheasant crest.

LADY GODIVA: Wing: red bucktail overwing, sparse white bucktail or polar bear underwing. Body: silver tinsel tag, yellow seal's fur, flat silver tinsel ribbed, red chenille butt. Tail: red and yellow hair or feather fibers. No hackle.

LORD IRIS: Wing: overwing of red, orange, green, and blue goose wing fibers married; underwing of orange hackle, peacock herl, badger hackle, and golden pheasant crests. Body: silver tinsel. Tail: golden pheasant tippet fibers.

OPTICS:

> *Red Owl-Eye:* Wing: red bucktail. Body: thick silver tinsel. Head: built up or bead lacquered black with orange eye and black pupil.
>
> *Wind River:* Wing: dark orange bucktail. Body: thick silver tinsel. Head: built up or bead lacquered black with red eye and white pupil.

Steelhead flies often are dressed on large, short-shank, up-eye gold-plated hooks for their keel effect and hooking power. The flies, themselves, range in size from 4 to 8, with a few in sizes 10 and 12.

The patterns listed represent a cross section only.

Salmon Flies

The range of salmon fly patterns has greatly increased in the past 30 years, particularly in the last ten, incident to the influences of American tiers who simplified the elegance of the old British standards. When the American hair-wing patterns proved more effective than standard stiff-wing styles, the entire perspective on salmon flies and fishing changed. The intricacies of "married" fiber sections and the use of exotic, expensive plumage lost favor. Emphasis also shifted to the low-water versions with abbreviated feather content; and, as the hair wings appeared more each season, the decades-old, difficult-to-tie classics of the Victorian period declined in use and effectiveness. Some prevailed, however and a few of them, together with a smattering of American creations appear in the following lists.

Low-Water Feather Wing Patterns

BLUE CHARM: Tag: silver tinsel, flat or oval. Tip: yellow floss. Tail: golden pheasant crest. Body: black floss, flat or oval tinsel ribbed. Hackle: bright blue (Silver Doctor blue, but not greenish) at throat. Wing: brown mallard flank feather sections with strip of darkly barred teal on each side. Topping: golden pheasant crest.

LADY CAROLINE: Tag: gold tinsel, flat or oval. Tip: yellow floss. Tail: golden pheasant crest or red body fibers. Body: olive-brown fur dubbing, oval gold tinsel ribbed. Hackle: blue dun at throat. Wing: brown mallard flank feather sections.

MARCH BROWN: Tag: gold tinsel, flat (or orange floss tip). Tail: brown partridge fibers, short. Body: brown fur dubbing picked out, gold tinsel ribbed. Hackle: brown partridge. Wing: brown turkey or hen pheasant fibers.

LOGIE: Tag: silver tinsel, flat. Tip: orange floss. Tail: golden pheasant crest. Body: brownish-red or claret floss, silver tinsel ribbed. Hackle: blue at throat. Wing: brown mallard flank feather sections.

SILVER GREY: Tag: silver tinsel, flat. Tip: yellow floss. Tail: golden pheasant crest. Body: black fur or ostrich herl butt; silver tinsel, flat; oval silver tinsel ribbed.

Hackle: teal or dark-barred mallard at throat. Wing: mallard flank feather sections. Topping: golden pheasant crest.

Low-Water Hair Wing Patterns

BLACK BEAR: An all-black pattern. Tail: black feather fibers. Body: black wool or fur. Hackle: black bear hair tied beard fashion at throat. Wing: black bear hair, long, to tip of tail fibers. A second but older dressing still is favored. Tail: gold pheasant tippet. Tag: gold tinsel. Body: green wool, gold tinsel ribbed. Hackle: guinea fibers tied beard fashion at throat. Wing: black bear hair.

BLACK BOMBER: Tag: silver wire. Tip: yellow floss. Body: black wool, oval tinsel ribbed. Hackle: black wound as collar and pulled down at throat. Wing: black squirrel or equivalent hair. Topping: golden pheasant crest. Cheeks: jungle cock.

BUTTERFLY: Tail: dyed red hackle fibers. Body: peacock herl. Wing: widely divided white hair wing (goat, calf, or polar bear). Hackle: sparse brown tied collar fashion.

COSSEBOOM: Tag: silver tinsel. Tail: green hackle fibers, blunted. Body: green floss, oval silver tinsel ribbed. Hackle: yellow tied collar fashion. Wing: sparse gray squirrel extending to tip of tail fibers.

MYSTERY: Tag: silver tinsel. Tip: yellow floss. Body: black chenille butt; silver tinsel. Hackle: brown. Wing: fox squirrel. Check: jungle cock eye.

ROSS SPECIAL: Tail: golden pheasant crest. Body: red wool, oval silver tinsel ribbed. Hackle: yellow. Wing: fox squirrel tail. Cheeks: jungle cock eye.

Salmon Dry Fly Patterns

COLONEL MONELL: Tail: ginger hackle fibers. Body: peacock herl, red floss ribbed. Hackle: grizzly tied palmer and full at front.

PINK LADY: Tail: ginger hackle fibers. Body: pink floss, gold tinsel ribbed. Hackle: ginger tied palmer and full at front, faced with yellow hackle.

SOLDIER PALMER: Tail: brown hackle fibers. Body: red fur dubbing, gold tinsel ribbed. Hackle: brown tied palmer.

RAT FACED MacDOUGALL: Tail: ginger hackle fibers. Body: deer hair trimmed egg shape. Hackle: ginger tied collar fashion. Wings: sparse white hair (calf, goat, polar bear) tied V-shape.

HEWITT SKATERS: All hackle flies. The hackles are white, brown, ginger, dun, or black. Tied toward the front of the hook. Supposedly, the originals were tied without benefit of cement or varnish so they could be moved back and forth on the shank, accordion-like, to suit the angler.

WULFF FLIES: These patterns are heavily tailed with bucktail, the butts of which, when tied to the shank, form the foundation for the wool or dubbed fur body. The bucktail wings are tied on ahead of the body then divided with the winding thread. The butts are left untrimmed. Two saddle hackles tied reverse, or facing toward the hook eye finish the fly.

Royal Wulff: A Royal Coachman tied with white (bucktail) tail fibers.

Grey Wulff: Tail: brown bucktail. Body: gray wool. Wings: brown bucktail. Hackle: two blue dun saddles.

White Wulff: Tail: white bucktail. Body: cream wool. Wings: white bucktail. Hackle: two badger saddles.

Shad Flies

Shad flies are slim, usually wire-weighted, size 6 and 8 regular and 3X-long. They seldom are hackled, although white- and yellow-winged trout flies which are, of course, have been effective for years. They definitely have their place in the shad-fly fly book.

These are some of the old and the new patterns. A single winding of lead wire around the hook shank quickens the sink rate, an important quality in shad fishing.

BUTT PATTERNS: These are tied with fluorescent chenille butts and collars. Bodies are floss, tinsel or Mylar ribbed. The wings and tails are goat, polar bear, or calf.

White and Orange: Tail: yellow. Body: white floss, silver ribbed. Butt and collar: orange chenille. Wing: yellow.

White and Green: Same as the White and Orange but with green chenille butt and collar.

ENFIELD SHAD FLY: Body: silver tinsel or Mylar. Wing: yellow quill fibers or hair. Red bead on snell in front of hook eye. Wing also orange.

MYLAR-BODIED PATTERNS:

Silver: Tail: red fur dubbing shagged out. Body: silver Mylar tubing counter wound with 10-pound monofilament. Wing: white goat, calf, or polar bear hair. Head: red tying thread about one fourth the length of the body.

Gold: Tail: red fur dubbing shagged out. Body: gold Mylar tubing counter wound with 10-pound monofilament. Wing: yellow goat, calf, or polar bear hair. Head: red tying thread about one fourth the length of the body.

YELLOW PALMER: Tail: yellow hackle fibers. Body: orange dubbed fur, gold or silver ribbed. Hackle: yellow tied palmer style.

WINGLESS PATTERNS: These are simple, consisting of the body and tails. The bodies are white, yellow, orange, and pink, silver ribbed.

Pike Flies

Size 1/0 and 3/0 long-shank hooks are best for pickerel and pike flies which, despite their size, are quite easy to tie. Red, yellow, and white, and their combinations, are the colors needed. Silver and gold tinsel (or Mylar) form the bodies. They are best counter-wound with monofilament or, even better, fine wire, to resist the needle-like teeth of the pike, pickerel and—hopefully—a muskie or two.

These are typical patterns that have worked well.

1. Yellow bucktail with a red center stripe, and silver or gold body.

2. White bucktail with a yellow center stripe, and silver or gold body.

3. Yellow bucktail with long white hackle streamers in the center and extending beyond the tips; silver or gold body.

4. Big Boy. This streamer is at least 6½ inches long and well worth the effort to tie it. Tail: 4½-inch yellow bucktail. Body: silver Mylar tube counterwound with monofilament or wire. Wing: 4½- or 5-inch bucktail, yellow over white. Head: red. This fly is a monster to cast and it takes some doing to get the feel of it.

Saltwater Flies

Like freshwater patterns, the patterns for salt water have become highly specialized. Many with new names follow the general lines and material selections of earlier patterns, or modify them slightly. As a matter of fact, I doubt that some of the tiers of the "new patterns" know they are virtually copies of flies developed decades ago. Several so-called "tarpon" flies, for example, are patterned largely after Loving's striped bass fly, originated about 50 years ago. And the dual-color type of streamer wing—the white and blue, white and red, and the like—is nearly as old.

The *type* is probably the most significant consideration. Tarpon flies are a good case in point. With few exceptions, they are tied with long bucktail or feather streamers trailing a full collar hackle. Flies for striped bass are more slinky, and only a few are collar hackled. Flies for bluefish are so like striper flies that they are hardly distinguishable, except by the name of the patterns. Flies for bonefish are of various designs and seem to be getting shorter.

Any saltwater pattern is best developed for casting, not for looks alone or exact imitation of a baitfish. When saltwater fish are "on the feed" they will take one pattern as well as another, provided the size is right and the lure is retrieved properly. The first consideration is tying the streamer to have a minimum of air resistance. Bulky hackles and built-up bodies increase it. White, yellow, and a little blue and red are the colors used in most saltwater flies; and they are successful from coast to coast. The following patterns are examples. They are not intended as the end to all pattern design for saltwater species. Sizes are generally 1/0 and 3/0, although there is a smattering of 5/0's. At times, the smaller sizes 2 and 1 perform better than the larger ones.

GIBBS' STRIPER: Body: silver tinsel. Wing: white bucktail with narrow blue feather strip up each side. Hackle:

sparse red tied beard fashion. Cheeks: teal breast or jungle cock feather (not eye).

LEONARD'S GALLI-NIPPER: Tail: short red imitation polar bear hair, shagged out. Body: silver Mylar tube, counterwound with 12-pound monofilament. Wings: yellow bucktail 3½ inches long, topped with 2 grizzly hackles, one on each side, 2½ inches long. Throat: short red imitation polar bear hair. Head: gold Mylar chenille lacquered.

LOVING'S STRIPED BASS FLY: Originally tied with no body or tails. Wings: white bucktail. Hackle: saddle hackle dyed red and wound collar style.

BROOKS' PLATINUM BLONDE: Tail: white bucktail wound over with tying thread to form the base for a full Mylar body. Body: flat silver Mylar, double layer wound. Wing: white bucktail reaching nearly to the tips of the tail fibers.

BONBRIGHT: Tail: white and red hackle tips. Body: silver tinsel (Mylar is better). Wings: four white saddle hackles. Topping: gold pheasant crest (also tied with red goose quill fibers). Shoulders: jungle cock eyes.

RHODE'S TARPON FLY: Tails: 10 white saddle hackles about 4 inches long. Hackle: orange tied palmer over rear part of hook, front part red tying thread.

LEFTY KREH'S COCKROACH: Tails: double paired grizzly hackle 2½ inches long. Wing: sparse brown bucktail trailing over hackles, completely around hook.

LEFTY KREH'S DECEIVER: Here again, the color schemes are all white or mixtures of red and white or yellow and red. Tails: eight hackles (long) with two or three strips of Mylar on each side. Body: double layer wound Mylar. Collar: calf tail tied completely around the hook and sloping back around the body. The calf tail is sparse.

LYMAN'S TERROR: This pattern is very similar to Hal Gibbs' Striper; the difference is the color of the center strip of bucktail which is red instead of blue.

Other than for the shrimp styles of flies, which have a place when fish are working in the shallows, the preceding list is a good one to follow or build on. When it comes right down to specifics, about the only thing a fly tier can do is to alter the color combinations, which is a matter of preference and experimentation. What evolves is up to the tier. The chances are good that he will be successful flyrodding with the patterns listed. They are good for every species, from weakfish to tarpon. For those tiers who wish to have a rather thorough listing of saltwater flies and the instructions on how to tie them, I suggest Ken Bay's book *Salt Water Flies*.

Flies, by J. Edson Leonard, is still considered by many to be a useful reference for patterns. The lists contain more than 2,200 individually described patterns for both freshwater and saltwater flies, some of which have been "re-invented" in the past 25 years.

Bibliography

BASHLINE, L. James. *Night Fishing for Trout.* New York: Freshet, 1973.

BATES, Joseph D. *Atlantic Salmon Flies and Fishing.* Harrisburg: Stackpole, 1970.

BAY, Kenneth E. & Kessler, Herman. *Salt Water Flies.* New York and Philadelphia: Lippincott, 1972.

BRADNER, Enos. *Northwest Angling.* New York: Barnes, 1950.

BROOKS, Joe. *Bass Bug Fishing.* New York: Barnes, 1947.

CAUCCI, Al & Nastasi, Bob. *Hatches.* New York: Comparahatch, 1975.

CONNETT, Eugene V. *Any Luck?* Garden City, N.Y.: Doubleday, 1933.

CROWE, John. *The Book of Trout Lore.* New York: Barnes, 1947.

HALFORD, F. M. *Dry-Fly Fishing.* Reading, England, Barry Shurlock & Co. (Publishers) Ltd. (Field and Stream Club Edition) 1973.

KOCH, Ed. *Fishing the Midge.* New York: Freshet, 1972.

LEISER, Eric. *Fly-Tying Materials.* New York: Crown, 1973.

LEONARD, J. Edson. *Flies.* New York: Barnes, 1950.

LYMAN, Henry & Woolner, Frank. *Striped Bass Fishing.* New York: Barnes, 1954.

NEEDHAM, James G. & Paul R. *A Guide to the Study of Fresh Water Biology.* Ithaca: Comstock, 1941.

NEEDHAM, James G. & Lloyd, J. T. *The Life of Inland Waters.* Ithaca: Comstock, 1937.

NEEDHAM, Paul R. *Trout Streamers.* Ithaca: Comstock, 1940.

RODMAN, O. H. P. *Striped Bass.* New York: Barnes, 1944.

SCHWEIBERT, Ernest G. *Matching the Hatch.* New York: Macmillan, 1954.

SCHWEIBERT, Ernest. *Nymphs.* New York: Winchester, 1973.

Figure

Index